Special Siblings

Special Siblings

GROWING UP
WITH SOMEONE
WITH A
DISABILITY

MARY McHugh

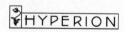

NEW YORK

Library of Congress Cataloging-in-Publication Data

McHugh, Mary.
  Special siblings : growing up with someone with a disability / Mary McHugh. – 1st ed.
    p. cm.
  Includes bibliographical references and index.
  ISBN 0-7868-6285-8
  1. Handicapped–United States–Family relationships–Case studies.
  2. Brothers and sisters–United States–Psychology–Case studies.
  I. Title
  HV1553.M38 1999   98–21165
  362.4'043'0973–dc21   CIP

Designed by C. Linda Dingler

First Edition

10 9 8 7 6 5 4 3 2 1

This book is dedicated to my brother, Jack Kennard,

who faces life every day with courage

and a smile. I love him very much.

ACKNOWLEDGMENTS

*T*here are a lot of people I would like to thank for their support, encouragement and help while I was writing this book: Stan Klein, former editor of *Exceptional Parent*; Don Meyer of the Sibling Support Project in Seattle; Debra Lobato at Rhode Island Hospital; Helen Gurley Brown; Lisa Glidden at the A. J. Pappanikou Center; Thomas Fish at the Nisonger Center; Thomas Powell; Milton Seligman; Bryna Siegel and Stuart Silverstein; Sandra Harris and Myra Bluebond-Langner at Rutgers; Alexandra Quittner at the University of Illinois; Ginny Thornburgh at the National Organization on Disability; Marty Krauss at Brandeis University, Julie Tallard Johnson; Lois Bonnell; Marylee Westbrook; Evelyn Hausslein; and Dr. William Bauman.

I also want to thank all the siblings of people with disabilities who poured out their hearts to me with great generosity. I promised them I wouldn't use their real names, so I can't list them here, but I couldn't have written this book without them.

And to my husband Earl who did everything he could to give me the freedom to spend every day at my computer writing this book, a special thanks. Thank you to the rest of my family–Kyle, Karen, Doug, Alex, Ian, and Michael–for their understanding and love.

But most of all, I want to thank my agent and best friend, Linda Konner, for loving this book and sending it to the right, caring editor, Laurie Abkemeier.

CONTENTS

FOREWORD

When I first met Mary McHugh as she was beginning the process of writing, I knew this book would be important. I was intrigued by her story of how she assumed responsibility for Jack though she herself was a mature adult, a parent of grown children, a wife, a grandmother, and an accomplished writer. She wanted to write another book—about the lives of "normal" sisters and brothers of individuals with disabilities in order to help other sisters and brothers share their stories and learn from one another.

I was delighted to try to assist Mary in this project by connecting her with people I had come to know over my forty-plus years working with children with disabilities and their family members. There have been several books on the topic of siblings of children with disabilities. I co-edited one myself. But Mary set about to do something very special and different from any other book thus far. As she tells us, in recent years, she has learned to love her brother, to appreciate him as a person of value and as someone who can teach *her* about herself and about life. Fortunately for us, she brings all of us into her life—and we learn from Mary and Jack and all the others we meet in this book. We learn and relearn together about how in the process of caring for one another, we need to listen and to talk with one another about uncomfortable topics with respect and empathy. As parents, we need to create a climate of openness for our children so that we teach by example how talking about difficult topics with compassion and understanding can help each of us master whatever may come our way in a world that is so often unfair.

I knew this book was important because as editor-in-chief of *Ex-ceptional Parent* magazine, I met many parents of children with disabil-ities throughout the United States each year. Typically, we met in small or large groups in which I invited the audience to bring up issues of importance to them personally for discussion. Concerns about their "other children" were always raised. Complicated questions were asked and powerful stories shared. I know that all those parents and thousands and thousands more will want to read this book, identify with so many of the topics that are discussed, and use this book to begin or continue important conversations with family and friends.

Today, our children know about children with disabilities because our world has changed. Most children with disabilities are now raised at home with their families by parents who can take advantage of a wide range of services designed to make it far more possible for chil-dren with disabilities to grow up, go to school, play with other chil-dren, and participate in community life. All of us, children and adults, are far more aware of people with disabilities than in years past. In fact, in the lifetimes of people like Mary and me, people with disabilities were once nearly invisible.

Mary McHugh and I both grew up in suburban northern New Jersey—Mary in the 1930s, I in the 1940s. I don't recall knowing any children with disabilities during my childhood. In fact, I don't remember even seeing any such children until I was about ten or twelve years old and attended a function in the nearby yard of family friends. Two of the adults in that family had muscular dystrophy. I have a very vague memory of seeing a few children with muscular dystrophy at this function, feeling upset when I saw them, and then leaving. As far as I knew, there were no children with disabilities at my school or in our community—or anywhere else. I don't think I ever met anyone like Mary's brother Jack until I began working as a camp counselor with children with cerebral palsy and other disabilities after my first year in college in 1954.

Mary's parents raised Jack at home at a time when most parents of children with physical disabilities and mental retardation were en-couraged to place their children in institutional settings. In those days, most well-intentioned professionals warned parents of the dangers to the rest of the family of raising a child with a disability at home. Usually based on no actual personal experience or research, it was believed that brothers and sisters of children with disabilities would be especially vulnerable to grave psychological harm if parents decided to raise a child with a disability within the family. Not only were most parents encouraged to place their children with disabilities, it was often suggested that after doing so, they forget about them. As a result, neither I nor most of my generational peers knew any child with a disability. And, in many families, the child who had been placed was not discussed openly and was a hidden family secret. Although Jack's disabilities were not exactly a secret in Mary's family, there was very little discussion in the family about them or any other related family issues. As Mary describes, her parents' way of coping with parenting a son with special needs was not an unusual one: her mother devoted herself to caring for Jack; her father retreated. Mary learned not to reveal her feelings about Jack.

Fortunately for all of us, Mary no longer keeps her feelings to herself. As she shares her interviews and research as well as her own personal experiences with us, we hear many perspectives. Mary gives us all a great deal of food for thought and even more important, food for appreciating the feelings of others and of ourselves.

When any of us look back on our lives, we have wishes about how people and events might have been different. I believe that all of us, like Mary, wish our parents had done certain things differently and been more aware of our needs. Often we believe that if only our parents had said or done some things differently our lives would have been better in some way. And those of us who are parents ourselves wonder how our own children will recall our parenting efforts.

Mary's parents might well have done things differently–just like yours or mine. Yet, I believe that all parents do the best they can within the contexts of their own lives. Sadly, the best some people can do leaves a great deal to be desired. But all of us can go beyond blaming our parents or other people's parents and appreciate how the incredible efforts of parents in years past have created the vast improvements in the lives of most people with disabilities today.

This book discusses many important topics in lives of families. I want to highlight several issues that are especially meaningful to me and to note some of the unfinished business that remains in our con-temporary communities.

Thank you, Mary, for writing about "forgotten" fathers. Although the roles of women and men have changed in many ways since Mary, Jack, and I were growing up, many fathers are still not actively involved in the lives of their children with disabilities. While there are many reasons for this, we need to reach out to fathers and encourage their participation. Our education and health care services need to be sure that fathers are invited and expected to participate in the challenges of parenting. And we need more support groups for fathers of children with disabilities.

Thank you for writing about support groups—for sisters and broth-ers as well as mothers and fathers and grandparents too. It has been truly remarkable to watch the development of more and more support groups and to appreciate how helpful such groups can be in the lives of children and adults. The support groups for siblings described in this book are relatively new. It is very important for siblings to have opportunities to participate in such groups—just like fathers. This is clearly an area of unfinished business.

The fact that this book includes sisters and brothers of people with mental illnesses is especially noteworthy. Appreciating the needs of these sisters and brothers is a unique contribution of this book. All too often, people with mental illnesses and their family members remain outside the systems of support, unacquainted with the books that have evolved in reference to people with other kinds of disabilities. This is another vast area of unfinished business.

For over thirty years, Jack has lived in a private residential program "run by kind, humane, compassionate people who truly care about the adults with mental retardation who live there." Some people will object to such a living arrangement and may be critical of Mary and her parents because they were able to choose such a setting for Jack. Safe, secure, and caring living arrangements for adults who are unable to manage their own care without assistance is another topic I hear from parents everywhere. I also visit many residential settings, some supported by public funding, some supported by families themselves. I believe that these settings are needed by some adults with disabilities and should not be dismantled. Rather, we need to continue to develop a variety of options for adults who need special supportive living set' tings and remain open to different models. Many current residential programs are doing creative things as they strive to create different options.

When I visit residential programs for adults or children, I shudder as I recall my first visits to the institutional settings of the past. I wish that I could forget the horrors I witnessed—human beings living under disgraceful conditions, ignored and seemingly forgotten. But, I believe these human beings were not actually forgotten. I have met many peo' ple who share with me their personal family secret—a family member living in a residential setting. Some, like Mary, have become more at' tentive and loving; others have not.

Jack began to live at the Duvall Home when he was thirty-seven. Many of the residential settings I have visited have described their typical current new clients as adults with significant disabilities in their thirties and forties who have been cared for since birth by their now aging parents—parents who can no longer provide the day-after-day care that is needed. I am troubled by these stories. As a society we need to create options for parents so that they do not need to be the primary caretakers of their dependent adult children until they "burn out" or die. Parents and sisters and brothers need not feel ashamed about seeking residential care for their loved ones. Jack has been for' tunate because his family has had the resources to support his adult living setting. Many families do not have such resources. So much unfinished business.

When we first published *Exceptional Parent* magazine in 1971, there was very little parenting information for parents of children with dis' abilities to share—about sibling relationships, or anything else. In 1972, when we published an interview with four college students, each of whom had a sibling with a disability, we realized that sisters and broth' ers did not have opportunities to talk with their peers about living in a family that included a child with a disability. Since those years, we have learned a great deal from parents, from sisters and brothers, and from people with disabilities. Today, we are ready to learn from Mary McHugh.

STANLEY D. KLEIN, PH.D.
Brookline, Massachusetts

Special Siblings

*O*ne January day a couple of years ago, I drove past the house in Short Hills, New Jersey, where I grew up. I hadn't been inside that house for over fifty years. I wanted to see it again. I wanted to go inside that red brick colonial and find the ghosts of my parents, my brother, and me when we were young.

I parked in the driveway and walked up the path to the curved steps leading to the screened-in front porch. A woman with a kind face answered the door.

"Hello," I said. "My name is Mary McHugh and I grew up in this house. Would you mind if I came inside for a minute, just to see it again?"

"Of course I don't mind," she said, smiling. "Come in. Please excuse the mess. We just took the Christmas tree down."

She stepped back. When I walked through the door into that familiar central hallway, I was overwhelmed by the memories in that house. I was seven years old again, back in the 1930s, safe inside with my mother and father. Safe from the frightening move to a new city when I was twelve, safe from my paralyzing shyness as an adolescent, safe from my embarrassment at having a brother with mental retardation, safe from watching my youngest child become blind, safe from the future.

The structure of the house was the same. The furniture and the wallpaper were different, of course, but I could picture the living room the way it had been when we lived there. The pale green and yellow wallpaper, the black velvet bench in front of the fireplace, the white mantel, the gold couch, and—amazingly—a piano in the same corner ours had been in so many years before.

I could see my father again, playing Strauss duets with me on our piano. He took lessons the same time I did and even played in a recital full of scrubbed eight-year-olds. My handsome, dark-haired father, trying not to smile, played the bass part of *Die Fledermaus* while I played the treble. An old lady in the audience said, "Young man, I admire your courage." He loved it.

I had forgotten until that moment how funny my father was. I tend to remember him as a dour man, disappointed with his life, angry at everyone, silent about his son who would never be a companion to him, never play golf with him, never talk to him about his dreams.

My father withdrew deep inside himself when Jackie was diagnosed with cerebral palsy and mental retardation. I never heard him cry, never heard him say anything about this deep hurt. I loved him so and ached to please him. But I was also afraid of him, of his anger. It felt like he didn't love me. I know he *did* love me, but he was buttoned up, a closed New Englander who couldn't say "I love you" easily. There wasn't a lot of hugging or touching going on in that house, but I do remember sitting on his lap while he read an alphabet book to me. "Here's your old friend A," he would say.

I could see my mother, smiling and pretty, pouring tea for a friend in the late afternoon before she picked up my father at the station. She was wearing a summer dress and small gold earrings. She was laughing, animated, free for a few moments from the worry of taking care of a child who had not yet learned to walk or talk at the age of four. She always believed he would be all right if she could just find the right doctor, the right school, the right expert, to help him.

I couldn't see my brother in this room at all. I have photographs that were taken of us every year, sitting on the bench in front of the fireplace or standing in front of the grandfather clock, so I know what he looked like as a little boy. He was beautiful. Blond, blue-eyed, sweet-faced. The retardation that would become more apparent as he grew older was hardly discernible in those pictures. But I couldn't remember him in this room at all. Just my mother and father and their friends.

I looked out the window at the backyard, but the magnolia tree was gone. I used to hide among its pink and white blossoms while I wrote stories about naughty children. When I asked about it, my hostess told me they had cut it down the year before. That was just about the time my mother died, I thought.

I crossed the hall into the dining room and saw once again the chandelier over the table, the china cabinet full of cut-glass bowls and Wedgwood plates. I could see my father there, the star of their dinner parties—smart, funny with a wry, offbeat humor. But he could also skewer someone if they said something he thought was stupid, including me. "You don't know what you're talking about," he would growl. And I believed him. I thought he was always right so he must be right about this. I carried that around for a long time, thinking my opinion didn't count.

In the breakfast nook in the kitchen, I pictured my father after work, drinking a Scotch and soda and reading the paper while my mother fixed dinner. I loved being with him then. After a day in New York, working at Bell Labs as an electrical engineer, his white shirt was rumpled and masculine smelling. He would ask me what I did in school and the words came tumbling out, "We made puppets and we're going to do *Peter Pan* and I'm going to be Mrs. Darling." He wasn't really listening, but he smiled and said, "Well, well." Just a "well, well" now and then was all I asked for.

"Would you like to see the upstairs?" the lady asked.

"Oh yes," I said. "Please."

I walked up those familiar stairs, touching the same walnut-stained banister that had been there when I was a child, remembering how big this house had seemed to me then.

At the top of the stairs, I stopped. There, straight ahead, was the door to my room. My clean, clean, blue-and-white room with the three large windows facing our front yard. I didn't see the three beds with rumpled covers, the basketball posters on the wall, the soccer ball in the corner. I saw my double bed with the white spread and the table covered with books. I saw the closet full of the smocked dresses my mother made for me. I remembered reading with a flashlight under the covers and my mother coming into the room and gently taking my book and the light away. "Time for bed," she'd say, and kiss me. I loved the touch of her soft hands. She was usually too busy to caress me. Jackie needed her. Jackie had to be dressed and carried and fed. But I needed her love. I'd give anything to feel the touch of her hands again.

I read Sherlock Holmes, Mary Poppins, *Just So Stories,* and comic books in that room. I wrote stories and learned French there. It was my refuge, my haven, my center of the universe, when I was growing up, and if I had had my way I would never have gone outside to play. I would have stayed in my room and been completely happy. The room I work in now is blue and white.

Reluctantly, I left this small piece of my childhood and went into my mother and father's room. I caught my breath. I could almost smell my mother's scent, the Coty powder she wore, the flowerlike perfume, her nail polish. I saw her sitting in front of her vanity with the three mirrors, wearing a black-and-white velvet gown, ready to go to a party with my father.

And I saw him too. In a tuxedo, handsomer than Clark Gable. He would say, "Doesn't your mother look sharp?" and I remember that there were times when he was nice to her. Usually he told her she didn't know what she was talking about or he didn't talk to her at all. I had forgotten the way he looked at her with pride and love. I had forgotten the times they were happy together, when they seemed to love each other. Most of the time I remember only his harsh words to her, his impatience with her. Maybe he blamed her for my brother's retardation. His mother did. She once said to my mother, "Wasn't there something wrong with your sister's child?" My cousin was born prematurely, but there was nothing wrong with him.

Down the hall was my brother's room. When I walked into it, I couldn't remember it at all. I couldn't remember my brother sleeping there or playing with his cars. I couldn't see him. I know we used to play school and I would be the bossy teacher who tried to teach him to read. When he got tired of my telling him what to do, he would just leave and go out to play. But I couldn't see him. The room didn't look familiar at all.

That's the way I've usually handled my brother's mental retardation. Most of the time I blocked it out, pushed it into the back of my mind. Why did I do that?

I thanked the lady who lives in my house now and left. Afterward, I began to think about my brother and my relationship to him. Was my reaction typical? Did other siblings of people with disabilities behave the same way? Was there something wrong with me that I didn't want to think about him? I decided to find out. This book is the result of my search.

The conviction that I wanted to write a book for other siblings started when I wrote about my relationship to Jack for the *New York Times Magazine*. I received so many letters that I realized there were a lot of siblings out there who feel exactly the way I do, and who have never had a chance to talk about their experiences growing up with a brother or a sister with a disability. One woman wrote me that she felt she had lived my life. "All my life," she said, "I suffered silently with the same kind of shame and embarrassment that you experienced. I also felt terribly guilty about having those same feelings."

After a fuller version of my story appeared in *Good Housekeeping*, a mother wrote, "I am giving copies of your article to my three children who have coped and will cope with the same situation concerning their youngest sister."

I realized that there was a need for a book on this subject and I decided to write my own story about growing up with Jack, combined with the latest research on the siblings of the 43 million people in this country who have mental retardation, mental illness, or a physical disability, and most important, the experiences of other siblings like me. I found these siblings by word of mouth and through letters they wrote to me. I found them on the Internet and at parties, through friends, everywhere. I talked to men and women in all parts of the country, ranging in age from six to seventy-six. They were all eager to help me with my book, and I thank them for their honesty and generosity. They don't all feel as I do. For many, their parents gave them a feeling of compassion without the resentment I feel. Somehow they talk about their siblings with love, as if they were blessed to have such a child born into their family. They think it was the best thing that could have happened to them because it made them into strong, loving, empathetic people.

I envy them. I wish I could consider my brother's existence in our family a blessing. But I miss the brother I could have had. We would be close now. Our children would play together. We would reminisce about our parents and our childhood. We would help each other in times of trouble, laugh at our early quarrels and fights, understand each other in a way nobody else could. Perhaps it was hard because there was only my brother and me, no other siblings for me to play with, defend Jackie with, get into trouble with. The people who have other siblings besides the wounded one often come out of their childhood with less resentment and anger, with more love and compassion.

This book is for all of us—the millions of siblings like me who want to love their brothers and sisters with a disability and feel guilty when they cannot, and for the fortunate siblings whose parents helped them to love their siblings with disabilities.*

When I talked to these other siblings—over a hundred of them—I discovered that we have a lot in common. Most of us are inventive problem solvers, compassionate, tolerant, responsible, often high achievers. We also carry around a heavy load of guilt because of the anger, frustration, and resentment we still feel because we lost out on a lot of the love and attention we craved as children living with brothers and sisters who needed so much time and care. We weren't allowed to grieve for our siblings who were born wounded in some way. The brothers and sisters who can't hear us or see us or play games with us. The siblings whose minds are slow, whose bodies were broken, whose spirits were crushed. We were told: "Think how lucky

---

*Note: All the experts and siblings I talked to emphasized one important point: When you are talking about those with disabilities, be sure and put the person first and the disability second. You talk about a person who is blind—never "the blind." You say "a person with mental retardation," not "the mentally retarded" or "the disabled." In other words, don't make the disability the most important thing. Emphasize the *person*. Other people often have to be gently reminded of this.

A young woman with loss of hearing explains it this way: "There is a difference between being 'disabled' and 'having a disability.' If I am 'disabled,' that defines who I am. If I 'have a disability,' I have certain choices as to how this physical and psychological reality limits what I do and how I live. If other people recognize and respect that disability, we can work together to create ways to stretch those limits."

you are that you can go to school, have playmates, do whatever you want. You can see (or hear or think or walk). Your brother can't."

We could never complain. We could never cause any trouble—at least not until we left home. We had to be good. Our mothers had enough problems. Think how monstrous it would be to add to their constant worry, their infinite sorrow, because they bore a child who was not perfect.

As I talked to the people who contributed so much to this book (I have changed their names and identifying characteristics) they expressed a great sense of relief that they could talk about all these feelings to me. More than anything else, I want this book to give other siblings the reassurance that their feelings are normal, that we all have them, to some extent or another.

When I was a child I thought that growing up with a brother with cerebral palsy and mental retardation was just a fact of life. A fact of life that I didn't like very much. I wanted a brother who could play Monopoly with me, could climb trees with me, could talk to me. I wanted my mother to pay more attention to me and less attention to him. I wanted a normal brother.

When I was an adolescent, lost in a new city, far from my friends who had accepted my brother as different, I was ashamed of my brother, embarrassed by him. I didn't want to bring people home. I didn't want my boyfriends to see him. I thought everyone would think there was something wrong with me too.

When I was an adult, I wasn't sure whether I should marry or not. Someday I would have to take care of my brother and I wasn't sure if it was fair to burden my future husband with this. Fortunately, I met a man who wanted to marry me no matter what.

After my children were born, I saw my brother when we went to visit my parents. My daughters seemed to accept him the way children do. He was just Jackie and they chattered away at him, kissed him, hugged him. He would smile when they came to visit.

My brother could read a little, dress himself, answer questions, say what he wanted and what he didn't want. But he couldn't live alone or earn a living. He stayed with my parents until he was thirty-seven and then went to live in a home for adults with mental retardation in

Florida. My parents wanted him to be happy and settled when they died. I didn't think about him often and I didn't feel much love for him. It never occurred to me that having a brother with mental retardation shaped my whole life. But of course it had an enormous influence on me.

Once I had children of my own, I understood my mother's dilemma. She ached for me. She killed herself trying to give me enough of her time, attention, love, care. But mothers are human. There were times when I had to spend more time with a sick child than a healthy one. And my mother had to spend more time with my brother than with me.

I yearned for her love as a child. She praised every sound, every physical move, every tiny step forward, my brother made. I wanted her to praise me, too. I wanted her to lavish extravagant praise on me for my A report cards, for the stories I wrote that were published in the school newspaper, for the puppet shows I wrote and directed, for my talent as a writer. I tried harder and harder to please her. The one time she did say something fairly positive to me, I treasured her words and remember them to this day.

When I was seven, I wrote a story about Sally Skunk, pasted it on construction paper, put clips through the sides, and showed it to my mother. "Look, Mommy, I wrote a book." My mother almost smiled. "If you keep that up," she said, "you'll have a real book published someday."

The memory of those words, of her almost-praise, stayed engraved in my mind and finally, at age forty-three, I did have a book published. I wrote five more after that, but she and my father never read any of them. They said, "Oh, that's nice, dear," and put them aside. When my brother bowled with the team in the Duvall Home in Florida, my mother sent me his picture with a bowling ball and said, "Isn't that wonderful!" I barely answered her.

When I wrote articles for national magazines, got a job as an editor at a magazine, stayed thin, married a good man, and learned how to develop my own photographs, she said, "That's nice, dear," and told me Jackie was singing in the church choir in Florida. "Great," I said.

When I went to a therapist in my forties, I didn't even mention my brother except in passing. "My brother is retarded," I said and rapidly moved on to my husband and my daughter. It never occurred to me that my whole life had been shaped by having a sibling with mental retardation. "I have no feelings for my brother," I said to the therapist. "Oh, Mary," she said, "you have very strong feelings."

Even then, I had no interest in exploring those feelings. I didn't want to think about him. Didn't want to accept his influence on my life. How could he affect me? I had ignored him for most of my life. My mother felt guilty about asking me to help, about crying in front of me, about admitting that it might be a slight strain taking care of a full-grown, retarded, helpless, disturbed man every day. She never said, "I can't do this all alone. Please help me." She never complained. Should she have? Probably.

I understand my mother much better now because one of my own daughters is blind and has had a leg amputated because of the complications of diabetes. As much as I wanted more of my parents' attention, resented the fact that our family was "different," and was embarrassed by my brother's retardation, I know now how hard parents try to be fair to their healthy siblings. Sometimes you feel shattered into a dozen fragments. But although I am a parent of a child with a disability, I am writing this book as the sister of someone who is disabled.

What is it like to be the sibling of someone with mental retardation, mental illness, or a physical disability? Very little has been written about it. The study of siblings most quoted was written in 1972 by Frances Grossman, a professor of psychology at Boston University, who concluded that half the people growing up with a sibling with a disability benefited from the experience and half were harmed by it. Research done in the last ten years leans more toward the positive side of the ledger, I'm happy to say, largely because people know more about those with disabilities than they used to.

In this book, I have included the latest positive steps taken to change things for the siblings of those with a disability and for their parents. The experts I talked to are working with healthy siblings in support groups, on the Internet, and in seminars to help them understand their strong feelings and to cope with them. The educator who has been the most active in this field recently is Don Meyer, director of the Sibling Support Project at the Children's Hospital and Medical Center in Seattle. He has started sibling support groups (Sibshops) all over the country and his SibNet on the Internet is a no-holds-barred place for siblings to vent their feelings about their brothers and sisters to others who understand exactly what they mean.

While doing research, I found that with all the sibling support groups and mainstreaming of those with disabilities, we healthy siblings still don't have the opportunity to talk to others about it very often. It's one of those things nobody really understands unless he or she has been through it, too. When I meet people like me, they say, "This is the first time I've ever talked to anybody else about this." This book will fill that void.

I have divided my book into three parts: Childhood, Adolescence, and Adulthood. As I talked to other siblings and experts in this field and read the latest research that has been done, I realized that each part of our lives has its own problems, and we need different information and help according to our age.

Children mainly need someone to listen to them, someone who will talk to them in words they can understand, someone who will welcome any questions, no matter how difficult the subject is. If there is a sibling support group nearby where they can play with other children in the same situation and talk about their fears, anger, and frustration, it can be very helpful. In Part I, I also explore the effect the parents' relationship has on the healthy siblings, and the psychological significance of a sibling's place in the birth order, his or her gender, and what difference the size of the family makes.

In Part II, I discuss the way in which adolescents are more sensitive to the reactions of their peers and how they can find help dealing with rude or insensitive remarks made by friends or strangers. During the teen years, everyone wants to fit in, to be like the others. It is a time to establish one's identity. Having a sibling with a disability makes them "different," and a therapist, an understanding parent or grandparent, or a support group can help them cope.

During adulthood, which encompasses everything from marriage and children to responsibility for a sibling with a disability when parents are no longer able to do so or have died, healthy siblings need much more complicated information: how to make room in their lives for the brother or sister with the disability when they have a family of their own; how to help their own children understand why their aunt or uncle is different from other adults; how to find a suitable group home for a brother or sister; how to provide for that sibling if something should happen to them. In Part III, I address the emotional issues, and I have included an appendix of resources to help with the more practical problems.

The information included in this book came from a variety of sources: research studies on sibling relationships in families where there is a child with a disability; books written by the leading psychologists and educators in the country; interviews with these experts; interviews with other siblings whose brothers or sisters have either a physical or mental disability; and visits to sibling support groups.

Most of the books that have already been written are aimed at other professionals to summarize the research that has been done, to help therapists counsel the healthy siblings, or to set up support groups. This book is for all of you siblings out there who want to hear my story and the stories of others like us. How have we coped with our ambivalent feelings, our anger and guilt? How has it affected our lives as adults? Are we more at risk for psychiatric difficulties than those who don't grow up with someone with a disability? Are the latest studies reassuring or pessimistic about our chances for happiness?

I have called this book *Special Siblings* to refer to those of us who do *not* have a disability as well as the ones who do. Our brothers and sisters with disabilities are often called "special"–even their Olympics are "special"–but I think it's important to point out that we are all special. I hope this book will show the rest of the world the qualities that make us that way.

I don't think I'm a bad person. I know I'm more sensitive, loving, and caring than I would have been if I hadn't had such a troublesome childhood. But if I come back again, I hope I don't have a brother like Jackie. I hope my parents love each other. I hope I have brothers and sisters who are normal.

PART 1

Childhood

1

YOUR NEEDS

I came into this world at the end of the jazz age and the beginning of the Depression. The only picture I have of me as a baby shows me more jazzy than depressed. I'm fat and happy, ready to jump out of my carrying basket and take on the world. When I look at that photograph of me at six months, I want to take that baby and run out of the house and find a place with no tension, no sorrow, no constant worry, anxiety, and grief. Maybe there's no such place, but I would love to have had the chance to grow up somewhere else.

All the other photographs of me were taken after my brother was diagnosed with cerebral palsy and mental retardation. He was born when I was two and diagnosed when I was three. In later pictures, there is not a glimmer of a smile on my face. Serious, solemn, such a sad child.

I don't know if that happy baby turned into that somber child because of my brother's disability or because my parents' marriage was almost destroyed by it. I just remember such tension and anger, such anxiety and worry, in that house. I must have thought I had done something wrong, as children often do.

My parents were good people. All they wanted was a chance to work, live in a house in the suburbs, have children, and be happy. My father was an electrical engineer, educated at MIT and Harvard on scholarships. His whole career was at Bell Laboratories, where he was a cable specialist who helped plan the first transatlantic telephone cable between England and the United States. The oldest of five children, my mother grew up on a farm in Maryland, went to New York when she was eighteen, and met my father when she worked as a secretary in his office.

When I was three, my parents bought the house in Short Hills, then a very small, quiet town way out on the commuter line. My brother Jackie was a year old, and by then my parents suspected that he would never be a normal child.

At first, he seemed like a perfectly healthy, beautiful little boy with white-blond hair, big blue eyes, and a smile that made you want to hug him. Then, gradually, my mother began to suspect that something was wrong. He didn't respond the way I had. "Don't worry," the pediatrician said, "boys always develop more slowly than girls." Still my mother knew there was something wrong. A mother's instinct beats a doctor's denial every time.

Feeding him one day, tears rolling down her cheeks, she said, "Oh, Jackie, you should be sitting up by now." Then, during his regular checkup, the doctor noticed that Jackie's feet turned in when he sat up.

"How long has he been sitting like that?" he asked sharply.

My mother's heart stopped. "For two months," she said.

"I think we have trouble here," he said, and all our lives changed forever.

After a series of tests, my brother's diagnosis was cerebral palsy with mental retardation—"spastic paralysis" it was called in those days.

When I was older and my mother could talk to me about such things, she told me Jackie's retardation was caused at the time of his birth. She said she was in the hospital and the baby started to come before the doctor arrived.*

I wish I could bring my mother back for a while and ask her to tell me how she could stand it when she found out that my brother would never be a normal child. After she died, I found her diary in which she had made a few entries. I pictured her young and healthy

---

*In those days an obstetrician didn't get his full fee if he wasn't there for the delivery, and my mother thinks the nurses held the baby back until the doctor arrived, resulting in a hemorrhage, which stopped the flow of oxygen to my brother's brain just long enough to cause his retardation.

and strong, married to a man she loved, the happy mother of a bright little girl and a ten-month-old baby.

"It was noticed that Jack evidently was suffering from some kind of injury," she wrote. "He was a perfectly splendid baby in every way. His food agreed with him and he behaved beautifully. He cut his first tooth at four months and all the rest came right along with no trouble at all. But at nine months he was not trying to pull himself up or get around."

At fifteen months Jack began saying a few words and, my mother wrote, "He would put his arms around us to hug us, particularly Mary. He also liked to mimic Mary when she was making faces or funny noises."

I can see him. That little boy with the sweet face imitating me. He was almost four before he walked. My mother never gave up. She went to doctor after doctor, consulted expert after expert, persuaded schools to take him in, found tutors to help him. But the older he grew, the more disparity there was between him and other children his age.

My mother was like many other mothers who find out there is something wrong with their child. She could not accept it. There had to be something she could do, some doctor who could fix everything, some way to help this child grow up to be normal.

I felt my mother's deep sorrow inside me and there was nothing I could do for her. Later in my life I would feel that same helpless grief when one of my own children became blind, and I couldn't stop it from happening. There is nothing more terrible than not being able to keep harm away from your child. And for a sibling, there is nothing more painful than watching your mother's heart break because one of her children is wounded.

IDENTIFYING WITH A MOTHER'S GRIEF

Psychologists tell us that a child can identify too strongly with her mother's anguish. She may develop an obsessive concern about her sibling with the disability and not want to leave her side to go to school or play with other children. Jennifer is like that. Eleven years

old, she is a little mother to her brother, who is deaf, blind, and profoundly retarded.

"I feed him and sit there and watch him so if he needs something,
I can get it," the little girl says. "Sometimes he cries because he's lonely
and I feel bad because we can't give him all the attention he wants. I
try to make him happy. Last week I felt so bad I didn't want to go to
school because he was having seizures on and off, every five minutes,
and I just wanted to be there with him because if anything happens,
I know what to do."

Debra Lobato, a developmental psychologist at Rhode Island Hospital, with a special interest in the siblings of children with a disability,
urges parents to do something right away if they see their healthy
siblings developing unhealthy concerns. She advises getting the child
out of the house for a while, away from the sibling who is ill. No
matter what, Dr. Lobato says in her book *Brothers, Sisters, and Special
Needs*, a mother or father should set a regular time to take the child
out and not talk about the sick sibling. The idea is to break the pattern
of obsession.

THE NEED FOR ATTENTION

A child's time alone with a parent goes a long way toward easing
the resentment a healthy sibling feels because the mother or father is
no longer concentrating on him. This happens whenever a new baby
is born, of course, but a sick baby greatly increases the amount of time
the mother must spend with him.

One of the best things my mother did was to take Jackie and me
to Children's Hospital in Boston to see Dr. Bronson Crothers, a pediatrician light-years ahead of his time in his understanding of children
with disabilities. He worked with a psychologist, Dr. Elisabeth Lord,
who also understood my needs as well as Jack's. I wish these two
doctors were still alive so I could talk to them and tell them how much
they helped all of us.

My mother would make that long drive to Boston once a year
over bumpy roads, before there were superhighways. I remember the
ten-hour trip through small towns and cities, stopping by the side of

the road to eat the sandwiches my mother brought. When I was sleepy, I would lay my head on her lap and take a nap. Every once in a while, she would take her hand off the wheel and gently touch my hair. Jackie was asleep in the back.

We stayed with my father's mother while we were in Boston. She was a mean old lady who was about forty when my father was born, so she seemed ancient to me. I can still see that white-haired old lady with a huge hearing aid that hung on the front of her dress. To entertain me, she would show me a little box of her treasures: a lock of my father's baby hair, a tiny wooden heart that she said was given to her by a man she loved (not my grandfather evidently), and the white ribbon from her wedding bouquet.

I used to sleep in a room with a white marble bust of Queen Victoria looking down at me disapprovingly. She's in my office now as I write this, reminding me of my grandmother, of my mother and father, of my little brother who couldn't help the way he was.

My favorite part of the trip was the visit to the hospital where Jack and I could play with the toys in a brightly lit room next to the doctor's office. We didn't know it, but there was a camera behind the glass window of the playroom that took movies of the interaction between my brother and me. As usual, I headed right for the books or the dolls, while Jack played with the cars. There were small chairs, child-size tables, cookies, and milk. The colors were vivid, cheerful. Blue and red blocks, yellow walls, orange chairs. Every once in a while the psychologist would come in and try to get me to play a game with Jack, to do a puzzle with him, to read to him. I liked reading to him for a while, but I would soon get impatient with my brother and go back to my table of books.

Dr. Lord was watching all this behind the one-way window and she would counsel my mother when she saw signs of trouble. I never hit my brother, but when he didn't understand what I wanted, I would slam a toy on the floor or punch the doll I was playing with. Dr. Lord helped my mother understand my frustration and suggested ways she could cope with my anger. My mother remembered her words many years later and told me what she had said.

"Mary doesn't understand why you have to spend so much time

with Jackie," Dr. Lord said. "It makes her angry, but she doesn't know why. Try to take time just for her. When you have a half hour free from Jack, take her on your lap and read her a story. Let her help you make cookies. Do anything just to give her your attention. She needs to know you still love her. I know you're worried about Jackie and want to do all you can for him, but Mary needs you too."

In those early years, I remember feeling that I had lost the mother I knew. She would look at me without seeing me. She didn't smile anymore. She always looked worried. I wanted my other mother back again.

How I wish my parents had picked me up, hugged me, and said, "We're worried about Jackie right now, but we love you very much and if you will just be patient, your turn will come." Because they didn't know how to do this, I crave love now. I *need* people to like me. I keep looking for that love and approval, the attention and understanding I wanted from my parents.

Many of the other siblings I talked to feel exactly the same way. "I felt so left out," they tell me. They say they needed someone to explain what was going on. Their whole world had changed. Everyone was sad and angry, but they didn't know why. They just wanted someone to tell them it wasn't anything they had done and that everything was going to be all right.

Even with the knowledge we have now that helps parents give their other children the extra attention they need, siblings of all ages still mention that they miss the time and love their busy parents cannot give them because of a sibling with a disability.

Ahadi was five when her sister with epilepsy was born. She remembers standing in the doorway with a blanket wrapped around her when they took her sister away in an ambulance after her first seizure at eight months. Now in her twenties, she mourns her lost childhood, too. "It's not just that I lost my mother's attention—you always lose that when a new sibling is born," she says. "But a great deal of my life was consumed by my sister's illness. I often woke up in the middle of the night to be sure she was all right. I went to the hospital with my mother, and later when my mother was with her in the hospital, I tried to take care of the house and myself as well.

"You're not only losing a parent, you're also losing some of your own time and your own experience as a child. I did lose an aspect of my childhood—some of the carefreeness. Most of my friends have never even been in a hospital. You realize that your life is so different."

Every mother and father is busy and sometimes unable to give children their full attention. But the difference in a family with a child with a disability is that the parents, especially mothers, focus almost their entire attention on the sick child. It's a focus so intense there is no getting through to them. Sometimes parents *must* concentrate that intensely on a child who is ill, of course, but it is very hard for the healthy child to accept. There's a vast difference between the way the parents acted before the child was born or got sick or was injured and the way things are afterward. The grim concentration on the child with the disability often takes away the laughter and the spontaneity that was there before.

Janet, a woman in her forties whose sister has mental retardation, says, "I feel like we were sacrificed for my sister because we could take care of ourselves. I was only eighteen months old when my sister was born. When my niece was that age, it was really difficult for me to see her because I would say to myself, 'That's how old I was when my sister was born. I was just a baby who needed her mother just as much as she ever did. I shouldn't have been on my own.'"

We all wish our parents had said they loved us more. But it's especially important to the sibling of a child with a disability. You sometimes get the feeling that you're just in the way, that your parents are so busy with the sick child that they wish you weren't there. A child is so attuned to the approval or disapproval of her mother and father that every time a parent brushes by a healthy sibling to take care of the one with the disability, it feels like the parent doesn't love her.

Often a mother is totally unaware that she is paying more attention to the child with the disability. She wants so desperately to be fair to each child in the family that she turns off some of the signals that alert her to the fact that the healthy child is being shortchanged. In an interesting study conducted in 1994 by psychologist Alexandra Quitt-ner and graduate student Lisa Opipari, mothers of children with cystic fibrosis reported that there was absolutely no difference in the amount of time they devoted to their healthy siblings and to their sick ones. But the diaries they were asked to keep listing their daily activities contradicted their oral interviews. It was clear they spent more time with the child with cystic fibrosis–not just in medical treatments but during playtime and at mealtime too. The control group of mothers who did not have a child with cystic fibrosis said quite matter-of-factly that of course they had to spend more time with a younger child. That meals took longer, toilet training took time, dressing the younger child was time consuming. They had no illusions that sometimes you must favor one child over the other.

In a follow-up study of older children, Dr. Quittner found that the healthy siblings in the cystic fibrosis families were affected by the fact that their mothers had to spend more time with their sick brothers and sisters. These children fought with their siblings more, were more likely to be anxious and depressed, and were disruptive in school.

"It's important for health care professionals to emphasize the fact that in *all* families, mothers and fathers sometimes treat children differently for a variety of reasons–age differences, developmental differences, personality differences," Dr. Quittner told me. "There's nothing wrong with spending more time with a sick child when you have to. But it's also important to try to find ways of spending extra time with the siblings who are healthy to make up for it. Let them know they are important. Ask for help from grandparents and friends. Look for ways to give them special attention."

When siblings can't find the love and attention they need at home, they often look for it elsewhere–from a teacher, a minister, a best friend. Allie, whose sister has Down syndrome, remembers that she and her two sisters found it in other people's families. "We all spent a lot of time with a friend's family. I was looking for an Ozzie and Harriet kind of home. My two sisters did the same thing. We practically lived in someone else's house."

Most parents *do*, of course, love all their children, but sometimes they don't take the time to show their love. Often, just a few minutes spent with a "normal" child alone makes her feel loved. When I asked siblings to tell me the moments they remembered most vividly as children, they always told me about the times a parent spent just with them without the child with the disability. One woman remembered a special, brief time spent with her mother when she was a child.

"There were five children in our family, including my sister with cerebral palsy," she said. "My mother was always busy, but I remember just as if it were yesterday the only walk my mother ever took with me. I was five years old. My mother was busy making dinner—I remember she had her apron on—but she took me down to the creek to go alligator hunting. We lived in New Jersey, so this was a totally fanciful thing, but it meant so much to me. It probably took ten minutes while Mom had the meatloaf in the oven. Just a short time, but I remember it to this day."

There was one place in the world where I could find the attention and approval I craved—school. I loved school. It was a place away from our house and Jackie and the worry and tension. I could read and write stories about "bad" children who learned to be good. I could be the narrator in the Christmas pageant. I could be Queen Isabella in a play I wrote about Columbus, and wear a deep purple velvet dress made out of my mother's old evening gown. I could shine in the classroom and bask in the warmth of my teachers' approval. Even in first grade, though, I knew I always had to be good, and I worried that I might not live up to the expectations everyone had for me. No child should have to worry about that at the age of six.

THE NEED TO ACHIEVE

The feeling that you must make it up to your parents for having a child who cannot achieve is a very powerful force in the lives of many children growing up with a sibling with a disability, especially if the healthy sibling is the only other child. That force can indeed lead to great achievements, but there is often a price to be paid. One study by S. V. Coleman in 1990 found that as "academic achievement increased, the self-concept (of the healthy siblings) decreased." The same study found a greater need to achieve among the siblings of people with mental retardation than those with physical disabilities.

This pressure to succeed may come from our own internal need to get attention by being "good," or from our parents. Parents may push their healthy children subtly by praising good grades above every-thing else, or not so subtly by spelling out their expectations.

Lydia's mother was explicit about her expectations for her daugh-ter. Lydia's brother was born with cerebral palsy, and she remembers vividly one Saturday she spent with her mother when she was six years old. It was always special to have time alone with her mother, and she had no idea what was coming. This is the way she describes that day in an article in *Glamour*:

> On the Saturday before I started first grade, my mother took me for an ice cream sundae. I should have known something was up, because she told me uncharacteristically that I could get all the extra goop I wanted. As I sat in that orange vinyl booth at Howard Johnson, digging into the extra hot fudge and cherries, she told me to listen very carefully to what she had to say.
>
> "You were born with the ability to do anything you want," she began slowly. "To ever do less than your best would be like throwing away a very precious gift."
>
> I remember thinking I must have done something terribly wrong, and now she was trying to make sure it would never happen again. I wanted to ask what I'd done, but felt too embarrassed. I stopped eating. "You may not understand ex-actly what I mean now," she continued emphatically. "But do anything less than your best and I will be greatly disap-pointed."
>
> It was a powerful charge for a six-year-old. And she was right—though I didn't understand her underlying message at the time—its meaning became all too clear as I grew older: You have to excel at everything because your brother can't.

Your parents don't always tell you as explicitly as Lydia's mother what they expect, but somehow you figure it out. Ginny knew instinctively that she must be the achiever in a family of three children, where one brother had mental retardation and the other dropped out of college. "I felt strongly that I had to be the good one," she says. "I was only ten and I remember saying to my mother, 'Well, Mom, I guess I'd better go to college. I'd better be good. I have one brother who has mental retardation and one brother who has dropped out, so I'll have to be the good one.' My mother said I didn't have to go to college if I didn't want to, but I still felt the pressure to go. As a compromise, I took a year off after high school and then went to college. I understood how hard it would be for my father and mother if I didn't go. I love my parents and I wanted to please them."

Ahadi, who watched her little sister suffer through epileptic seizures, grew up to attend Yale Law School and work for a Ph.D. in political science. She sees her need to achieve as having different roots:

> I think perhaps I am motivated to achieve because I never had this concept of immortality that a lot of people my age have. I remember people in high school playing stupid games with cars, which I thought were dumb because I knew what it would be like if you did survive an accident. I think my drive is partly because of never knowing in my heart of hearts whether something might happen to me. Maybe my time wasn't when I was a child but my time will be when I'm older.

THE NEED FOR INFORMATION

In addition to the need to achieve, we siblings have a hunger for information about our brother's or sister's disability. When we are very young, we need to know the basics: "What's going on here? What happened to the new baby? Why are you always going to the hospital? Why didn't the new baby come home when Mommy did? Why can't the baby see when her eyes look just like mine? Will I catch it? Did I do anything bad that made him sick? Why is everybody so sad and angry and tired? Aren't you ever going to play with me again the way you used to? Why don't you read me a story anymore when I go to bed? Why do you push me away when I try to hug you? Why are you always telling me to be quiet?"

Later on, when we can understand more, we want information that is clear, structured, and definite. No vague, simplistic answers. We want our parents to help us find the books, magazine articles, videos, and professional counseling to give us specific answers to our questions. Something like:

Your brother has a disease called _____. The symptoms are
_____. He will need an injection of _____ every day. He
will always have this disease. These are ways in which you can
help with the management of the disease. Doctors tell us he will
probably be able to _____ as he grows older. He will never
be able to _____. We have made the following provisions
for your brother when we are not here to care for him...

We need to be armed with specific information so we can explain
to our friends exactly what is wrong with our siblings. It will make
them more comfortable if they understand the limitations and abilities
of our brothers and sisters. It takes the mystery, and therefore the fear,
out of the situation.

Fortunately, times have changed since my own parents' silence
about Jackie. We know so much more now about how children learn
and what they are able to absorb at different ages that the healthy
siblings need no longer wonder what is going on in the family when
a child with a disability is born.

Dr. Lobato explained to me the different techniques she advises
parents to use with their healthy children to help them understand:

> Just as you say "I love you" to an infant before she can un-
> derstand what you are saying, parents should start explaining
> a sibling's disability, trying to put it in words that a three-year-
> old will understand. They should tell the child their own re-
> actions at a very concrete level, trying to be matter of fact
> about it, if possible. If parents are very emotional, I encourage
> them to practice until they can give children the information
> they need in an unemotional manner.
>
> I work with parents whose kids have cancer, whose kids
> were born with a disability, or who acquired an injury later
> on. They're thrown into it, and they don't know where to
> start.
>
> For example, the parents of the child with cancer can't
> say the word "cancer." They get choked up. They can't say
> the words "mental retardation." So they approach the healthy
> child carrying all their personal concerns about a particular
> word or diagnosis. The child comes to understand that word
> as being something that causes tension.

What I encourage parents to do is first rehearse how they can have a conversation with their child. I tell them to constantly make comments about the way people are. "That woman has lovely blond hair." "This child is using a brace on her right leg." It's not a value judgment. It just gets the child used to the idea that her family talks about behavior and characteristics of people. Or parents can ask them questions, "How do you think that little boy in the waiting room feels when he uses that machine?" They don't have to answer the question, but they are setting a tone for the child that it's all right to talk about it.

Because the thinking of a four- to seven-year-old child is so different from the thinking of an eight- to twelve-year-old, they won't even remember what they learned at the age of four. It's the process that is most important. A parent might say, "Your sister has what some people call mental retardation and others call a developmental disability." Then if the child hears those words outside the home, she understands what people are talking about. Parents should make talking about a disability a natural, easy thing for the child to do.

Children eight to twelve are much more aware of the reactions of other children to their sibling with a disability. Dr. Lobato helps them figure out what to say when someone says something derogatory about a brother or sister. She says:

I work with kids to fortify them, and I think it does them no service to pussyfoot around words that other kids are going to throw at them in school or in the street. I get them to rehearse what they will say. They run the gamut from explaining in a very diplomatic way, "Well, my brother was born that way," to "I would just punch him in the nose and say 'don't use that word.'" I'm trying to help them find a response that they feel comfortable with.

Kids around twelve are sensitive to even minor differences. If they don't have the right pants or the right shoes, they feel vulnerable to peer rejection. So if they also have a brother or sister who might do something offensive, it puts them on the defense.

Children under the age of eight especially need information about their siblings with a disability because they interpret everything personally. They often think something they have done or said caused some catastrophic event in the family—such as the illness or disability of a new baby. They think they caused the drastic change in the atmosphere in the family because they were bad. They need to be reassured they haven't done anything wrong. One of the saddest stories I heard was about a little boy who thought he had caused his baby sister's blindness by kissing her on the eyes when she was born. "I made the baby sick," he said. His mother had no idea he was carrying this horror around with him until she heard him talking to a counselor.

Sometimes children are afraid that they too will develop a disability. Psychologists call it "magical thinking." One little girl thought she might have epileptic seizures if she stood too close to her sister.

A child keeps many of her fears to herself because she's afraid people will laugh at her or tell her she's stupid. One five-year-old boy thought his mother gave birth to a child with mental retardation because she ate a pickle when she was pregnant. A little girl was sure that God knew whenever she was mean to her sister who had autism. "I thought God put her there to test me," she says. "No one explained anything to me."

When parents don't give their children a chance to ask questions, don't set the tone in the family that no subject is taboo, it affects the way a healthy child reacts to his brother or sister with a disability for the rest of his life. He may resent his sibling without understanding why. He may be more subject to depression and anxiety because of all the unanswered, repressed questions he carried around as a child and adolescent. He may think of his sibling with the disability as a burden, as the person who changed the family from "normal" to "different." Open, frank communication gives the sibling the feeling of participation in the management of the disability, a healthy interest in ways in which the family can work together to lighten the load of everyday household chores and medical treatments.

WHY PARENTS HAVE DIFFICULTY TALKING ABOUT DISABILITIES

There are many reasons why your parents may not be able to talk to you about your brother or sister with the disability. They may be reluctant to discuss it because they want to maintain the illusion of normalcy to themselves and the rest of the world. They want to believe that this situation is not really as bad as they think it is, that somehow things will get better with time, that there was a mistake in the diagnosis, that researchers will discover a cure for whatever the child has. If they say, even to themselves, "This is a hopeless situation. We are going to have a terrible life because this child will never walk or talk or feed himself or dress himself," they have given up before they even try, and most parents refuse to do that.

Some psychologists use Dr. Elisabeth Kübler-Ross's five stages of grief—denial, anger, bargaining, withdrawal, and acceptance—to explain parents' reactions to the serious illness of a child. They tell us their reluctance to discuss the disability honestly and openly with their healthy siblings is because they are stuck in the first stage—denial. Allison's mother is a good example of that.

Allison, a thirty-six-year-old real estate broker from Dallas, with a sister with Down syndrome, remembers her mother saying to her when she was a child, "We really have no idea what Down syndrome is. It's a complicated set of symptoms that means that your sister is good at some things and bad at others, slow in some areas and needs more time to learn. To say that she is retarded and has Down syndrome is a mistake because that would mean reacting to her in a single way."

"To this day—she's thirty-eight now—my sister has never been formally told that she has mental retardation," Allison says. "You can imagine how confusing that was for me. I knew there was something wrong with my sister, but my mother was telling me she was fine. I didn't know how to deal with it when I was with my friends."

Other parents may find any discussion of the disability so painful that they avoid the whole subject or answer a healthy sibling's questions so minimally that it is clear that this isn't a subject to pursue.

Jennifer's mother could not bear to talk about her child who couldn't walk, think, talk, or see. She knew that Jennifer was very bright and assumed that she would understand all by herself. But Jennifer was only five when Jimmy was born. How could she understand the loss of her mother's attention, the tension in the household, the arguments between her mother and father, her father's anger, her mother's grief? Because her mother's signal was, "I don't want to talk about this," Jennifer kept her questions and fears to herself, and as a result is overly worried and protective of her little brother, as I discussed earlier in this chapter. Children need to be able to ask.

Theresa *did* ask questions about her brother Daniel's autism, but her parents had to get through their own pain before they could help their daughter. Theresa was only six when her brother's illness was diagnosed. Until he was three, he talked, responded, seemed to be a normal child. But then he regressed and Theresa was heartbroken. Daniel began to lose the words that he had learned, and worst of all, he rejected his sister. Theresa did not understand. She kept crying, "Why doesn't he want me? Why won't he play with me? What did I do?"

Theresa kept asking questions. Her mother Evelyn did her best to reassure her. "Of course he loves you," she said. "But it's hard for him to show it right now."

"It took a long time to get our lives back on track," Theresa's mother said. "Just as everyone remembers the moment he heard that Kennedy was assassinated, I remember vividly the day the doctor first said the words 'life-long disability' to me. It was a long time before I could have a conversation without crying. I think that's probably true with anybody in a situation which causes you so much pain. If you're going to help somebody else through it, you have to get to a certain place yourself first."

With her parents' help, Theresa has come to terms with her brother's autism. This is the poem she wrote about him:

MY BROTHER
by Theresa Basile

No one understands him.
No one knows what's on his mind.

He is very secretive. He can't say how he feels.
He wants to
but he can't.
With chestnut brown hair
and bright blue eyes,
and a happy, cheerful face,
he laughs like a baby boy.
Sometimes his face is a dark, rainy cloud,
but sometimes a bright yellow sun.
Sometimes he giggles and runs around
and sometimes he sobs
hiccuping, gulping sobs,
for a very long time.
My brother, Daniel
is his own twin.

You may not have received the information you needed when you were a child, but whatever age you are now, you can learn much more about your siblings with a disability than I could when I was little. You can join a sibling support group, where you can often find out answers to your questions from other siblings. You can go to SibNet on your computer and ask experts and others like you for information. You might be able to persuade your parents to talk to you about your family situation. Get them to face the problems that loom in the future when they are no longer around.

One of the primary needs of all children is a family where the mother and father have a good strong marriage, but when there is a child with a disability in the family, that need is more important than ever.

2

YOUR PARENTS' MARRIAGE

*M*y mother knocked herself out trying to follow the advice of the doctor and psychologist in Boston and give Jack and me what we needed, as well as taking care of my father, who was a difficult, demanding, often selfish man, who hadn't a clue about what to do with a child who had mental retardation. He was silent, grim, locked deep in his own grief and worry. He always seemed angry, and as children often do, I thought he was angry at me. I was afraid of him and at the same time I adored him. I thought he was the handsomest, smartest, funniest, most wonderful father anyone ever had. But I bit my nails and had stomachaches after the long, silent meals at the dinner table. My mother told me later that he often stopped talking to her for two weeks at a time and she had no idea why.

YOUR FAMILY'S "PROBLEM-SOLVING STYLE"

Experts refer to "the family problem-solving style" as one of the determining factors in the health of a household. One researcher, D. Baumrind, identifies three types of parenting: authoritarian, authoritative, and permissive. Our family's style was definitely authoritarian. I was supposed to keep quiet, to pretend there was no problem. There was never any discussion. My father laid down the law and that was it. "You're just a little potato," he would say. I learned to shut up, to keep my feelings to myself.

That's the way I react today. Instead of speaking up when something bothers me, I stifle my feelings just as my mother did. Then I explode over some irrelevant issue.

I remember long periods of silence in our house. A tense, angry silence from my father. A crushed, hurt silence from my mother. I didn't know why my father was angry and neither did my mother. I thought I had done something wrong. And to this day, if everything isn't going well, I assume it's my fault.

How much of my father's anger was because he had a son with retardation? How much was because he drank too much before dinner? How much was disappointment that his life was all grim responsibility? There is no way to prepare a man for a son who is brain damaged. How could he cope with it? His way was to numb his brain with alcohol and golf. Never to talk about it.

Drinking turns up in a lot of the stories I heard when I talked to other siblings for this book. Tracy, a twenty-six-year-old stockbroker living in Chicago whose sister has mental and physical disabilities, became an alcoholic when she was eleven, just as her father was becoming sober.

"I think one of the reasons I started drinking," she says, "was because I had been holding our family together for so long that I was burned out. It was like I knew that my father had stopped drinking so it was okay for me to fall apart."

Tracy became sober in her teens and it strengthened the bond with her father. "I respect and love him deeply. We're very much alike. We even look alike. I can talk to him about business and about sobriety—it's sort of like we have a 'topic' relationship. He's close to my sister now, but while she was growing up, he was very much hands off. He goes to visit her in her apartment now, and he calls her on her attempts to manipulate him, but he finally understands that he cares about her, which is just amazing because he had almost no relationship with her before.

"My mom and I have a much different relationship. I took care of her emotionally when I was growing up. I don't think my mom has ever been my mom. I think she has been a friend and that's not always good. I was her pal in trouble more than her daughter."

My mother would never have dreamed of turning to me for any

kind of help—emotional or otherwise. She yearned for my father to help her with Jack, but she didn't know how to ask. She thought he should offer. It didn't help that the psychologist in Boston told her to "keep everything on an even keel." So my mother turned herself inside out trying to keep the household calm. Everything had to be pleasant—no fighting, no arguments, no screaming. I learned this lesson well.

In my mother's day, doctors almost always advised parents to put a child with a disability in an institution, and many followed that advice. When I was doing research for this book, I came across a paper written by Dr. Groves B. Smith in 1937.

"I feel that in the beginning all these children should be removed from the home," he said. "The oversolicitude of the parents during the actual illness is one factor. In the majority of these children, there is this abnormality of behavior which the average parent doesn't understand."

This doctor represented the thinking of the 1930s. I was surprised to find out that it persisted for several decades after that. Paul, a forty-nine-year-old lawyer, remembers the agony his parents went through in 1965 when they reluctantly decided to place their baby with Down syndrome in foster care rather than bringing her home to a house with four other siblings. Paul was sixteen when Patty was born, and the prevailing attitude of most doctors and counselors at that time was the same as it was when Jackie was born.

"My parents consulted our rabbi," he says, "who advised them to place my sister in a foster home because my little brother was only four and all the energy devoted to Patty would take away from my brother's development. My other siblings were much older. Later on, I found out that the rabbi had a secret of his own. He had a child with Down syndrome in a state institution.

"My parents definitely did not want to put my sister in an institution, especially the one in our state which was infamous for its treatment of those with retardation. And they didn't want to jeopardize my brother's future. So they found a foster home for her, where she lived for six years before returning home to live. It was very difficult for them to make that decision, and I know they have wondered whether it was the right thing to do many times."

The doctors didn't diagnose my own brother's cerebral palsy until he was almost a year old and by then, my parents would never have considered putting him in an institution. When my brother was in his teens, my mother investigated several state and private institutions to place him in when my parents were older, but she considered them totally unacceptable. All my life she would say to me, "Mary, I don't want Jack to go into a state institution—*ever*." And he never will.

Today, with early intervention programs that help parents cope with a child with a disability right from birth, the tendency is to keep a child at home unless his behavior seriously disrupts the household or if he needs more care than a mother can provide. In many states there is respite care that entitles families to a certain amount of help per month so that a mother will have more time for her other children. They provide trained people who will come in to help.

There are also community resources to help parents now. They can contact the special education department at a college nearby and find students who welcome the chance to sit with children who have the same problems they will encounter later in their teaching. Sometimes student nurses are available.

But my mother had no one to turn to. She was doing her best to keep everything "normal," struggling to find ways to help her broken child and trying to follow the psychologist's advice to give me extra attention and love. And all the while she was dealing with a husband who withdrew into Scotch and soda and weekend golf, with one child who couldn't quite understand what was happening around him, and a daughter who tried so hard to be good she felt as if her smile was frozen on her face.

It is to my mother's great credit that our house was often full of their friends laughing, drinking, dancing, playing bridge, eating dinner, trimming the Christmas tree, playing Ping-Pong. It was the Depression, so dinner could be scrambled eggs and bacon or hot dogs, but I remember the laughter the most. My parents' friends accepted the tragedy of Jackie's mental retardation and when I ask them today what they thought about our household from hell, they tell me, "Your mother was wonderful. Always smiling and gracious. You would never have known she carried such a heavy burden. She was the one who helped me when my husband lost his job. She was the one who offered to help when one of my children was sick. I don't think your father was able to cope with the whole situation, so your mother handled it all."

If my parents' marriage had been better, I would have had an easier time growing up with a sibling with mental retardation. But my parents rarely talked to each other except for an impatient "You don't know what you're talking about!" from my father or a "What time will you be finished playing golf?" from my mother. They hardly ever sat down and had a conversation about anything. There was no easing of the tension in our household because a child with cerebral palsy and mental retardation lived there. No attempts to solve problems together. No understanding that I might have a few questions.

MARRIAGES IN TROUBLE

When I asked one "normal" sibling whether she would have preferred not to have a brother with mental retardation, she said, "What I really wanted was for my parents to have a good marriage. My brother's disability drove them farther and farther apart until they finally divorced. I don't think the marriage was very good in the first place."

In the few studies done on the marital relationships in a family with a child with a disability, the conclusions are just what you would expect. If the parents fight most of the time, are hostile and aggressive toward one another, the children in the family will follow their example. Boys, it seems, are more likely to be aggressive in their behavior toward the sibling with the disability and their own peers.

Girls, as you might expect, tend to become withdrawn and anxious. None of this is exactly startling news, but it does help us understand how much our relationship with our sibling with the disability is affected by the way our parents treat us. Often parents take out their frustration, anger, and fear on healthy siblings, not only because of the brother or sister who is sick, but also because their marriage is in trouble. Marital unhappiness leads to "increased punitiveness, decreased use of reasoning as a discipline strategy and fewer parental rewards," according to researchers Zolinda Stoneman and Phyllis Waldman Berman.

It takes a strong marriage to withstand the drastic changes in daily living that occur when a child is born with a serious disability. When any baby is born, it affects the marriage because the mother's time is taken up with the new child—time that she used to spend with her husband. So you can imagine the amount of time a child with an illness can take up. That's hard for a man to deal with. He has lost much of his wife's companionship and he has lost the healthy child he expected to enrich his life. The mother has lost too, of course, but somehow she is expected to cope and handle her marriage, a child who needs her twenty-four hours a day, and the other siblings. Many of the siblings I talked to mentioned the strain on their parents' marriage, and many said their fathers left because of it.

There is often a clash between the mother who is determined to help her child with the disability achieve his full potential and the father who resents the time and energy she takes away from him. Gwen's parents were divorced partly because of the battle of wills that took place after her brother's autism was diagnosed. Gwen, a twenty-three-year-old special education teacher in Baltimore, describes the struggle between her parents:

> My mother devoted her energy entirely to Simon because he needed twenty-four hours of attention. She was determined to get him to stop being self-abusive, to get him to speak and communicate, to bring him into the world and help him be a functioning member of society, to give him integrity and dignity. My father was left out of the loop. He's one of those people who is not very social to begin with. He isn't good with kids at all. He loved me, but he didn't enjoy the grunt work of bringing up his children.
>
> My mother taught Simon sign language and that was another thing that further separated my parents. She and Simon could connect, but my father wouldn't learn to sign, so he was left out. I'll never forget the first time Simon communicated with us. My mother taught him how to indicate, "I want," by putting one hand on top of his fist. One night we were sitting

at the dinner table and Simon pointed to the freezer and made that sign for the first time. My mother cried, and the next day she went to school to learn signing. My father was removed from all that.

I think my father is the biggest unresolved anger I have. That is something I need to work on. He and my mother were divorced when I was four, partly because he couldn't handle having a son with autism and my mother was totally involved in the fight to help her child in every way she could. My father says the most insensitive, uncaring things to my brother and I can't stand it, but I try to restrain my anger with him. I have a long way to go in dealing with this.

My own parents' marriage lasted until my father died, but the stresses on that marriage were tremendous. Perhaps they would have divorced if my brother had not been mentally retarded, but my father was too responsible to leave my mother with that burden.

Family counselor Lois Bonnell told me, "Marriages seem to go from one extreme to another. The couple are either closer because they are working together on this problem and are supportive of one another, or it divides them to the point where they get divorced."

I've concentrated on marriages that were in trouble because of a sibling with a disability. There are, of course, many marriages that not only survive but are strengthened by a child with special needs. Usually that's because the father in the family is supportive and loving and doesn't expect his wife to carry the full load. Shelley talks about her parents' marriage with pride, but has reservations about the support group her mother went to when her severely disabled son was a baby.

My mom and dad have a good marriage, but Mom needed a little help dealing with a child who was so sick all the time. She went to a support group for the mothers of children with disabilities, and the first woman she met said to her, "Oh, you're new here. How old is your child?"

"A year and a half," Mom said.

"He's still young," the woman said. "Just wait. Are you married?"

"Yes," Mom said.

"You won't be for long," said the woman and walked away.

"And that was a support meeting!" Shelley says, shaking her head and laughing.

FATHERS

I often think now that I'm older, how hard it must have been for my father to realize that his only son, named after him, would never be able to go to college, or have a family, or be a comfort to him when he was old. My father's way was to grit his teeth and keep it all inside. Never to show that he was grieving. Maybe if he hadn't had all those Scottish and stiff-upper-lip English ancestors, he could have let it out, cried and stormed and raged. Maybe if his mother had let him make noise in the house when he was growing up or let him be a child when he needed to be, my father could have been more of a help to my mother—and to me.

What makes so many fathers withdraw from the grisly dailiness of caring for a child with multiple physical and mental problems? So often they just aren't there. They try, but it's often easier to escape into work or drinking or bowling or something to get them out of the house.

Fathers, more than mothers, evidently, are more likely to consider their children an extension of their own egos so that when a child, especially a son, is born with a severe disability, they are "more apt to become more isolated, to reduce or withdraw from social interactions," according to recent research by Don Meyer.

Anne, a woman in her thirties with a brother with mental retardation, has a complicated relationship with her father. She resented him for sending her brother away when he was only four and she was eight. She still struggles with the feeling that she abandoned him, that she shouldn't have let her father send him away.

When she had lunch with her father last year, she tried to tell him how she felt. "He looked at me with astonishment," Anne says, the pain evident in her face. "He said, 'You haven't gotten over Jimmy yet? You're kidding, Anne—we've all gotten over this.'"

Anne knows nobody in the family will ever get over it, her father most of all.

Naturally a father's withdrawal from the family affects everybody. His reaction affects the marriage, the adjustment of the other siblings, and his wife's ability to cope. Mothers too often assume that their husbands cannot care for a sick child the way they can. They may shut the fathers out, make them feel unwanted. It's easy to lose perspective when confronted with a child who needs so much attention and care.

All of these factors affect the healthy sibling: a father's withdrawal, the strain on the parents' marriage, the tension in the household, the loss of time and attention from both the mother and father.

So for everybody's sake, it seems a good idea to encourage fathers to help. The only problem, according to Don Meyer, is that when fathers are present at meetings to discuss the child's disability and ways in which the whole family can work together, some of the mothers are intimidated by the presence of the men and don't talk as freely, and some of the fathers are not willing to share their feelings in a group. Don suggests that fathers and mothers may be served better in separate programs.

Jim May, Director of the National Fathers' Network in Seattle, has been working with fathers of children with disabilities and their siblings for over ten years. He told me:

> I tell people they can't build their families around the child with the disability. You have to take all the children into account. And help them understand that's the way life is. It isn't always fair.
>
> There is an underlying assumption that Mom will be the designated family nurturer. Men in our society aren't given a lot of strokes for being a nurturing family kind of guy. You get strokes for working hard, staying late, and being highly competitive, taking charge.
>
> For many men, we're our own worst enemy. We're scared to admit out loud that we don't know as much as we should,

and we don't know how to ask for help. We stumble along trying to fool everybody that we're fine. All that blows up when you're trying to deal with a child with special needs and his brothers and sisters. When they get help, most guys say, "I've become a much better father because I've had to relearn certain values. I found out that I can't take charge of everything."

Jim suggests several ways fathers can help the other children in the family.

You can take over for Mom with the child with special needs so she will have more time with the other kids. And of course, the more time you can spend with each of the other children yourself, the better it will be for them. Help educate them about the disability of their brother or sister. A lot of kids just don't have a great understanding of that. Tell them how they can help. They want to know. And work on showing them how to create a really nice connection with the other kids in the family. That will help them feel good about themselves, and about their other brothers and sisters too.

Men also often feel they must be the strong one in the family. Gina Shulman, a social worker at the Cerebral Palsy Center of Ocean County in Lakewood, New Jersey, runs support groups for the siblings of people with disabilities.

"The fathers I've spoken to feel like they have to hold it together," she says. "They think that if they fall apart, their wives will have no one to lean on. You think of the birth of your child as a time to celebrate, and they're not sure if they should celebrate. They have a tendency to be very stoic and together. They don't allow themselves to let out the sadness, loss, regret, and fear."

Julie Tallard Johnson, a psychotherapist and author of *Hidden Victims, Hidden Healers*, told me, "Read *Men Are from Mars, Women Are from Venus* by John Gray to understand why men react the way they do when there is a crisis in the family, such as the birth of a child with a serious disability or the onset of mental illness in a previously healthy child.

"Men try to find a solution for everything. A woman is more

concerned with the process of dealing with a difficult situation. I see this all the time in marriage counseling. The mother just wants to express her feelings and work with the situation. Men put the disability in a box and say 'This is what it is, and this is what it needs.' Women have more of an emotional response."

Angela's father couldn't turn to his daughter for help with his deep sorrow about his sons. Angela talks about her father with an ache still strong many years after his death. Her mother was an alcoholic. Angela, who is fifty-two now, remembers her childhood in the 1940s as a horror story, not because of her two brothers with mental retardation, but because of her mother's drinking:

> I was the son my father didn't have, until I started to become a young woman. And then things with my mother started getting very bad. So when I was twelve, my father sat me down one day after dinner and said, "Look, it's too upsetting to your mother for me to spend a lot of time with you."
>
> At that point he had not admitted that my mother was an alcoholic. He felt a terrific amount of guilt because my mother convinced him that it was his fault that his sons were mentally retarded. She believed that God was punishing them because they had sex before they were married. So my father really abandoned me at twelve. I felt orphaned. I loved him so much. To this day I can see him at night sitting at the kitchen table with his coffee Royale, staring out at the darkened bay with tears in his eyes.

It must have been devastating for Angela to lose her father's support and love. According to a study by J. Markowitz in 1983, in which early childhood special education program representatives talked about the positive effects of a father's involvement, there are benefits for the whole family, including "improved family communication, reduced stress and tension, more sharing of burdens and responsibilities, enhanced family support system, increased acceptance of the child, more consistent discipline, and more harmonious family functioning."

A father's positive effect is evident when you talk to Jayne Abbot, whose face glows with pride when she talks about her father, Quincy

Abbot, the national president of The Arc (formerly known as the Association for Retarded Citizens). Jayne's sister Becky has mental retardation, lives in a supervised apartment, and has a job at Cigna.

Jayne is the youngest of Quincy's four daughters. "My father's dedication and the kind of energy he has put into his work with The Arc has affected me and the rest of the family," she says. "It's inspirational to see him work that hard and have that kind of focus, that kind of drive to get something done. I'm really happy that Becky is in our life, and she has made me a better person, able to look at people differently, not just see them physically but to see what they can do."

Professionals do sometimes inadvertently overlook fathers. Linda Fox works with early intervention programs in Massachusetts and she remembers one father saying to her, "You need to make sure you include fathers."

"I said, 'Of course we're including fathers in our family groups.'

"'You don't understand,' he said. 'You have to say "fathers" in your flyers announcing meetings, because there is such a long-standing tradition of "parents" really meaning "mothers." So if you don't actually say "fathers," we often don't feel like we are included.'

"It was like a knife in my heart," Linda says. "I thought, 'My God, we have this supposedly family-centered system in place that has systematically excluded dads.' I realized we had to bend over backward and say, 'Okay, fathers, come in! We want you.'"

Any sibling will tell you how important a father's presence is in a family with a child with a disability. Every child needs a father's attention, understanding, compassion, love. If only I could do it all over again, I'd try to connect with my father and ask him all the questions I didn't have the courage to ask him when I was a child. "Do you love me?" "Do you love Mom?" "Do you love Jackie?" "Why don't you ever tell us you do?" "Why are you always mad?" "Why don't you talk to me?" I'd tell him how much I need him.

When I think about it now, I can't imagine how my parents managed to maintain a household where we were all supposed to pretend that nothing out of the ordinary was going on. The whole atmosphere, desperately fostered by my mother, was: "We are an absolutely normal family. We might have a slight problem here with a child who can't do everything other children do, but aside from that we are fine, fine, fine."

Repression of strong feelings can cause guilt and adjustment problems for the healthy siblings. Let's take a look at our feelings.

3

YOUR FEELINGS AND HOW TO

COPE WITH THEM

I grew up thinking I should never complain, never do anything bad, never cause my parents a minute's worry because they had so much to concern them as it was. A child needs to be naughty sometimes. A child needs to stamp her feet and yell and scream. A child needs to say, "Hey, I'm here and you're not paying any attention to me and I'm mad!" A child needs to be able to punch her brother sometimes. Other kids could get mad at their siblings, yell at them, hit them once in a while. I would never have dreamed of hitting Jackie. What kind of a person would hit someone with mental retardation? I suppressed all my anger until it was buried so deep I could not express it unless driven to the wall. Then I would explode, crying and yelling, usually because of some minor incident that didn't warrant such a violent reaction.

I can tell you—with the help of psychology courses in college, articles in women's magazines, and a skilled therapist—some of the reasons for this. My parents were of Scottish, English, and German descent; my father was from Boston; I grew up in the thirties when children were expected to be quiet and good, *especially* girls; anger and grief were unacceptable emotions in a household with a child with mental retardation; my father did not approve of expressions of emotion, nor did he allow them.

ANGER

So there you have the logical reasons for my stifled feelings. But that doesn't help much. I still can't deal with the anger that results from it. Anger is a terrifying emotion for a child. You don't know what to do with it. You sense that it is unacceptable in a household under siege, where everybody is holding on by the skin of his teeth to keep everything manageable. But anger doesn't go away. It just grows inside until you explode.

There are many reasons why we siblings of people with disabilities get angry and often suppress it. One major reason for resentment among siblings of those with disabilities is an early collision with the fact that life is unfair. We all find that out sooner or later, but it's sad when you have to learn that lesson so young.

"The whole situation is profoundly unfair," says psychologist Helen Featherstone in her book, *A Difference In the Family*. "It is unfair that one family must live with schizophrenia, autism, blindness, or retardation while others do not. It is unfair that some children must function as adjunct parents even before they go to school, while others successfully avoid responsibilities of all sorts well into their second decade. The brothers and sisters of the handicapped child learn to cope with this unfairness, and with their own response to it, the sorrow and the anger."

In my first chapter, I emphasized our need for attention and love. Even though we know our parents try their best to keep everything equal in a family, we are angry when we feel neglected for our siblings with the disability.

It has taken Alicia, a thirty-five-year-old nurse who lives in Chicago, many years and a lot of therapy to get over her feelings of anger at her parents because she felt they often ignored her. "My brother showed signs of mental illness when he was very young. I'm two years older than he is and I was a neglected child. I was angry that my parents had to spend so much time and energy on my brother. Once he was born and started having problems, all my parents' resources were directed into that child. And I was expected to take up the slack.

"As a young child, I was expected to do things that children shouldn't have to do. My mother sent me food shopping when I was three years old. She was so obsessed with my brother's illness that she often wouldn't leave the house to buy things that we needed, so she sent me. Three years old."

Many of us siblings knock ourselves out trying to please our parents, but sometimes it seems the harder you try, the less appreciation you get for your accomplishments. That can make you very angry, but you feel like a spoiled brat if you say, "Hey, I did something really good here. How about a little appreciation—the kind you give my brother for tying his shoes?"

Ahadi, now in her twenties, expresses the yearning of all of us when she says, "I would come in and be so excited about an A on my test. I worked so hard and I studied for days and I wrote this paper. The teacher loved it, and my parents would say, 'Oh that's great.'

"But my sister would come in with a B or a C and my parents said, 'Wow, that's wonderful! Let's take her out for dinner.' So sometimes I felt that what I was doing was kind of overlooked. That can be upsetting, it can make you angry. It can make you just want to scream and yell."

One particularly guilt-making cause of anger is noticing that a lot of the money available in the family is going to take care of the brother or sister with a disability. If anything can make you feel selfish and greedy, it's resentment of the family's resources pouring into the medical, educational, and therapeutic needs of the child with the disability. You feel like a thoroughly bad person, and when you're a child, you don't know that you *aren't* bad.

Dana still carries her guilt around to this day. She is thirty-eight and a teacher in a private school in San Francisco. She grew up with two brothers, one mentally retarded, the other mentally ill. She remembers her anger at the unfairness of life when she was a child:

There wasn't a lot of money in my family, but I remember the year my mother collected all these glossy brochures about wonderful sleep-away camps, and I got very excited about them. I know she thought they would be able to afford it, but something happened to my brother, who had mental retardation and required a lot of medical expenses, and she told me they wouldn't have enough money for my camp.

I remember feeling so angry about the unfairness of it. Here was this child who was taking so much of their time, so much of their attention and so much of their money. He tormented me and made my life hard and embarrassing and kept me from having some things I wanted. I grew up in a family where you thought everything should be equal, everything should be fair, but it wasn't. I think that's hard for a child to accept. The hardest part, I think, was that I was expected to be "a good girl," but even though my brother was behaving badly, he still got more of my parents' time and attention.

You will certainly feel angry if your sibling destroys your belongings when you are away from home. You know a child with autism can't help it, but it doesn't keep you from being furious. Gerri Zatlow, director of Siblings for Significant Change in New York City, is eloquent on the subject of accumulated anger when you grow up with a sibling with a disability. Her brother has autism and it is obvious how much she loves him and how proud she is of him. But she doesn't deny the problems of growing up with him. Gerri was pummeled, bitten, and screamed at by her brother. Her records and possessions were thrown out the window of their apartment building. Gerri's life was chaotic because of her brother's illness.

"I learned not to value possessions too much," she says. "Any property I loved, my brother would destroy. He threw my favorite records out the window, a first edition of *Candide* that could not be replaced. I learned if you want something very badly, it may not always be there. I learned there's no use being angry at someone who can't help his behavior."

Dr. Sandra Harris, a specialist on autism told me, "Children with autism don't understand the notion of personal property or what might be valuable to someone else. They get very upset when there is a change in the environment, so if a brother or sister leaves a toy somewhere out of place, that interferes with the comfort of the child with autism. It's not a willful wish to make the brother or sister unhappy, but when their anxiety is triggered, they have to recreate a stable environment."

No matter how logically someone explains all this to you, you are going to feel angry when your prized possessions are destroyed. Lydia remembers her favorite gift from her father being smashed by her brother with cerebral palsy who couldn't help his clumsiness. Lydia was only six when she was forced to hand her brother her treasured ceramic replica of the Liberty Bell her father bought her from a visit to Philadelphia. She wrote about her anger and frustration:

" 'Lemme see,' my brother said. I hesitated, afraid he might break it, as he had accidentally broken several of my more fragile toys at home. 'Let your brother see it,' Mom instructed. As I grudgingly gave it to him, it slipped from his hands and crashed to the floor. I couldn't stop the tears. It wasn't just the bell. I felt that all my things, and even myself, were vulnerable to Phil, never safe, never protected."

Many healthy siblings talk about their resentment when eagerly anticipated plans had to be canceled because of the illness of their brothers and sisters. Cassie remembers all the trips to restaurants, toy stores, and movies that had to be put off because of her sister's seizures. "A million times we pulled out of the drive to go somewhere," she says, "and my sister would go into convulsions, and we'd go straight back into the house and that was the end of that trip. You learn not to complain. How can you complain about something that your sister can't help? You learn to soldier on in a way that's not normal. You're supposed to throw tantrums and be annoyed and be selfish sometimes when you're a kid, but I never could. It's not a normal way to grow up."

You may be angry at your parents for bringing you into this abnormal family in the first place. That's certainly an irrational feeling–after all, would you rather not exist–but who said feelings are rational? Marsha is eighteen and a freshman in college, but she remembers yelling at her parents when she was a child because she felt frustrated at having an older sister with spina bifida:

I was almost mad at my parents for having me. I didn't think it was fair, and it was their fault. I felt like I didn't deserve to come into a family like this. I didn't ask to be born into a family that was so different. I didn't want it, so if something bothered me, everyone knew about it. I have my dad's temper, and we still clash every once in a while just because we like to yell at each other.

It got better because I learned to calm down as I got older—especially after my sister moved out. She was too old to be living in our house and she didn't have a job. It bothered me that she wasn't doing anything. I couldn't understand how she could just do nothing. It really frustrated me. That was when I fought with my family. Then she moved out and every-thing became a lot better. I've worked on trying to be more patient, to calm down, because it doesn't really help to get angry. I'm a lot more laid-back than I used to be.

Healthy siblings are often angry at their parents because they think they are spoiling the child with the disability. They think the parents are making it more difficult for the sibling in the long run because other people will not be as indulgent, and the sad fact is that someday the disabled sibling will have to live with someone else.

Ellen wishes her mother had let her brother be more independent. He had retinitis pigmentosa that was gradually robbing him of his eye-sight. "She would pack his suitcase for him when we were going on trips. I remember thinking, 'Just let him do it.' And I resented the fact that my mother had to spend so much time with him and not enough with my sisters and me."

Often siblings are angry at their fathers because they let their wives do all the work when there is a child with a disability in the family. They realize this isn't fair and it affects their feelings toward their fathers.

Alicia, thirty-five, whose brother has manic depression, says, "My father was sometimes physically abusive to my mother and she was so angry with him all the time that she shut him out of our upbringing. My father was never really there. He would go to work, come home, read the paper, eat dinner, go to sleep. All my mother's energy went into taking care of my brother. She really suffocated him.

"I still don't have a clear understanding of how it all fits together. I'm not sure what it had to do with my brother, their own screwed-up marriage, or the toxicity with which they related to each other. But I know it spills out over the kids. And I'm still angry at my father for not being there for us."

In addition, you may feel anger when your peers reject your sibling. You may be angry at them, but at the same time you're probably thinking, "If I didn't have this sister, everyone would want to play with me. No one would be afraid to come to our house. Why can't we be a normal family?" Again, that's not a very comfortable feeling for someone who loves her family and feels like a traitor for having these feelings.

Sarah Lowry has a couple of practical suggestions for dealing with this whole subject. She is ten and her brother Jeff, who is thirteen, has mental retardation and epilepsy.

"My family likes to go on ski trips," she wrote in *Views from Our Shoes.* "Once, my brother and I were skiing ahead of my dad. We took a wrong turn onto the black diamond expert run. I started down the hill thinking Jeff was following me–but he wasn't! He had just quietly sat down in the snow. When I got to the bottom, Jeff wasn't there and my dad blamed me! I tried to explain that I thought Jeff was following me, but Dad still got mad! It's not fair. If that happened to me, Jeff wouldn't have gotten in trouble. My dad wanted me to be Jeff's baby-sitter. But I'm younger than Jeff!

"I have a suggestion for anybody else who gets the blame: tell your parents what you think–but don't yell! If they don't listen, write them a letter–DON'T WHINE!"

Squashing your anger can lead to suppressing your other strong feelings as well. "Inhibition of anger also means that other forms of spontaneity–such as kidding, humor and 'messing around'–get squelched," say psychologists Stephen P. Bank and Michael D. Kahn in *The Sibling Bond.*

Maybe we wouldn't feel so guilty if we understood more about anger when we were children. Instead of feeling that it is a bad emotion, it would help to know that it's just another way of feeling, and we are not wicked for experiencing it. As Sandra Harris, an expert in this field, told me, "Anger is a perfectly legitimate emotion. The feeling of anger is often constructive. It tells us there is something that we need that's being thwarted. Some frustration that's there. If we can get at that and try to find some solution that meets our needs as well as the other person's needs, that's very important. Anger is a signal of a problem to be solved and not something to be hidden or avoided."

GUILT

Why do we all feel guilty about being angry at our siblings with a disability? Because we know those feelings are unacceptable. Bank and Kahn explain it this way:

> We are all taught that we should not entertain these invidious feelings about people who are "less fortunate than we are," in this egalitarian society where the underdog is supposed to be given more than a fair chance. This is a "Catch-22" to be sure.
>
> Guilt over angry feelings is often combined with guilt for hostile actions that may actually have harmed the weaker sibling and been instrumental in making that unhappy brother or sister slip a few steps farther into difficulty. Many people feel acutely guilty about having directly contributed to the problems of a brother or a sister.

I remember teasing my brother when we were children because he couldn't do things as quickly as I could. When I think about that today, I cringe at my cruelty. I suppose I wasn't really that different from other big sisters who teased their little brothers in "normal" families, but the realization that I was taking advantage of someone vulnerable and helpless doesn't do much for my self-esteem. Even the youngest children know this.

Richard feels guilty about tricks he used to play on his brother, who is deaf. "I used to trick my brother into thinking that I could see through the wall and he could not," he says in *It Isn't Fair*. "He honestly believed that, and now I feel kind of guilty for having done that kind of stuff. I took advantage of him and I really should not have."

Ellen wishes she had not teased her brother when she was little. He was losing his sight gradually, and she and her sisters hid his things and chased him around when they knew he couldn't catch them. "It's awful to think back and know that you did that," she says, echoing the guilty feelings of most siblings, whether they have a brother or sister with a disability or not. "We knew how to push his buttons and how to take advantage of him."

The worst part is that many of us feel we are "bad" because we have these feelings. It's really awful to grow up thinking you're a terrible person because you have mean thoughts sometimes. A recent study of people with disabilities by psychiatrist John S. Rolland found that these feelings of guilt can result in withdrawal, depression, suicidal thoughts, self-destructive and aggressive behavior, and declining school performance.

Psychologist Milton Seligman tells us in *Ordinary Families, Special Children*: "In instances where a sibling's guilt is unbearable, that child can become isolated from his or her own feelings. Guilt over such emotions as anger, hostility, resentment and jealousy may be so excessive that the sibling's true feelings fail to surface. Such a situation may occur in families where negative thoughts about a handicapped sibling are prohibited or punished. Anger may seemingly be unattached to a handicapped brother or sister, but hostile feelings may be deflected onto others, such as parents, school officials, or other persons."

There are all kinds of guilt that we siblings of people with disabilities torture ourselves with. My own particular brand of guilt comes from running away from my brother, pretending he didn't exist, blotting him out of my mind—or trying to. I'm lucky. I have the chance to include him in my life now.

Psychologists talk about something called survivor's guilt. This results in sabotaging your own efforts so that you will fail and not outshine your brother or sister with the disability, like the man with a brother with mental retardation who was eligible to compete in the finals for the Olympic games as a squash player, but fell and couldn't compete in the finals. He didn't know why he kept himself from winning, until a therapist pointed out that unconsciously, he was asking himself: "How come I don't have all those problems my brother has? How come I got away so easily? I can't win. I'm not going to win because look at my poor brother. I can't achieve what he can't achieve."

Dr. William Bauman, Director of The Spinal Cord Damage Research Center at Mt. Sinai Hospital in New York City, conducted a study of twins, one of whom had suffered a spinal cord injury. He told me some classic examples of survivor's guilt in the people he studied.

"In some sets of twins, the able-bodied sibling showed deference to the injured twin in some of the tests we ran. For instance, we did exercise challenge testing, and in some cases, the able-bodied twin would not surpass the injured twin in upper body exercises. It was as if he were saying, 'You win.'"

Some people have learned to deal with guilt better than others. Gwen is one of them. She is two years older than her brother with autism.

"I feel guilty about everything," she says. "But not in a bad way. I don't think it's pathological guilt. I feel responsible for everything and guilty when I can't do more. But I do realize that I can't do everything. There are some battles that I believe in but can't fight because I'm fighting other things. You've got to be good at what you do and not spread yourself too thin."

EMBARRASSMENT

I was especially plagued by embarrassment when I was a child and teenager. I blushed easily, so I felt the whole world knew that I was embarrassed and was laughing at me.

It was in elementary school—my sanctuary away from the tension in my house—that I first became vividly aware that Jackie was different. Until then, it was not so obvious that he was not like other children. My friends in the neighborhood just accepted him as slow, but they played with him and teased him and treated him like everybody else. I wasn't embarrassed when I was with him then.

But after my mother persuaded the school principal to let Jackie come to the first grade class, things changed. I walked past the open door of the first grade classroom one day, and there he was, sitting on the teacher's desk, his feet turned in, staring out into the room while the teacher taught the other children to read. He wasn't part of the class. He was different. Everybody would know he was my brother, and I was sure they would think there was something wrong with me too. I felt ashamed of him and even more ashamed of myself.

I was also embarrassed when I went shopping with my mother and Jack and people stared at him. It wasn't just that they stared. It was the expression of fear on their faces. They pulled their children away from him as if Jackie could hurt them in some way. I wanted to shout at them, "My brother would never hurt anybody. You don't have to be afraid of him. You're really stupid to look at him like that." But, of course, I didn't.

It's especially embarrassing when a sibling does something out-of-the-ordinary in public. Behavior that doesn't bother you at home is humiliating in public. If your brother or sister approaches someone just wanting to be friendly but the stranger backs away in fear, you are angry at the stranger and angry at the sibling for embarrassing you. If your sibling is afflicted with Tourette's Syndrome and lets loose a stream of curses at a bus driver, it makes you angry that you have to deal with the embarrassment of the situation. You aren't really old enough to know that people don't think less of you; they are just reacting to the strange behavior of your brother or sister.

"It is easier to extend oneself to a sibling who is depressed than to one whose florid psychotic break is expressed by winding up completely nude in front of a church on Main Street, trying to crawl into the cradle of the infant Jesus in a nativity scene," Bank and Kahn say in their book *The Sibling Bond*. "Guilt by association depends on whether the family perceives the sibling's behavior as socially disgusting or socially acceptable. Most commonly, the well sibling sees, in a disturbed brother's or sister's eyes, a frightening shadow of what he or she might have been or might still become, and flees."

Donald was nine and his sister with mental retardation was twelve when they were swimming in a hotel pool one day. He wrote about his experience in *Boy's Life*:

> We were having a very good time. One thing Lillian and I can do together is swim. She loves the water. Suddenly one of the grown-ups who had been at the other end of the pool came down to our end. Lillian pushed him. He pushed her back. I immediately told him about her and said that was her way of saying hello. He answered, "Well, if she's retarded, she doesn't belong here." I was so angry and so frustrated I got out of the pool and ran back to our room.
>
> Later when I didn't want to go out to dinner with my parents and Lillian because I didn't want to have another experience like that, my mother understood. She said I was em-

barrassed by my sister. She told me that it was all right to feel
that way, but she did think that we could go out and have a
fun time. She wanted me to give Lillian a chance. Mom said
she would work hard to make sure that Lillian behaved herself.
We did go out and we had a happy time, but I can't help
worrying about what other people will think. I don't like to
be stared at and I get very embarrassed. What hurts the most
is not Lillian being the way she is, but the way other people
behave toward her. I love Lillian because she is my sister, even
though sometimes it is very hard to love her.

It's not so easy to express your anger when an adult outside your
family does something stupid. Donald was too young to know that the
adult was at fault here, not Lillian, but luckily his parents were good
at helping him through times like that.

Some siblings hang tough when the world attacks their brothers
and sisters. Gwen, whose brother has autism, was sometimes a little
embarrassed when her brother acted out in public, but for the most
part, she says, "I had an us-against-them mentality. My attitude was,
'See, world, this is what some people have to deal with.'

"One time when I was six years old, I was out with my mom and
Simon when he behaved inappropriately. Everyone was staring at him.
I turned to him and said in a loud voice, 'Simon, don't stare at all the
normal people.' I was a very fierce child."

It's much harder for a child to deal with her brother or sister's
disability if parents are not honest. Ellen remembers how embarrassing
it was for her as a child: "My brother had a disease that was causing
him to lose his sight and as a result, he was slower developing in other
ways. My parents chose not to tell him that he had this disease for
quite a while. That made it very awkward for my sisters and me because other children often asked us what was wrong with him right
in front of him, as children do. We wanted to protect him, but we
didn't know what to say."

Julia Ellifritt wrote about being mortified by her younger sister
with Down syndrome in *Exceptional Parent* magazine:

My friends would come over to play, take one look at her,
and some would actually turn around and leave. I felt like

everything I did, Bonnie had to do also. I could not get away from her. If I took piano lessons, she had to take piano lessons. When I was in Girl Scouts, she was in Girl Scouts. She wanted to be like me.

I wanted so much to be accepted by my peers, and yet no one would play with me because of my shadow–my "social disease" that would not go away. The kids at school would tease, take advantage and play tricks on her and the other "special kids" in the lunchroom.

I wanted a party on my sixth birthday without my sister. She loved parties and would be upset if she knew she was miss-ing mine, so Dad took her to a movie while Mom had my party. I feel bad about that now. I know how much my actions hurt my parents, but why should I still feel guilty about wanting my own identity, wanting a time when I was the special one?

Little children don't even have a name for their resentment of a sibling with a disability. They just know they are mad at their parents and mad at the sibling with special needs and mad at life in general because things seem so unfair. It's a hard feeling to deal with because it makes you feel miserable and you don't know where to turn for help. That's why sibling support groups are excellent outlets for all of these emo-tions. Children hear others their own age expressing feelings they can-not tell their parents about, and it's a great relief.

HELP FOR HEALTHY SIBLINGS

No one can really understand your problems as well as somebody who is going through the same thing. Until recently, though, there were no support groups for siblings of people with disabilities. Now, thanks to the Sibshops all over the country started by Don Meyer in Seattle, Debra Lobato's support groups in Providence, the A. J. Pappanikou Center at the University of Connecticut, the Nisonger Center in Ohio, and many others, there are groups available for children as young as four years old. There has been a gradual awakening to the fact that healthy siblings are an important part of the family and can contribute a great deal to the well-being of the family if they are included in planning activities and help for the disabled child.

Don Meyer's Sibshops have given the siblings of people with disabilities the chance to talk about their feelings in a safe place. They meet with other children who understand exactly what they mean when they speak about being embarrassed, angry, sad, or worried because of a sibling with a disability. I had the chance to talk to some of the people who run the Sibshops and to watch them in action. Each facilitator has a slightly different approach. Some encourage children to discuss their feelings. Some devise activities that give them a chance to express their emotions in nonverbal ways. But whatever method they used, it was obvious the children benefited.

Psychologist Claudia Sabino Benowitz set up a Sibshop for the siblings of children with autism at the Allegro School in Cedar Knolls, New Jersey. When her program was in danger of being canceled by the school, the children protested to their parents so vehemently that the parents arranged for Claudia to continue by paying her themselves.

Through play therapy, the siblings in her group, aged eight to thirteen, can ask questions about their brothers and sisters or not talk about them at all. Claudia is a gifted psychologist who can interpret subtle signs of confusion or anger or resentment expressed in play therapy to help the children work their problems out. The dancing, writing, painting, acting, and other activities often reveal the children's feelings about what is going on at home, in school, with friends, with their disabled brother or sister.

The techniques she uses to help these children are typical of the kinds of activities used in Sibshops across the country, but I think Claudia is particularly creative and innovative. She uses everything–a little yoga to stretch and feel in tune with the body; a few meditative oms while sitting in a circle; self-portrait collages; magazine pictures to illustrate an autobiography; parties; murals; making board games to play with the sibling with autism; writing love letters to yourself: "Dear Rachel, I think you are a very sweet person. I think one day you will be able to do something no one else can do."

One exercise was especially helpful to the siblings of brothers and sisters whose autism often denies them access to the words they need to express their feelings, needs, and desires. "I gave each child a sentence to act out without using words," Claudia says. "Things like,

'Close the door.' 'I like you.' 'You make me mad,' 'I like to play baseball.' 'I get scared when people yell.' Afterward the children discussed how frustrating it was trying to convey a message without talking. In this way they experienced how hard it could be for their siblings. How often people imagine you are doing a completely different thing from what you are doing."

She also has children act out situations that might occur at home. "You are going to a party and your mother says you cannot go because your brother is having some difficulty. What would you do? The children can say anything they want: 'I don't like my brother.' 'I hate this.' They are safe because the other children understand. They all have had the same feelings."

Claudia told me about one child whose twin is autistic. Their mother had been dressing them alike, cutting their hair the same way, buying the same kind of glasses for each child. And the nondisabled child, understandably, did not like this but did not know how to complain about it, so one day he slashed a picture of both twins, screaming "I'm different, I'm different, I'm different!"

"It really scared his mother," Claudia says, "but I helped her to understand that it was a good thing he could express his anger like that. I suggested to the mother that it was not a good idea to dress them alike. She was relieved."

Other Sibshops, especially for older children, are discussion groups that deal with what it's like to be the youngest child in the family, the oldest, or the one who does most of the baby-sitting. Gina Shulman, social worker at the Cerebral Palsy Center of Ocean County in Lakewood, New Jersey, uses that approach too. "These sessions lead to good interaction with their parents too," Gina says. "It makes their parents touch on things they don't want to deal with. The children will say, 'I don't want to have to baby-sit so much,' or 'I don't always want to take my brother along when we go out.' The parents have to face this and talk about it."

Psychologist Debra Lobato schedules support groups in Providence for children aged four to eight. She set up her first sibling workshops over the opposition of some academics who feared it would make children more anxious to talk about their disabled siblings. "But the parents welcomed the idea," she said. "Their second question, after 'What can I do to help my child with a disability?' is often 'What does this mean for my other children?' I realized the need for sibling groups, but it took me years to overcome the opposition to the idea. When I did, it was clear that children benefited from it." Dr. Lobato gave me an idea of what happens in her group sessions:

Sometimes we get a group of little angels in here. It's not that we want to turn all saints into devils, but one of our objectives is to give them permission to complain, and to complain without guilt. You can get anybody to say, "Yes, my brother is a pain," but then if he goes home and feels he betrayed his loyalty to a brother or sister, we haven't accomplished anything.

There's always some kid in the group who has no guilt whatsoever and just spits it right out and then that kid's parents come in the room and hug him. The other kids see that and realize it's okay to say something negative. You couldn't do that in individual therapy. You always have the child who is going to say nothing bad about his brother or sister because he feels his role in the group is to defend his sibling, and you always have somebody who thinks this kid with a disability is a royal pain in the neck.

In one of the first groups I ever ran, I had a five-year-old girl whose brother had multiple medical problems–he was on a respirator, tubes all over him, and he cried all the time. Her parents had to spend most of their time taking care of him. But she would not make a peep about this brother. She would not complain. Yet every time she would go near him, there was turmoil because she might trip over a tube. There were many reasons she could have complained. But she wouldn't.

Then another little girl in the group who complained about everything found out that the first little girl had a brother with brain damage and she said, "Your brother has brain damage? So does mine. What a pain in the neck!" She just spewed out all these negative feelings about her brother.

At the next session, the little saint said, "He's cranky sometimes." And I thought, "Hallelujah!" That's a much more realistic perspective. No one could criticize her for saying he's cranky. Yes, he *is* cranky and sometimes you can't go to the zoo because of him. She took everything on herself. She tried to be the rudder in that family. The parents were the sails. Her brother was the ship. She was trying so hard to keep them all afloat, but everything was going on beneath the surface.

I've kept in touch with that family and that girl is a graduate of an Ivy League college, a wonderful young woman, extremely accomplished. Because her family had the strength and courage to allow her to participate in our sibling support group in those early days, we could help her shake things loose a bit and give her and her family a little support and information so she could find her own path.

The Kennedy Krieger Institute in Baltimore has offered a Child and Family Support Program since 1979. The sibling groups they run give children from eight to fourteen years old the chance to ask questions that have been gnawing at them but they haven't felt comfortable enough to ask their parents about. Some of those questions are based on misconceptions that can lead to agonizing guilt for a child. One twelve-year-old, for instance, thought his sister's brain damage was caused by an argument he had with his mother when she was pregnant. He carried this worry around until he went to a support group and the leader of the group assured him he could not be responsible for his sister's retardation.

Betty didn't go to a sibling support group until she was twenty-two. "All siblings should go when they are five years old, when their personality is being shaped," she says. "I grew up saying, 'My brother is slow' instead of 'My brother has mental retardation.' My parents could never say that he was retarded. They always told people, 'My son is a little slow.' And until I was twenty, I said the same thing. Now I try to tell my father, 'Dad, he's more than a little slow. He is mentally retarded.'"

"Siblings of people who have a disability need a place that's just for them," Joan Charlson, manager of social services for the Easter Seal Society of Western Pennsylvania in Pittsburgh told me:

Kids who come to our groups cannot get enough of them. They ask if we could have them more often. They need a place that no one else can invade. The child with the disability isn't allowed to come, and the parents can't come either.

The siblings have a sense that Mom and Dad are giving more time to the brother or sister with the disability. It's just one step beyond normal sibling rivalry. Often they feel as if they are being displaced or forgotten or ignored. So much time is spent taking the child with the disability to doctors or a clinic, worrying about this or that. Therapists may come to the house, or their mothers have to take them to special education classes. These children know that a lot of energy is being expended by parents on behalf of the sibling with special needs. We offer them this wonderful experience in a place that's just theirs alone. They sometimes talk about their siblings or their parents, but the important thing is some recognition of their own uniqueness as an individual."

An excellent source of information for siblings all over the country is the A. J. Pappanikou Center on Special Education and Rehabilitation at the University of Connecticut. It is a clearinghouse of information that relates to brothers and sisters who have a disability, publishing a quarterly newsletter called the *Sibling Information Network Newsletter*, with many of the articles written by siblings.

The newsletter also includes information on conferences and new books that are being printed about siblings. "Sibpage" is specifically for younger kids, with names of pen pals, letters from other children their age, books, puzzles, and games, and even recipes. Bibliographies list books helpful to families: one dealing with family issues, one with sibling issues, and one with children's literature. There is also a list of videotapes.

To give you an idea of the kind of articles siblings write for their newsletter, this is an excerpt from an open letter to her parents by Maryjane Westra:

No, I didn't resent Martha. I didn't resent baby-sitting for her. I would cancel my plans if there was no baby-sitter for Martha. I loved her. I would do anything for her. She taught me how to love without reservation; without expectation of returned love. She taught me that everyone has strengths and weaknesses. She taught me that human value is not measured with IQ tests.

As children, I know I was a very important part of Martha's life. I was the only one who could braid her hair, take her into a store, and stop her tantrums.

Sometimes I mourn the loss of the ideal sister, but I remind myself that other sisters fight, argue, and even hate each other. I have a much better relationship than that.

And that relationship continued long after Maryjane wrote that letter. Her sister Martha has been living with her for seventeen years, and Maryjane says, "I continue to be amused, tolerant, and sometimes frustrated by her autistic quirks. But, above all, I love her fiercely and owe her my life for the gifts she has given me and the lessons she has taught me. One of those gifts is tolerance and acceptance of people with differing abilities." And Maryjane adds something that didn't surprise me at all, "I have adopted five children with disabilities."

There are many factors that determine our adjustment to life when we have a sibling with a disability. I'll explore some of them in the next chapter.

4

HOW DID YOU GET THAT WAY?

*S*oon after I saw Jackie sitting on the teacher's desk in school, the teacher realized she couldn't keep him in the class-room anymore and my mother hired a tutor to teach him at home. Sometimes Jack and I would play school. I had an easel black-board and I would be the teacher and Jackie was my student. He did eventually learn to read, and I always thought that I had taught him. Of course, looking back, it seems more likely that the tutor was the one responsible for Jackie reading and writing. My little brother would often get sick of my bossiness and just walk out of the room, but I loved being a teacher and for a long time I thought I would grow up to be one. Instead, I became a writer, and here I am writing a book about Jack. Our siblings with disabilities have a much stronger influ-ence on our lives than we realize.

I've tried many times to figure out how those early years of living with a brother with a disability shaped me. How am I different now from what I might have been had I not grown up with him? For one thing, I am completely comfortable with people who are different from me. I know what to say to them. I connect. I have great respect for every human being I meet. I am interested in that person and endlessly fascinated by the differences in people. Without Jackie, I don't think I would be like that.

I also think my love of solving puzzles and problems has something to do with growing up with Jack. Because he didn't speak until he was four, I had to figure out what he wanted in other, intuitive ways. He would point or make noises and by the process of elimination, I knew what to do for him. I became quite good at guessing on the first try. I was his interpreter with the outside world and often, with my mother. If Jack cried and had a temper tantrum, I knew it was because he wanted to do whatever I was doing. He didn't want to be left behind when I went to play with my friends. He wanted to talk and walk and do what the rest of us did, but he couldn't. Instinctively, I tried to help him. I was his mother as often as I was his sister. I protected him, ran interference for him, smoothed over his retardation with other children. I grew up too fast in some ways. I think I missed the silliness, the goofing off, the fun that my friends had. If they had younger brothers and sisters, they didn't have to explain them to anyone.

I wanted to find out what factors decide whether we siblings of people with disabilities grow up well-adjusted or are, as the psychologists say, "at risk." And if so, at risk for what? Divorce, prison, psychiatric wards? Or just a minor neurosis that we can take off to a therapist to fix. Is it harder when the disability is severe or when it's not as noticeable? Is it better to be younger or older than our sibling with the disability? Do males or females have an easier time? Is it better to be the oldest child or the youngest in the family? Is it easier to deal with the disability if you have other brothers and sisters?

I read books by the experts in the sibling field, studied research by psychologists, sociologists, and psychiatrists, talked to people leading sibling support groups, and I must say I didn't find any clear-cut evidence that would tell me exactly why some of us function well, some of us are a mess, and most of us are somewhere in between— slightly neurotic but doing all right.

Psychologist Debra Lobato was reassuring about our prospects for a fairly well-adjusted life. "The way I look at it," she told me, "the brothers and sisters of people with disabilities are normal kids in often stressful situations. They are at risk for more adjustment problems than other children, but they are *not* at risk at all for having major psychiatric illness—clinical depression or true anxiety disorders.

"A good number of these siblings tend to be more altruistic, more understanding, less driven by petty issues, more tolerant of others, and they are able to see the optimistic side in a situation. In character development, the people we respect, people of fine character, didn't become that way by chance. Something bad has befallen them and that often makes them wonderful people. We never look at it like that, but we judge people's characters on how they handle adversity. Brothers and sisters of kids with disabilities have learned that lesson very well and have come to others' aid with great maturity well before other kids can do it."

"Siblings of people with a disability are tenacious," Gerri Zatlow, who has a brother with autism, says. "Some people think we're too tenacious. If I have a problem, I don't stop until the problem is ended or the solution is there. Hey, what do you expect us to do? We have been given something that is not going to be fixed, not going to be cured. Right away, somebody has given us a toy that doesn't work and the warranty has run out. Do we throw it out? No, we find other ways to make it work. That carries over into our daily lives. But that doesn't hurt us. We do this all the time. Other people are not like that. They say, 'We have a problem and maybe we'll fix it and maybe we won't.'"

When Dr. Lobato first started her research in the 1970s and early 1980s, most of the scientific literature reflected the opinion that the siblings of people with disabilities would have serious problems. "There was a tendency to interpret achievements and wonderful characteristics in a normal sibling as negative fallout, that the person was achieving as a reaction to the disability in the family, that she was overachieving to compensate. I started a campaign to describe strengths as well as problems."

The studies I read showed conflicting results about how we would turn out, but that there were a few factors that might make a difference. Let's start with the *type* of disability that our brother or sister has.

TYPE AND SEVERITY OF THE DISABILITY

Psychologists tell us something that seems quite obvious: the more severe the disability is, the harder it is for the other children in the family to live with it. A child with serious physical problems naturally takes a greater toll on the family's resources than a child whose disability is not so severe. When a child needs constant physical care, the mother in the family will get less sleep at night, the parents' marriage will be under a lot more stress because of the unrelenting needs of the child with the disability, and the healthy siblings will feel the effects of the strain on the household.

When you say, "I have a brother with cerebral palsy," "a sister with spina bifida," or "a sibling with mental retardation," other people cannot really understand the full implications of that diagnosis for the rest of the family. It's not just the fact that someone is unable to learn or walk or talk or see. The hardest part is all the emergency trips to the hospital, the injuries from seizures, the medication that doesn't work, the life-threatening physical problems that can erupt at any time—in the middle of the night, during a birthday party, in school. It's the fact that a parent or a healthy sibling never knows when a sudden crisis will suspend the life of the whole family. You're always waiting for the next emergency. It keeps you anxious, on edge. Serious physical symptoms accompany many disabilities, and most of the outside world doesn't have to live with problems like this.

CYSTIC FIBROSIS

With a disease like cystic fibrosis, which varies in its severity over the course of the illness, the healthy child's behavior changes according to how sick the sibling is. Over a two-year period, Myra Bluebond-Langner, professor of anthropology at Rutgers University, studied in depth forty families where there was a child with cystic fibrosis and discovered that when the child with the illness was doing well, the healthy sibling felt free to voice his demands for attention.

"When the child's condition started to deteriorate or the treatment changed in some way," Dr. Bluebond-Langner told me, "the well sibling did not make these demands directly. The healthy sibling had a vested interest in helping others see the brother or sister as well and normal. As long as they did that, the well sibling could make more demands. If the brother or sister was not seen as well by parents and others, it was more difficult to make demands since society makes it clear that the needs of the ill child must come first."

Dr. Bluebond-Langner emphasizes that the illness is not an isolated entity but is woven into the very fabric of family life. "Just as fabrics wear and tear differently under different exposures, so too does an illness." She points out an important fact to keep in mind when talking about disability in a family: attitudes, relationships, and the illness itself change over time in the life of a family, and the family must adjust to the varying demands of a chronic disease.

CEREBRAL PALSY

Cassie's sister has cerebral palsy, but those two words don't begin to describe her sister's problems. "She has diabetes and cataracts," Cassie explains. "There was pressure in her brain from a shunt, and she would have two or three days when she didn't really sleep and would just flail her arms. My parents would be up night after night after night. Naturally this affected my brother and me, too. Because she couldn't sleep at night, she often slept all day, and we had to tiptoe up and down the stairs. We couldn't talk in loud voices the way children naturally do. I always felt stifled. Until I was forty years old, I tiptoed when I went back to visit my parents and kept my voice low."

Cerebral palsy can take many forms in the half-million people who have it. It can result in physical impairment or mental retardation or a combination of the two. My brother is more mentally affected than physically impaired, but his weak muscles affect his walk and the strength in his arms. Lydia Ross's brother Phil has a more serious form of the condition.

"Phil is a hulking man/child whose speech is slurred and halting, whose gait resembles that of a drunk trying to navigate a straight line," she writes in *Glamour*. "He suffers bouts of frustration when he can't express a simple thought, and embarrassment when he trips over his feet or loses his balance, slamming sideways into the nearest wall."

INVISIBLE DISABILITIES

But of course, there is the other side of the coin, too. When the disability is barely noticeable–autism, epilepsy, cystic fibrosis, hearing impairment, a learning disability, attention deficit disorder, diabetes–it is harder for the outside world to understand and be compassionate because your sibling doesn't *seem* disabled. Therefore, it is more difficult for the healthy sibling because strangers often make cruel comments that wound the sibling as well as the person with the disability. Yet, the healthy sibling can't go up to someone in public and say, "He acts that way because he has autism." The healthy sibling just wishes he were somewhere else. And then he feels guilty.

I wanted to see if every kind of disability–mild or severe–caused the same reactions in the healthy siblings I interviewed. When I asked them about it, I found that most of them do indeed experience the same feelings of resentment, guilt, embarrassment, and anger, as well as pride, to the same degree, no matter what the disability of the brother or sister.

This was confirmed by Thomas Powell, dean of the College of Education at Winthrop University in Rock Hill, South Carolina, who has been studying siblings of people with disabilities for seventeen years and is himself the father of a child with a disability.

"I have talked to the siblings of brothers and sisters of people who have a mild case of learning disability," Dr. Powell told me, "and they tell me the same story. They talk about the same issues with parents and about wanting to be involved in family plans, with the same anxiety, fear, hope, and joy that those whose siblings have serious disabilities report. It doesn't matter what the label is. By and large that experience is going to have more common elements than different ones."

Sue Levine, social worker and co-founder of Family Resource Associates in Shrewsbury, New Jersey, whose support groups give siblings a chance to express their feelings, told me about one of the children who had great difficulty accepting his brother's disability:

He was one of the angriest children who was ever in one of my groups. His brother was born with four fingers missing. His mother was so distraught and had such difficulty dealing with this that she could barely attend to the needs of this other sibling, who was five years old. He actually wanted a disability too so he could get some attention. I hear that from a lot of kids.

The siblings of children with a learning disability are often very confused and resentful. They don't understand why their mothers have to spend so much time with the brother or sister. "Why does my older sister need more help with her home-work?" they'll ask in a support group. "She talks fine, she looks fine, she can take care of herself. Why does she need Mommy to sit with her and do her homework every night? I'm younger–I should need more help. It's not fair."

The role of the support group in this situation is to affirm the child's feelings–"You're right. It doesn't seem fair"–but also to point out that the disability is real. "It's very hard for your sister to learn. Mom needs to give her that extra time." The support group also encourages the child to discuss her feelings with the parent and perhaps to find a solution that will help her feel more involved or will allow for some one-on-one time with the parent at a later time.

Attention deficit disorder (ADD) is another disability that the other siblings in the family find hard to understand. They get mad because this kid is always messing up their toys, punching them, or can't sit still. To them, it's a behavior prob-lem that should be punished by the parent.

DEAFNESS

Having a deaf brother or sister may be more difficult for healthy siblings because the sibling with the disability is so isolated from the rest of the world. They usually go to special schools for the deaf and it is harder to include them in social activities in the hearing world. Carey is a thirty-six-year-old psychiatrist born into a family with two deaf parents and two deaf brothers. "I was a big disap-pointment to my family," she told me with a laugh. Her parents and brothers were a part of the "deaf world," and she was a member of the hearing community. There is a wide gulf between the two worlds. Carey became a fluent signer and today she says she "passes" in the deaf community. There were many conflicts with her brothers. She says:

> Growing up, I was not very close to my brothers. They really didn't take an interest in my schooling or my friends or even my career. For the most part, they are completely immersed in their own world and I don't fit into it. When we were children, they expected me to interpret for them. They would pick up the phone, dial a number, and tell me to talk to the person they were calling without my even knowing who it was. I was happy to interpret for my parents, but I rebelled against doing so for my brothers. They resented me because I didn't have to do any of the chores around the house. My parents felt that my chore was being their ears twenty-four hours a day and they didn't ask me to do other things. My brothers couldn't understand this at all. They thought it wasn't fair. They didn't understand me.

It really wasn't until one of her brothers had a hearing child that Carey became closer to him because she was able to help her brother and his wife understand their child better.

BORDERLINE MENTAL RETARDATION

It's also very hard for healthy siblings whose brother or sister has borderline mental retardation, as Alex can tell you. At thirty-six, he is a year and half older than his brother Tom, who functions well in many ways. "It's sort of a blessing and a curse when someone is high functioning and can communicate his feelings very well, but with that same intelligence understands what he is missing," Alex says. "My brother wants the same things my sister and I have. He lives in a group home with four other adults who are about his same intelligence level, but he wants his own house. He wants to live alone. He wants to go to college. But he can't do those things."

Rosalie is in her sixties now and worries that her brother will have trouble finding friends when she is no longer alive. "It would be better if he were a little more retarded. He doesn't fit into a group home because he's not retarded enough, and he doesn't fit into normal society because he's slow. When I'm not here, who will call him up and take him to the movies? Who will invite him over for the holidays?"

However, while mild mental retardation can be harder for the sibling with the disability when it comes to dealing with the outside world, there is usually less stress for the family than when the retardation is severe, according to a recent study of 461 families with an adult child with mental retardation conducted by Marty Krauss, director of the Starr Center for Mental Retardation at Brandeis University, and her colleagues.

"The families of people with Down syndrome were less stressed, had higher support services, and adapted better to the situation than other families," Dr. Krauss told me. "We think that is because there is more understanding in society about people with Down syndrome than other kinds of retardation."

All you have to do is talk to some siblings of people with Down syndrome and you *know* their brothers and sisters have brought warmth and love into their homes that would not have been there otherwise. Pammy was born into a family of three boys and one girl and she has enhanced all their lives. Graham, one of her brothers, says:

> Pammy is very bright, articulate, sociable, gregarious, vocal. We didn't know what to expect when she was born, but she learned to read and write, lives on her own, has a boyfriend, and is very independent. Because of her, I specialized in early childhood education and Pammy has enriched my life in every way. Some people have value because of their cognitive achievements, but many people who have high cognitive achievements use them for what I would consider socially destructive purposes that do not enhance our lives. Other people may not have a high rate of cognitive achievement, but they bring warmth, companionship, a loving, accepting attitude with them which does enrich our lives. That's how I feel about Pammy.

I remember when my grandfather was in his last year and pretty feeble. He couldn't hear that well, so it was hard to have a conversation with him. He and Pammy would sit on the front porch chit-chatting away. He probably didn't understand a lot of what she was saying because of his hearing, and she probably didn't pay that much attention to what he was saying, and they'd be laughing and talking and smiling. It was wonderful to watch. We have to understand that people can contribute to our lives, our families, our society in a lot of different ways.

AUTISM

Autism seems to be one of the most difficult disabilities to live with because of behavioral problems. It's a disability that is uneven. A person can be gifted in one area, extremely retarded in another. It shows up before the age of three. One-third of all people with autism never speak. Two percent have above average intelligence, but their autism doesn't allow them to live independently. Fortunately, we know enough about it now so that we no longer blame "refrigerator mothers" for causing the disability by not relating to the child.

Children with autism are often destructive. Gerri Zatlow says, "I hate his autism, but I love my brother." Describing life with Douglas she says, "We don't grow up like other people. I didn't really know that until a friend pointed it out to me. She described what it is like being around Douglas. She said, 'I compare it to different record speeds. In my house, we kind of went at thirty-three and a third. But with Douglas, you jag up to seventy-eight. Your heart pounds. You think, 'How does Gerri stand it on a daily basis?'

"It's like a three-ring circus day to day. There is no way you can ignore somebody who has motor oil for blood, doesn't sleep so nobody sleeps. There's constant turmoil in the house. It's not a healthy way to grow up, but you learn to cope with it. You either accept it or you flail against it your whole life."

Recently, early intervention in the form of many hours of physical therapy has made a difference in the lives of some children with autism.

But the emotional toll for the siblings is often high. Sandra Harris, dean of the Graduate School of Applied and Professional Psychology at Rutgers University, says,

> The benefits can be dramatic. But early intervention calls on tremendous family resources. We're talking about forty hours a week of very intensive work in which the parents are called upon at the very least to be the coordinators and oversight supervisors, which is very demanding.
>
> The rest of family life is on hold, and the other siblings have to struggle with that. In most families there is a risk that they will be shunted to the side. They might be able to take part in some play sessions and encourage their brother or sister to learn, but very young children would not be capable of the kind of meticulous method that has to go into the teaching. Of course if the child with autism is one of those kids who benefits from all those years of intensive training, the end product is a brother or sister who is more responsive, more fun to be with, but not every child benefits. The cost to family life is substantial.

CANCER, AIDS, AND MENTAL RETARDATION

There are three kinds of illnesses that are very difficult for the other siblings in the family to cope with, according to psychologist Debra Lobato: cancer, AIDS, and mental retardation. She feels this is a reflection of society's attitude toward these illnesses. "Kids will come into my support groups and say, 'Melissa used to be my best friend until my brother got cancer and then her mother wouldn't let her play at our house anymore.' It's as if the entire family took on a stigmatized role and the child felt it. If a sibling has AIDS or is HIV positive, Dr. Lobato says, "the other siblings are extremely reluctant to have that information out among their peers. Mental retardation is difficult, too, because sometimes those afflicted can exhibit significant destructive behavior."

Barbara, who supervises workshops for siblings with disabilities, suddenly understood their problems directly and painfully when she was faced with the unexpected reaction of her younger son to his brother's cancer diagnosis.

"Our son was being treated in another state," she says. "So we had to literally abandon our sixteen-year-old son to be with our oldest child. Our younger son had been an A student all his life. I started getting phone calls from teachers saying he was disruptive and his grades were going down. I found out what it's like to have your other children's lives disrupted by the serious illness of one of them. I helped him through it the best I could, but after our older son was successfully treated for the cancer and back in college, our younger son began developing symptoms that were very similar to what our first son had undergone. I rushed him to a surgeon, and thank God, there was nothing wrong with him, but it was obvious he had this need to mimic his brother's original symptoms for some psychological reason."

MENTAL ILLNESS

Being the sibling of someone with a mental illness may be the hardest disability to deal with. Dr. Krauss and her colleagues also conducted a study in which she compared the effects of mental retardation and mental illness on healthy siblings, which indicated that "the vast majority of siblings of people with mental retardation felt that the experience of having a brother or sister with a disability had been mostly positive, whereas over half of the siblings of those with mental illness felt that it was mostly a negative experience."

Mental illness seems to cause the most pain because those outside the family have so little understanding of it. There is much more of a stigma attached to it than to a physical disability or mental retardation. It's also much harder for the healthy sibling to deal with because his help is often violently rejected.

In her book, *The Four of Us: The Story of a Family*, Elizabeth Swados evokes the atmosphere of a home where one member is seriously ill:

The effects of mental illness became a dominating force in our home because no one could face that it existed. The strain on my parents' marriage intensified the mental illness and weighted every dialogue. Yet no one acknowledged the unhappiness. Everyone was part of a conspiracy that couldn't be detected or unwound. The sporadic and passionate love that we four individuals felt for each other caused confusion and then un-expected tenderness. This love motivated terrible mistakes and was the force behind heartbreaking gestures of reconciliation.

There are no rules in a family with a mentally ill child. You have to make your own as you go along, and very few young children are equipped to do that. Most people don't realize until years later that every family doesn't live in the same state of tension and anxiety that they do.

WHEN THE DISABILITY OCCURS

In addition to the type of disability in a family, another major factor that affects the adjustment of siblings is the age of a sibling when the disability occurs. In Dr. Krauss's study, she and her col-leagues found that siblings of those with retardation are much more affected than those whose siblings were mentally ill, in their career choice, decision to have children, feelings about themselves, romantic relationships, plans for their future, and feelings about people with disabilities.

"We concluded that one of the main reasons for this difference in attitude was the age of the sibling when the brother or sister was diagnosed as having a disability," Dr. Krauss told me. "For most siblings of adults with mental retardation, the only life they have known is as a sibling of a brother or sister with mental retardation. However, for nearly three-fourths of the siblings of the adults with mental illness, the brother or sister was diagnosed after the sibling reached adulthood. Thus, siblings of adults with mental illness were more established in their life domains prior to the onset of their brother or sister's disa-bility."

Bank and Kahn tell us that a sudden appearance of a disability, as in an accident where the child is paralyzed, or when a sibling becomes subject to seizures or loses his sight or hearing due to a disease, "allows more sympathy than does a chronic illness which pounds at the family for years, draining everyone's energy without relief. Far more prevalent are disturbances that have a slow rate of onset and last for years. This situation actually makes it more difficult for the sibling...to deal with. There is no clear cause, no moment when the person is struck with a disease. The awareness of a good relationship turning bad ferments gradually, as the family grows ever more miserable. If the disturbance lasts many years, hopelessness, pessimism, and cynicism can paralyze the sibling relationship."

Or it can forge a strong, loving relationship. Mark is fifteen and his brother Tim is twelve. They talked to me about their older brother Andrew who has cerebral palsy and whom they love very much. They obviously ache for Andrew because he has severe seizures and can't do the things they do, but they can't imagine life without him because they've never known anything else. "If you've lived with it since you were born, it's just part of your life," Mark says.

When an accident results in a serious injury to a previously healthy child, it's an entirely different story. The whole family is thrown into turmoil. The child may come home from the hospital looking the same but acting like an entirely different person. For example, nothing was the same in the Greer family after one of their children was hit by a car when she was nine years old.

"We didn't even know if she would live," Maureen, the mother, says. "When she did come home from the hospital, she was fine physically, but because of her traumatic brain injury, her emotions, her ability to concentrate, to take information and synthesize it, were all affected. She had tremendous fluctuations. One minute she'd be fine and the next minute hysterical. For our other three children (ages four through twelve) it meant that they could be playing with her and suddenly she would be crying. They couldn't figure out what was the matter. It was very hard on them and we had to help them understand that it wasn't anything they had done, but a result of the injury."

But what if you are a twin and your sister is paralyzed at the age of four months in an automobile accident and you are fine? A baby probably feels the loss of attention and care even more than an older child. Dr. Bauman, at Mt. Sinai in New York City, told me the story of a twin's reaction to her sister's disability as they were growing up:

> One of the twins was in a bassinet in the front seat of a car and was thrown against the dashboard. Her back was broken. The noninjured twin spent her entire life in the shadow of her injured sister because the sister who was paralyzed took attention, love, time away from her. The injured twin was incredibly independent, learning to climb onto counters just using her arms. She used her arms as we use our legs.
>
> And her sister hated her. It was seething. To this day— the sisters are now in their twenties—the healthy twin hates the sister in the wheelchair.

BIRTH ORDER AND GENDER

In addition to the age you are when your sibling becomes disabled, it also makes a big difference where you are in the birth order and whether you are a boy or a girl. If you are born before your sibling with the disability and have to cope not only with a new baby in the family but a new baby with serious problems, it will be harder for you than if you were born *after* the child with the disability and accept his condition from the beginning.

Some of the research indicates that older sisters, especially in families with only two children, grow up with more resentment toward their siblings with a disability because they often must bear the brunt of baby-sitting and household chores. In a family with several other children, it is still the older daughter who is often given more responsibility for the sibling with a disability. Though we like to think we are long past the time when girls are expected to do the housework, the cooking, and the baby care, while boys wash the car and take out the garbage, a mother still looks to her daughter to help her with the child with the disability. And the healthy sibling often carries a hidden resentment all her life for the extra responsibility.

Many siblings complained to me that they had to come home right after school to look after a sibling with a disability. This kept them from seeing friends or participating in after-school activities. This feeling of forced servitude, of deprivation, of not having as much fun as your friends, can cause an anger that has no place to go. You feel like an ingrate if you complain. You see your mother struggling to juggle all the needs of the family. She's tired and overworked and you want to help. At the same time, you don't want to feel you *have* to do it.

Thirty-seven-year-old Julia Ellifritt still resents the baby-sitting her mother expected of her when she was a child. It was Julia's job to make sure that her sister with Down syndrome got on the bus after school each day. It was never her younger brother's responsibility. "It wasn't because I was older than my brother, it was because I was the female sibling," Julia told me when I called to talk to her about the article she had written for *Exceptional Parent* fourteen years earlier when she was twenty-three. In the article Julia wrote:

> It wasn't a problem until one day I could not find her. I panicked. She was not on the bus or in her classroom. I ran back to the bus, but the bus was gone. I was so upset. I cried and cried. I would have to call Mom and tell her I had lost Bonnie. Bonnie was gone and it was my fault. I tearfully got through to Mom on the phone, just as Bonnie was stepping off the bus in front of our house. My mother wanted to know where I was. Why had I missed the bus?

To this day, Julia resents the amount of responsibility that was placed on her shoulders, and that she felt such guilt at the time.

Psychologist Milton Seligman agrees that it is still older sisters who end up doing most of the caretaking. "But," he says, adding a new twist to old research, "brothers are sometimes discouraged from caretaking when they would like to."

A study done by S. M. McHale and W. C. Gamble in 1987 of siblings of people with disabilities found that older daughters are indeed at risk for adjustment problems later on in life, but that older brothers have problems too. They are often more anxious and have more difficulty getting along with other people.

Sandra Harris found in her recent study of the siblings of children with autism that younger brothers too have adjustment problems, but she is cautious about making generalizations. She told me:

> The two groups that have been highlighted for adjustment problems are older sisters and younger brothers, but I wouldn't bet my life savings on those findings.
>
> Younger brothers seem to be vulnerable because boys in general are more vulnerable to psychological problems than girls. They have a harder time, probably because they have to learn to manage their aggressive impulses as well as learn to be sufficiently masculine. In other words, boys have a narrower line to walk than little girls. Girls can be tomboys or very feminine and either one is fine, but little boys can't be too girlish or they are in trouble. You've got to be clearly a boy in our culture.
>
> In general, boys seem to need more active parenting than girls, and if parents are absorbed in the needs of their child with a disability, they are going to have less time to direct to that little boy. He may get less of the help that he needs in learning to walk that relatively narrow line of appropriate behavior for a boy. That's my explanation, but as I say, the data are equivocal. Not every study finds that little boys have more problems adjusting to a sibling with a disability.

And we have to take into account that society is changing. Developmental psychologist Bryna Siegel, associate adjunct professor at the University of California in San Francisco, points out that the proliferation of day-care centers and preschools makes it possible for younger children to be out of the house for several hours a day. "The younger brother, for instance, can have his own life," she told me. "He can develop his own identity and not be adversely affected by his sibling with the disability. I think some of the older research that put younger brothers at risk assumed that these children were home with Mom and the disabled child all day long."

Betty has both an older brother and a younger brother, in addition to George, who has mental retardation. She says both her "healthy" brothers had a much harder time adjusting to their sibling with retardation than she did. Betty is an introspective woman of fifty, who

works as an editor in San Francisco, and she told me about the reactions of each of her brothers:

> My oldest brother is the most damaged of all of us. I never
> disagree with him anymore because he explodes. Even a bas-
> ketball game can set him off. He's three years older than
> George, and he was no longer the center of the universe when
> George was born. He was Peck's bad boy. He always resented
> me because I could do no wrong and he could do no right.
>
> I was sixteen months old when my brother came along. I
> was the good child. I had to be the achiever, the I-won't-give-
> you-any-trouble, you-can-count-on-me child.
>
> My other brother is five years younger than I am. He's a
> person who can't really feel. He has what I call foxhole family
> feeling. Just keep your head down and ignore what's going on
> all around you. He was angry at my father because he couldn't
> afford to send him to law school. He had the highest law
> boards on record, but there wasn't enough money to send him
> because we had to keep George in a private facility from the
> time he was eight. He left all responsibility for my brother up
> to my parents and later, after they died, to me.

Janet, too, says that her older brother was much more affected by the
birth of their sister with mental retardation than she was. Janet is in
her early forties now and is a computer programmer in Houston. She
was eighteen months old when her sister was born, and her brother
was three and a half. "My brother has always been a much angrier
person than I was," she says. "I thought he wouldn't be affected the
way I was because he was three and a half when my sister was born.
He had a solid home life for a good amount of time, but after she came
into our family, he was quiet, inhibited, always causing trouble.

"When he was fourteen, he ran away from home. He came back,
but he was resentful of our parents. We didn't really reconcile until
he got married and had a child. He needed to be noticed. That was
his way of asking for help, for attention. My reaction was just the
opposite—I wanted to help my mother."

Middle children, too, often have a hard time adjusting to a child with a disability. They seem to have a precarious role in any family, with or without a disability, but when you add the complication of a disabled child, it's an even harder role to adapt to. Being in the middle of the sandwich between the oldest child who has had time to endear himself to his parents without any competition and the youngest child with serious health problems who needs a great deal of time and attention, can be a difficult position to be in.

Lisa Haebler, a social worker, told me about one family she counseled where the children range in age from one to twelve. "The oldest boy is probably better adjusted to his brother with serious physical and mental problems than the others," she says, "because he had his mother to himself for eight years before the next child was born. It's that next child, the middle child who is nine now, who is having the most difficulty dealing with it.

"He is intensely jealous and resentful of the child with the disability. This boy needs help, but his mother does not have the energy or the will left to get this child to a therapist or to a sibling support group."

So what can we conclude here? Can we say that all older sisters of children with disabilities turn into caretakers and martyrs, exploited by friends, husbands, and children? Of course not. Speaking as an older sister myself, I can assure you that I am no martyr, even though I sometimes put other people's needs ahead of my own.

Will older brothers of people with disabilities join a cult or turn into heroin addicts because of their position in the family? Will younger brothers run away from home and become hermits? Will middle children turn into serial killers? Not likely. They may have a tougher time adapting than siblings who do not have a disability in the family, but it's a problem of adjustment, not a serious defect.

According to Dr. Thomas Powell, the latest research is still inconclusive on the subject of birth order and gender. "There are pop psychology books which claim that the oldest child is more apt to be a leader and the last born child is overdependent," he asserts, "but I know of no scientific data that supports any of that. It makes for nice television but you can't make generalizations.

"There may be some tendency for the oldest female in a family to have the burden of the caretaking in the family, but if parents and professionals are aware of this tendency, they can guard against it. We want siblings to have responsibilities, but we shouldn't go overboard with it. Sometimes parents err on the side of saying they don't want to burden the healthy siblings with responsibilities at all."

WHEN THE YOUNGER SIBLING SURPASSES THE OLDER

In many families, problems often arise when a child younger than the sibling with the disability surpasses the disabled child in achievement. When the younger one talks before the older one, or walks, or goes to school, she may feel guilty at leaving her sibling behind.

Marge, a woman in her forties, says, "I'm four years younger than my brother. He sees himself as my older brother and he resents the fact that I have to be a parent to him. I have to pay the rent, see that he goes out with friends, has a social life. I say, 'What do you mean you lost the money order?' and he hates it."

Many younger siblings are sensitive about surpassing their older brother or sister with a disability in achievement and they learn kindness and diplomacy at an early age. Robert, for instance, still remembers the day he discovered that he could do some things his brother, brain damaged in an accident, could not. He was six years old, and his brother was thirteen when his mother gave the two of them twenty cents to buy gum at the store down the street.

> When we got to the store, I started to pay twenty cents for four pieces of gum, but there was a penny tax. So I realized we could only get three sticks of gum. I understood then, at the age of six, that it would be difficult for my brother to figure that out, so even though he was older, I took over when we got to the cash register. It was the first time I realized that I had gone past my brother in some things. He was my playmate, my friend. I loved him very much. The change in the relationship is still vividly marked in my mind.

Jenny, who is four years younger than her brother with cerebral palsy, remembers the first time she was aware of passing her older brother in achievement. She was eight years old and had learned to ride her two-wheeler. She had tried to teach Billy to ride, without success. But one day she came home from school and saw her older brother riding his bike around in a tight circle in the driveway, his knees all skinned because he wanted desperately to do what his little sister could do. "Then I realized how hard it must be for him not to be able to do what I could do. I hugged him and told him how wonderful he was."

Julie Tallard Johnson counsels families that part of the healing process when there is a child with a disability in the family is to be aware of the age difference and honor it.

> For instance, I have a lot of the characteristics of the oldest child even though I'm second to youngest in a family of five children, because my older brother is mentally ill. He became more like a younger brother to me. I had to learn to allow him to be my older brother instead of me always being the social worker or the older sister, which is humiliating for him. I had to respect the fact that he's my older brother. It made a significant shift in our relationship when I learned to do that.

SIZE OF THE FAMILY

The size of the family is often a determining factor in the way healthy siblings adjust to a child with a disability. I wish I had other brothers and sisters to talk to when I was growing up with Jackie. I wouldn't have felt so alone. When I was angry, embarrassed, resentful, or guilty, there would have been someone else who understood what I was feeling. We could have joined forces to face the world and it would have been a lot easier.

Donald Meyer and Patricia Vadasy, authors of *Sibshops*, tell us that feelings of resentment and shame like mine "usually seem to occur in families where there are only two children, one who is affected and one who is not. Additional children in the family appear to dilute the negative consequences of growing up with a sibling who has a disability or an illness. Other siblings can provide a typically developing child other children with whom he or she can identify and a built-in, informal means of support."

Ellen D'Amato, educational psychologist at the Harry W. Kohler Child Development Center in Winfield, New Jersey, agrees. "The situation is more difficult in families where there are just two children. The healthy sibling may feel intense responsibility in caretaking and also may have the feeling that 'I am the one who must achieve, I am the one who must be perfect. I must compensate for this child.' When there are a number of siblings there may not be that sense of burden."

That certainly seems to be true in Liz's family. Liz is thirty-six years old and a police officer. She is the oldest of six children in a close, loving family. When her mother was carrying her fifth child, she contracted German measles and the baby was born deaf. Doctors told her he had mental retardation, but Liz's mother knew there was no way this bright little boy was retarded. Finally when he was two, a doctor figured out that he was deaf and he went to a school for the deaf to learn sign language. Liz is unequivocal when asked if her brother was a burden on the family.

"No way," Liz says. "He was our little brother and we learned sign language to communicate with him, told the other kids in the neighborhood to knock it off when they teased him. We played with him, baby-sat for him, and loved him. My mother did spend more time with him, but he made the sign for 'Stop it! I'm fine,' and she left him alone. He's very independent today."

Can we say that it's a little easier growing up with a sibling with a disability if you live in a big family? Probably. Brothers and sisters can be very annoying sometimes, but they often understand you a lot better than your parents do, so they know how you feel about your disabled sibling.

No matter what the research shows about the type of disability, the age of the siblings when the brother or sister becomes disabled, the place in the birth order, or the size of the family, the one thing most experts agree on is that a sibling of a child with a disability who grows up in a loving family where the mother and father are open to questions and discussion has a good chance of being well adjusted when he grows up. This is not exactly startling news. Such a child would be well ahead whether she had a sibling with a disa-bility or not. Strong, loving families are obviously the best place to grow up.

To sum all this up, we have to be very careful about generalizing when we look for clues about how we "healthy" siblings got this way. Milton Seligman, coauthor of *Ordinary Families, Special Children,* and one of the leading specialists in the country in this field, told me, "I think there's only one conclusion you can come to when you're talking about the siblings of people with disabilities. And that is that there are so many factors involved in family adjustment that you can't make definitive statements about who will be well adjusted and who will not.

"You have to take into account life cycle changes, other problems in the family such as drug and alcohol abuse, other illnesses, how the mom and dad deal with it, what their relationship was like before the disabled child was born, whether the grandparents are involved with the family in a positive or negative way, whether the family lives in a rural community without a lot of early intervention programs available or in an urban community where help is offered. There are too many variables."

And to make things even more complicated, Thomas Powell points out that it's important to remember that a sibling of someone with a disability can have positive feelings about his brother or sister at one phase of his life and negative feelings at another. In fact emotions can run the gamut in a single day from anger, resentment, embarrassment, and guilt to pride, love, protectiveness, and joy.

"It doesn't really matter what the research says," Dr. Powell tells us. "The big issue in our society is, what are we doing about it? Now we have many more services. People aren't going to institutions any-more. We have the advent of the Education Act, we have supportive employment, supportive living, families getting subsidies. We have shifted from doing research which just describes the problem to re-search which is focused on action. 'Let's do something about it. Let's change the world.' And to me that is the excitement of this field of study."

The change in attitude toward those with a disability has made it easier in some ways for healthy siblings to deal with adolescence, but there will always be problems for all of us during our adolescent and teen years.

PART 2

Adolescence

5

ADOLESCENT ANGST

*a*s we grew older, the difference between Jack and other children became much more apparent. My mother still believed she could help him reach the top level of ability of which he was capable, and she probably did that. The only problem was that it wasn't a very high level. Jack could dress and feed himself, read and write on a very basic level, was toilet trained, but he couldn't carry on a conversation or live by himself.

As long as we lived in New Jersey with friends I'd known all my life who accepted Jackie as a little slow but not someone to be shunned or derided, I was all right. But when I was twelve we moved to Baltimore and everything changed. I left my friends in New Jersey who accepted Jack. We had all grown up together. Nobody rejected me because I had a brother who was mentally retarded. Nobody thought there must be something wrong with me too. But in Baltimore, neighbors stared at Jackie and kept their children away from him.

I was a very small twelve-year-old. I looked about eight. When we first arrived in Baltimore, I remember going to a party to meet other people who would be in my seventh grade class, and a really cute boy leaned over and said, the way you would to a child, "What grade are you in, little girl?" I was mortified.

I was also dressed all wrong. My mother had put me in a white organdy dress with a huge blue bow while every other girl was wearing a sweater and skirt and saddle shoes.

To make matters worse, I also blossomed with acne and my nose grew. Pimples, a large nose, and a brother who was mentally retarded did not make me the most popular girl in my class. I felt ugly inside too, unlovable.

The neighbors shunned us because we were "Yankees" and because they were uneasy around Jackie. He was ten now and his disability was more apparent. He ran awkwardly, his hands turned in. He wasn't an adorable little boy in a sailor shirt and navy blue jacket. Neither one of us was adorable anymore. I was embarrassed to be seen with him.

EMBARRASSMENT WITH NEW FRIENDS

Even people without a brother or sister with a disability are sometimes embarrassed by their siblings. But a disabled sibling who looks different is especially embarrassing to a teenager who wants to be like everyone else.

The adolescent years are a vulnerable time, particularly if you have just moved to a new place, as I had. You never really know how friends will react the first time they meet your sibling with a disability. You hold your breath waiting to find out what they will say—or not say. Will they find an excuse to leave and you'll never see them again? Will they pretend everything is all right, but never come back? Will they value your friendship enough to return? You never know.

I was recently reminded of my embarrassment when someone in my family said angrily to me, "You sound just like Jackie." I felt like I had been punched in the stomach. I didn't realize until that moment how much I was afraid that people would think I was like my brother. That's how I felt as a teenager in Baltimore, trying to make new friends. I remember worrying that if I didn't make sure they knew right away that I was smart, they would think I was retarded, too, that it ran in the family. I did *not* want to be identified with him.

I felt a strong kinship with Julia Ellifritt when I read her story in *Exceptional Parent* about moving to a new town when she was a teenager. She decided not to tell anybody about her sister, Bonnie, who has mental retardation.

"This was my chance to start over," she writes. "I was starting high school in a new town where no one knew me. I swore to myself that I would not let Bonnie embarrass me anymore. In my mind Bonnie suddenly disappeared."

When her new friends asked her if she had any brothers or sisters, she said no.

"Bonnie was not going to be my problem; she was not my sister. I would simply lie. It was easier to lie than to explain," she writes.

Her plan worked until the night she went to a church meeting and the leader introduced her as the sister of a girl who was mentally retarded.

Julia struggled alone at first to come to terms with her embarrassment, her guilt about her angry feelings toward her sister, her resentment toward her parents who never explained her sister's retardation or allowed Julia to express her frustration or confusion. But therapy and sibling support groups helped her resolve the embarrassment and anger that had built up for so many years. Hearing others talk about their own negative feelings about a retarded sibling was an enormous relief. "The joy I felt was indescribable," she says.

Gerri Zatlow understands Julia's feelings all too well. "It's cruel to make healthy siblings feel there is something wrong with them when they are embarrassed," she says. "Don't tell your other children they have no right to be upset when their sibling is undressing in public. Don't say, 'What's the matter with you? Don't you know he can't help it?' It's insane, crazy behavior, but parents expect you to ignore it and act like it's not happening. And that's wrong!

"You're making them feel crazy. They think: 'My mother isn't upset, my father isn't upset. Maybe I'm crazy for getting upset. Tell them it's normal to be embarrassed, that you're embarrassed, too."

Betty's brother, who has mental retardation, also has Tourette's Syndrome. When he's in a large crowd of people he gets anxious and starts cursing. She has given up taking him places. "I just can't take him anywhere he doesn't want to go. We don't force him. It's not worth it. He can't handle a whole bunch of people—especially at big family gatherings, like weddings. It's too embarrassing."

MENTAL ILLNESS

As I pointed out earlier, the disability that can cause the most embarrassment to the healthy siblings is probably mental illness and it is also the most distressing during adolescence. According to the study by Jan Greenberg, Marsha Seltzer, and Marty Krauss comparing the effects of mental retardation and mental illness on families, "The siblings of people who are mentally ill have very little positive to say because their brothers' and sisters' behavior is so erratic. The community services are just not there, and the stigma is so strong they just want to flee. They can't get away fast enough. They worry about the safety of their parents—and they should."

"I never know when my sister is going to do something crazy," says Carla, who is twelve. "She'll be fine and then we'll be out with friends and she'll start taking her clothes off. I just want to crawl in a hole and die. And I hate the way she treats our mother. I know it's her illness that makes her act like that, but she is always blaming her for everything and once she even hit her. My brother told her if she ever touched our mother again, he would kill her. All the rest of us in the family are sort of holding our breath all the time waiting for her to do something terrible. As soon as I'm old enough, I'm moving far away."

Margaret Moorman, in an eloquent and moving book, *My Sister's Keeper*, about her sister with mental illness, writes:

> I was entering adolescence, and I wanted friends—neat friends. I was afraid that Sally's strangeness would get in the way of my social life. For me, Sally was a liability and I all but stopped speaking to her. If I could behave as if she were invisible, she might disappear.
>
> As a teenager, I earnestly pursued the fantasy that I was an only child. Denying Sally's very existence enabled me to concentrate on trying to make my own life seem as normal as possible, but it eventually took a toll. I couldn't bear to be alone, and I was often unable to concentrate. In my early teens I began to have trouble studying, and by the time I reached high school, I could barely keep up with my classes. I was often deeply depressed.

FITTING IN

Margaret Moorman's phrase "trying to make my own life seem as normal as possible," epitomizes my struggle to be like everybody else. In addition to my embarrassment about my brother, I was in culture shock when I started junior high in Baltimore. In 1940, there was still a North/South war going on in this border city. On my second day of school, a classmate said to me, "I hate Yankees. A Yankee soldier pushed my grandmother down the stairs." I had no idea how to cope with this—or anything else. For the first time in my life, I got Cs on my report card. I was a mess.

My mother found an excellent school for my brother—the William S. Baer School for Handicapped Children, as they were called in those days.(The word "handicapped" is no longer used in the name of the school.) For the first time, Jack wasn't the only one with physical and mental problems. As part of my research for this book, I asked the William S. Baer School to send me Jack's records. There wasn't much there, but I was moved by the notation, "Boy is rather playful and does not help when given direction regarding relaxation." I never thought of him that way at all.

While Jack had found a place that he fit right into, I felt left out, ignored, just like a person with a disability often does. I didn't know how to cope with new people.

When I was thirteen, World War II started, but I was waging my own inner battles. I was full of adolescent angst, and my mother didn't know how to handle it. Once, she and my father went away for the weekend and left us with an aunt. I teased Jackie and he chased me around the house with a hammer. I was so afraid that he might kill me, I completely forgot that I was supposed to go to dance class.

When my mother returned, I ran to the car to hug her. She reached for Jackie first and then asked me if I had gone to dance class. Those were her first remarks to me. Not "I love you and I missed you," which I wanted to hear. No, she asked about the dance class. When I said I forgot to go, she scolded me and paid no attention when I told her Jackie had tried to kill me. I thought she was very unfair, and it must have affected me deeply because I'm still mad at her to this day. Jackie never got punished for anything, but I was supposed to be good all the time.

LIFE IS UNFAIR

This sense of unfairness runs like a scar through all of the literature about the siblings of people with disabilities. When I talk to other siblings, a trace of bitterness often creeps into their voices when they talk about their responsibilities during adolescence. It's not easy to find someone who will change an incontinent fourteen-year-old in a wheelchair. What mother would let a neighborhood teenage girl sit for a retarded young man? Who would take care of a child with a disability for a week so the parents could take a vacation by themselves? It's hard to go out for dinner, much less take a vacation.

Gerri Zatlow remembers having to sit with her brother who has autism:

> From the moment my parents divorced, I was Douglas's other mother. Who was going to baby-sit for my brother? He had temper tantrums that could last an hour, biting, breaking plates, ripping, destroying. Who are you going to find who will handle that?
>
> I had to be home every day after school because my mother worked. If I missed the bus, I heard about it. I had no time for myself. I was twelve years old and I did the grocery shopping with Douglas. I wanted to be with my friends hanging out. I never hung out. I never got into trouble. I looked at people doing dope in front of me, and I thought, "My parents didn't do any drugs and they had Douglas." If I did drugs, I'd have a kid with six heads, four ears, and eight arms.
>
> It's not fair to make a child be her brother's keeper. It distorts and twists the sibling relationship, makes you think of the disabled child as a burden. And you'd be surprised how often people forget to say please and thank you when they expect the other children in the family to do something unpleasant or difficult for the child with the disability.
>
> One mother of a fifteen-year-old said to me, "I asked my daughter to stay with her brother so we could go out, and she

did it but she didn't do it happily." I said, "Happily? She gave up going to a party to stay with her brother so you and your husband could go out and you want her to be happy? At least say thank you."

Dr. Debra Lobato says that siblings in her support group often complain that their parents just expect them to help and then don't show enough appreciation for that help, which is the bigger issue. She cites recent studies that show that children in a household with a child with a disability only spend seven more minutes a day on chores than children in a house where there is no disability. She says:

> When the healthy child feels resentment, it's usually because of the way they are asked to help, not the amount of time. Children who are the most resentful are those who are given responsibility for a child who is antagonistic and irritable. There is probably a good reason why Mom and Dad don't want to do it. They are shifting it onto another child who does not appreciate that. The children who are given responsibility for more neutral, non-child-care tasks don't have any more resentment about their responsibilities than others.
>
> Kids need to learn responsibility and there's a great sense of self-esteem that comes from knowing that you have made a positive contribution to your family. When they are praised and not asked to do child care unless they volunteer, there is less stress.
>
> A household can't go the way children want it. It has to go the way the parents want it. If you are in a family where everybody has to pitch in, and tasks are assigned fairly and consistently, without acrimony, without feeling that you are obligated to work, there is less resentment.
>
> Siblings usually respond positively to a legitimate request for help. They want to contribute to the family, and like every other sibling, they want to be appreciated when they do help.

Because the older sister is so often expected to help when there is a disability in the family, other siblings may not realize until later how unfair that decision can be.

In one family, the two oldest sisters took a semester off from college to help their mother care for a brother who was paralyzed in an automobile accident. Their younger brother didn't really appreciate their sacrifice at the time. Now in his thirties, he says, "If anybody got the short end of the stick it was my sisters. They gave up their own ambitions for a time to help around the house, to take care of Pete, to take care of all of us. I don't think we understood what they gave up. I sometime wonder if I ever let them know how much I admired them for doing that."

Andrea, whose twin sister has epilepsy, was put in an unusual position during adolescence because her sister's seizures usually occurred at school during athletic events, or at dances or social events on weekends. When she had a seizure, Andrea was paged to come and take care of her twin.

"I ran track," she says "and I would be pulled off a race when my sister had a seizure. As if I were the only one who knew what to do. Anyone could have helped her, but they paged me over the intercom whenever she was in trouble. And I accepted that role. Everyone depended on me."

Being given too much responsibility because of a sibling's disability can often lead to the feeling that what you do best in life is take care of other people, says psychologist Bryna Siegel. "When mothers say, 'I could never cope with Billy if I didn't have Mary here to help me— she's like his mother,' Mary may grow up getting involved with alcoholics or other kinds of not-too-competent people. She will feel she is worthy of love only when she is in a caretaking role."

Angela, whom we met before, grew up in a home with two siblings with a disability *and* a mother with alcoholism. She had to become her own mother during adolescence because her mother could not handle the situation:

> I felt, as the eldest, like the back-up mother, not only for my brothers, but for my parents, too. Mom's alcoholism often interfered with normal family life, and being a part-time mother was often a necessity for me. I might have to prepare holiday meals at the last minute because Mom was "tired" (which meant she was drunk), or I would have to get the boys ready for school in the morning because Mom had a "rough night,"

or wash and iron their clothes and dress them for an outing when Mom couldn't get herself together. I developed a way of withdrawing and separating myself to survive.

Things were so bad that I had a breakdown at nineteen and married early to get out of that house. My marriage ended in divorce.

Not all healthy siblings resent the caretaking they had to do during adolescence, of course. Psychologist Milton Seligman feels that one of the things that has changed over the last twenty years is a new and more positive attitude toward caretaking on the part of some healthy siblings.

"It was once considered a pretty negative behavior by the siblings who had to engage in it," he told me. "but now that isn't necessarily so. Some siblings actually enjoy it if it's not overwhelming and not a replacement for the parent. A lot depends too on the number of kids in the family. In a large family the sharing of caretaking responsibilities is dissipated because one person doesn't end up doing it all. In extended families, there may be help from a grandparent or aunt or uncle."

Peggy, now in her forties, grew up as the oldest sister in a totally chaotic household because of the mental illness of her mother and two brothers. She happily took over the caretaking responsibilities of her younger siblings and her mother. "I knew instinctively that my job was to take care of everyone from the time I was a little child because my mom had so many problems. I actually loved being at home taking care of things. It made me feel important and valuable. I always felt I was the one who had to fix things. I didn't leave home until I was thirty."

It's not always the older sister who is asked to take on adult responsibilities. In some families an older brother is asked to carry part of the burden. Paul will never forget having to lie to his mother when he was sixteen after his sister with Down syndrome was born. Paul's father told him that there was something wrong with the new baby but that his mother didn't know it yet. He asked Paul not to tell her when he spoke to her on the phone in the hospital. "It was definitely one of the most poignant moments of my life," Paul says. "It was really sad because she was just bubbly and happy. It was the easiest of her five deliveries. She was delighted that she had another girl with three boys and one girl in our family. And I was trying not to cry while she was so enthusiastic."

There's no forgetting such an experience, and today Paul has a doctorate in special education and has played a large part in his sister's development.

For most teens who have a sibling with a disability, the sense that life is unfair is strong and pervasive and can often lead to some kind of rebellion during those difficult adolescent years. Today that rebellion might be taking drugs, promiscuous sex, or piercing some part of the body, but in the innocent 1940s, we had to settle for pretty tame acting-out.

One day I rebelled in my own way against the whole unfair adult world. I was around thirteen and was like a fierce little ball of anger by this time. Every morning, a whole battalion of school children got off the trolley car and walked up a long hill to the junior high. We walked in the street because the only sidewalk was a stone footpath on the other side of a wall. It was uneven and we couldn't walk side by side. A policeman we called Smoky Joe because of his sunglasses, drove by and told us to get out of the street because we were a hazard to the cars.

For some reason I spoke up and told him the sidewalk wasn't big enough and we weren't going to move. Me. Good little Mary. Everyone cheered and Smoky Joe followed us into the school yard. All the kids were on my side and it was my first recognition since we had moved to Baltimore. I kept arguing with the policeman and he reported me to the principal. I had never in my life been in trouble, and here I was defying the police *and* the principal. When I was called to the prin- cipal's office, several of my classmates came along to back me up, and of course, I crumbled. I apologized and cried and my tiny flame of rebellion was squashed forever. My mother was appalled, but neither she nor I made any connection whatsoever between my behavior and the reality that I was very angry and sick of being good.

ANGER AND FRUSTRATION

There's no way around frustration and anger when you live in a house with a brother or sister with a disability. Adolescence is a difficult time for most people anyway, but when you add a disability to the family, there are bound to be times when you just can't stand it another minute.

"You're confused," says one fifteen-year-old girl, whose sister has epilepsy, "because you know you should be feeling one way because of what your parents are telling you—more tolerant, more understanding, because my sister is going through a hard time. But at the same time, you're thinking, 'No one understands that I'm really upset, I'm really angry.'"

Julie has learned to just leave the room and even the house when her twin sister Janna with cerebral palsy is in a bad mood. "I can't stay in the same room with her," she says. "If I do, I'll probably lose it. I used to think that it was not good to be angry, that it was wrong, and that it was a sin, and I was never to do that. Well, that's not true. That was the hardest thing for me to accept as a sib because I used to get frustrated a lot."

Julie and Janna's father understands how difficult it is for the twins and for their older brother Brad. "There are times when it is frustrating for them, I'm sure, and for us. There is a need for them to be in their own worlds. And Janna is not part of that world really. It's tough to know when it's okay to split and be in your own world, and when you sort of owe an allegiance to stay home."

Diane, a college student whose sister has mental retardation, remembers wanting her parents to come to see her play basketball in high school. "It always hurt me when my parents were never able to come to watch me participate," she says. "I felt that they did not care about what I was doing, what my so-called accomplishments were. Of course the excuse always was, 'Well, you know we cannot find a baby-sitter, and you will just have to accept that.' But I really did not accept it at the time, and I thought, Well, they do not care. They just do not want to go, they could find a baby-sitter if they really wanted to."

Deep down Diane knew that her parents would be there if they could, and that it was only the seriousness of her sister's condition that kept them away, but she still felt resentment and then felt guilty for the resentment.

GUILT

Guilt is the most useless of feelings and also the hardest to get rid of. It starts in childhood, continues through adolescence, and stays throughout adulthood. When you are a child, you feel guilty about teasing a sibling with a disability or being afraid you have caused the illness or about being "bad" and disappointing your parents. As an adolescent, you feel guilty about wanting to get away from your sibling and your parents, not realizing that the teen years are the times when you are *supposed* to separate from your family and establish your own identity. When you are an adult, you can dream up all kinds of reasons to feel guilty.

If I talk about guilt a lot in this book it's because most of the other siblings I speak to are tormented by it. There's always a variation to the theme, as many reasons for feeling guilty as there are siblings with a brother or sister with a disability. Ahadi, whose sister has epilepsy, graduated from Yale with a Ph.D. and a law degree. She told me about her own guilt during adolescence:

> I felt guilt on so many levels—especially when I was a teenager. I felt guilty about feeling resentful. How did I have the nerve to even begin to say that I've had a difficult time? Look what my sister had to go through. I felt the guilt of not having epilepsy, at being angry at Tia because my mother wasn't there, the guilt of wanting my mother to be there when she couldn't be.
>
> I remember one trip we took to Hershey Park. It took us forever to get there. We rode for hours in the car. As soon as we got there, my sister had a seizure and we had to turn around and come home because she could have another seizure at any time. I was so angry that we had to leave without seeing anything after that long ride. Then, of course, I was terribly guilty because I was angry at my sister who couldn't help it.
>
> The trick is learning to work through the guilt and mini-

mizing it in such a way that you are productive as opposed to incapacitated by it. I've pretty much learned to do that now.

Twins of someone with a disability often feel a heightened sense of guilt when their sibling cannot do all the things they can. The feeling "Why should she have a disability and not me when we were born at the same time?" causes that guilt.

Andrea says her relationship with her twin began to change when Andrea got her driver's license and her sister could not get one because of the frequency of her epileptic seizures. Until that time, Andrea says, she actually tended to depend on her twin.

"I was quiet and shy," she says. "She was more outgoing. I was nervous about college and chose the same school she was going to. She had a hard time adjusting to college life, largely because of her seizures, and she dropped out. Our lives changed just that much more because I graduated and she didn't. I got a master's degree, married and had children. She has decided not to have children and that makes me very sad.

"Do I feel guilty because I was able to do all those things and she couldn't? Oh yes. I wonder, How did I luck out? We were twins, born at the same time. It could have been me."

Brian's mother helped him understand that it wasn't his fault that his little brother was hit by a car while Brian, twelve, was taking care of him, and now Shawn is unable to walk or talk.

"My brother broke away from me and ran into the street to get to my other brother standing on the other side," Brian says. "I tried to hold him back but he just broke away. He got hit by a car and it dragged him down the block. I thought it was my fault. But my mother told me that it wasn't my fault."

Even so, you know that Brian will see the image of his little brother being dragged down the street for the rest of his life. You can see it in the tenderness he shows when he feeds his brother and in the haunted look in his eyes when he talks about the accident. When he says, "It just feels like I'm doing what I'm supposed to do," when he helps his mother with Shawn, you know that it helps him too.

Psychiatrist John S. Rolland warns in his book *Families, Illness, and*

Disability that parents must be careful to encourage a child to express feelings of guilt and not reassure them too quickly: "When sibling guilt is not openly addressed, a child can harbor fears, such as of losing control of his or her anger and physically harming or killing someone."

Katie was careful to let her daughter Chris talk about her guilt when her younger sister Gina was seriously injured by a car when the two girls were at a Halloween festival. Chris was twelve and Gina was nine. "I knew it was important to let her work through her own feelings," Katie says. "My first instinct was to say, 'Of course it wasn't your fault.' But that wouldn't have helped Chris. It would have shut our conversation off. I made sure she knew I was listening to her. Then she came to her own realization that it wasn't her fault."

Glenn, now fifty-four, took on his mother's guilt after his brother was born with Down syndrome, and it affected his life profoundly. He grew up a Catholic in a small town in Iowa in the 1940s. His mother divorced his father when Glenn was ten and then remarried, earning the disapproval of the small, closed-in, religious community where they lived. A year later his mother gave birth to a child with Down syndrome.

"Our relatives said, 'This is God's punishment for marrying outside the church,'" Glenn says. "I felt judged too, for being part of this family. I went into the Catholic seminary when I was fifteen, and I think part of my decision to do that was to make amends for my mother marrying outside the church."

Glenn became a priest, but later left the priesthood to marry, have children, and work in a home for people with mental retardation. And though he doesn't realize it completely, the fabric of his life is woven inextricably with threads of his brother's retardation. It has made him stronger, but also, he says, "a little suspicious. I need to know a little bit more before I trust people and life. Some of that comes from the fact that I know things can pop up in your life that can be pretty brutal, so I'm less likely to assume the best."

He is also more compassionate, more tolerant, more open to people with disabilities and problems than other people. "I tend to judge people very much on personality, character, attitude, rather than the way they look on the outside," he says.

When parents don't tell their other children the truth about the sick brother or sister, it can cause devastating guilt later on. Brenda's sisters both had cystic fibrosis, but because her parents didn't tell her how life-threatening the disease was, Brenda, now in her twenties, is left with a consuming guilt after the death of one her sisters. She talked about it on a videotape, *Keeping the Balance*:

> I kick myself now. I remember saying to Jody when she complained about having to go to the hospital, "Oh, I'd love to go to the hospital for a week, getting candy and presents and being with Mom and Dad, watching TV." She was getting a lot of attention, getting served her meals in bed. I didn't understand the severity of this disease. My parents didn't tell my sister and me a lot. I wonder, was that right of them not to tell us anything?

Brenda's eyes fill with tears as she struggles to understand why her parents didn't tell her that her sister might die:

> When my sisters were diagnosed with cystic fibrosis, their life expectancy was five years, and then it got a little bit better gradually. I don't blame my parents for not telling me because why would you tell somebody your sisters might not be around in five or ten years? I'm glad in some respects that they held that back from me so that I could live a normal life with my sisters. I wish that as I got older I had learned a little bit more because I don't really feel I was as sympathetic to my sisters' situation as I could have been had I known more. And I think it would have changed a lot.
>
> Jody really took it hard when I said I'd love to be able to go to the hospital. I never realized until years later when she said to me, "You didn't really understand what I was going through." Now I wonder how I could ever have said that, but if you look at it from a young child's perspective, you really don't understand what they're going through. I wish now that I . . . it's too hard to talk about it.
>
> The day before Jody passed away, I was with her in the hospital and I said, "Jody, I'm really sorry for everything that I did. I know that I wasn't the best sister to you."
>
> She said, "But Brenda, you're making up for it now," and she put her hand on my knee and she said, "When I get out,

we're going to crack open that bottle of liqueur I gave you, and we're going to celebrate because we finally got our relationship back to where it was."

I really cannot thank God enough for that day because then it really hit home that we finally were the sisters I had always wanted us to be. I know that she left feeling like she and I were very, very close.

I remember saying to her that if we could have switched roles, if I could have taken her pain away and she could have lived my life, I would have gladly done it. I guess you look at, Why was I so lucky? And why was she unlucky? Things happen for a reason. I guess it's the way it was meant to be.

Would it have been better if her parents had told her from the beginning that her sisters would not live long lives? Would Brenda have had a normal, give-and-take relationship with her sisters? Or would she have worried all the time about losing them? It's hard to fault her parents, but if she had understood the seriousness of her sisters' plight, she would not have to live with the guilt she carries with her now.

Cassie is grateful that her mother saved her from guilt about her sister with cerebral palsy. "My mother sent me to college at sixteen. She said, 'Get out of here and don't move back home because this is not a good life for you. You've got to go out and make your own life.' She never made me feel guilty for a millisecond. She was amazing, and I'm grateful that she did that."

My mother certainly didn't mean to make me feel guilty. She took Jackie to school, struggled with the rationing of gas, meat, sugar, and butter, volunteered in the community, waited for the weekends when my father came home from Washington where he worked for Vannevar Bush in the Office of Research and Development. She assumed I was all right because I didn't talk to her about my problems.

The trouble was I wasn't all right. I had few friends, felt scared and lonely, ugly and different. My father was no help. He didn't have a clue as to how to make a teenage daughter feel loved and secure and pretty. And it didn't help that I could never talk to him.

I was so unhappy and lonely during those adolescent years. I know I'm not the only person in the world who had a horrible adolescence, but having a brother with mental retardation certainly didn't make it easier. If there had been someone I could have talked to about it, it would have helped a lot.

GETTING HELP

Obviously, you can't go through life without feelings. Nor do you consciously summon up feelings of anger, shame, embarrassment, resentment, and guilt. They just work their way into your heart and mind and you're stuck with them. They can do harm to you, though, if you don't ask someone for help. They will eat away at your self-esteem and warp your behavior later on, so you can't ignore those feelings. Talk to someone who can reassure you that your feelings are normal and that you will come to terms with them someday.

Lucy found a sympathetic therapist when she suffered a serious depression in college. The therapist helped her understand that she had stifled her feelings of anger and grief during her adolescent years after her sister with Angelman syndrome (a disorder that interferes with the ability to speak) was sent to a boarding school when Lucy was twelve. During those teenage years, she pushed her sister to the back of her mind, trying to forget her:

> My sister had been such a crucial, daily part of my life until then, and all of a sudden she was gone. My therapist helped me deal with the feelings I had suppressed. It was a painful but incredibly rewarding experience. It was like the fog was lifted. Things looked sharper, crisper, than they had before. Or more accurately, it was like somebody took away a glass that was in front of me my whole life, that I could see through but which kept some kind of distance between me and the world. I never realized it was there until it was taken away. I thought I was a very well-adjusted person emotionally, but now I know I had a lot of problems I never faced because of my sister.

Most of us don't suffer major psychiatric breakdowns, as Lucy did. We all have problems of adjustment, especially during adolescence, but psychologist Thomas Powell reassures us that, "The majority of siblings will *not* need psychotherapy to handle their feelings and concerns or to learn new ways to solve their problems. Less intense, more informal, counseling is recommended for most siblings who have brothers and sisters with disabilities."

What should you look for in a counselor besides maturity, honesty, empathy, acceptance, and ethics? Dr. Powell tells us to look for someone with a solid knowledge of "social services and community resources available, as well as being cognizant of state-of-the-art philosophies concerning human development, behavioral principles, and disabling conditions. Successful counselors are fully aware of current research related to siblings as well as innovative service programs aimed at meeting their needs."

"You get through all your difficult feelings," Ahadi told me. "It's hard to believe that you will mature and live through the resentment and anger and embarrassment, but you do. There were so many times when I wanted my mom to go on school trips with me but she couldn't because my sister was sick. Naturally I was resentful and angry. But it's not something I dwell on now. My mother and I have such a tremendous relationship and we reconnected from those times when she was so busy and so focused on Tia. It's not as if those connections are permanently frayed. It goes in spurts."

I transferred to Friends' School in my sophomore year of high school. I did not mention my brother to my new classmates. I felt different enough. I only had one friend who might have understood. Her sister had Down syndrome and Florence never talked about her either. She was also a good student and a good girl. When I went to her house and saw her sister, I felt a deep bond with Florence, but we never discussed it. She just filled me in on the essentials: Anne was older than she was; she was sick a lot. That was it. She never expressed any resentment for having a sister with a disability. She never said, "I wish I lived in a normal family." And I never said any of those things to her about Jackie either. It was understood that you didn't talk about it.

We could have helped each other a lot if we'd known enough to admit that we felt ashamed, resentful, and guilty about our siblings. We each fit the profile Don Meyer describes of those healthy siblings most likely to feel shame: someone born before the 1960s when John

F. Kennedy spoke openly about his sister with mental retardation and Hubert Humphrey talked lovingly about his granddaughter with Down syndrome; someone who grew up in a home where there was no discussion or opportunity to ask questions about the disability; and someone in a family of only two children, without other siblings to share the load.

I called Florence while I was writing this book and we connected as if we hadn't been out of touch for forty years. That bond was still there. She said she wished we could have talked to each other about our siblings when we were adolescents. "The hardest thing about being a teenager," she said, "is that you think you're the only one with a problem. Then when you grow up, you find out that everyone had some kind of difficulty to deal with in their families."

She remembers thinking how nice it would be to have a regular family vacation. "I would go somewhere either with my mother *or* my father, but we couldn't leave my sister alone for any length of time for a real vacation."

Then she remembered something so painful that we both started to cry when she told me about it. "My mother said that if she had known Anne was retarded, she never would have had me. She became pregnant with me soon after Anne was born, before the doctors had diagnosed her Down syndrome. My mother loved me—I know she did—but it was so hard having a child like Anne that my mother wouldn't have had another child. That hurts so much."

When I told her I always felt I had to be good all the time, so good that my smile felt frozen on my face, she agreed. "That's a terrible thing to put on a kid," she said. "Why *shouldn't* we have been a problem once in a while? You feel you have to be really good because your mother and father have this tragedy to cope with. You couldn't let your parents down because they had a terrible kick in the teeth."

Friends' was a wonderful school with gifted teachers. But I was so lonely. Nobody would come to my house after school. I assumed it was because their mothers didn't want their daughters in a house with a teenage mentally retarded boy, but it might also have been because I was a little strange in those days. I was certainly mordantly shy. I would blush if anyone said "Hello." I had no self-esteem whatsoever.

The walk home from school was a long one–I was almost always alone, stumbling along the rough path in my blue-and-white uniform carrying a heavy bag filled with the books that were my only friends. My thoughts were gloomy. I wanted friends. I wanted to be popular. I wanted boys to like me.

Twice a week I worked at the local library putting books back on the shelves. It was a perfect job for me. I was almost happy surrounded by all those books. Books were my substitute for friends, family, popularity. When there was a lull I would sit in a quiet corner and read everything from *Dr. Dolittle* to Shakespeare. I was inside those books, caught up in the story, totally involved with the characters. I lived vicariously through them. To this day I have a love affair with reading and still get lost in books when I want to escape.

At home I would go to my room, do my homework, avoid my mother, pick at my dinner, do more homework, and go to bed. I actually typed up my notes from all my classes every night. What kind of a life was that for a fourteen-year-old?

LOVE AND PRIDE

I'm happy to say many of the siblings I talked to told me a different story about their adolescence. It was not exactly their favorite stage of life, but they had more help from their families and friends than I did and usually didn't have to cope with a new place to live. These siblings talk about their brothers and sisters with love and appreciation for the added dimension they have given to their lives.

Ahadi, who has talked many times in this book about her sister, Tia, who has epilepsy, takes great pride in her sister's accomplishments and character. She feels Tia has overcome great odds in life. "Tia has her own strengths. I remember one time when she went to get her blood work done in the hospital–she had to go so often–and a little girl was crying because she was afraid to go into the doctor's office. Tia automatically, without even thinking, took the child's hand, walked in with her, calmed her down, and played with her until she was okay. Tia is a lovely person. I'm so proud of her. I love her so much that it's hard to express. She inspires me every day. I would like others to know that with all of the hardships, we have been truly blessed in so many ways. I honestly believe that God never gives us more than we can handle. The stressful times make us stronger in the end. Yet my sister's constant gentleness and care prevents my skin from becoming too thick. She reminds me to keep loving."

Mark and Tim are teenagers who have an older brother, Andrew, with cerebral palsy. "Having Andrew for a brother has made me a better person," Mark says. "The doctor told him there wasn't too good a chance that he would walk, but he's walking fine now. It shows you can do anything when you actually try."

"In many ways my brother is smarter than I am," Tim says. "I can talk to him about things I can't talk to my parents about and he always helps me. My brother understands people's problems more than anyone else. He remembers everything. He can't read because he doesn't see print the way you and I do, but if you read something to him, he remembers every word. That's why it's very hard now when I've started getting brochures from colleges and I know he can't go. I hope someday he will be able to go."

Megan is seventeen, and in *Views from Our Shoes*, she writes that her brother Andy, who has Down syndrome, has taught her a lot—that she's a better person because he was born into her family.

> I became a more accepting person after the birth of Andy. I became more accustomed to seeing people with disabilities and not staring like I did before. I see Andy as a totally typical kid, not as a kid who needs a lot of help, or even as a kid with Down syndrome. Because of Andy I have learned how to cope with things in my life. My friend John died the summer before my junior year. Andy helped me through that too, when he said, "Don't cry Meg, you'll make John sad. He doesn't want to see you cry."
>
> Every day Andy teaches me not to give up. He knows he is different, but he doesn't focus on that. He doesn't give up, and every time I see him having a hard time, I make myself work that much harder. He teaches me to be dedicated to my work and to be proud of all I do, just as he is.

If I had not grown up with him, I would have less un-derstanding, patience, and compassion for people. He shows us that anyone can do anything.

Susan's sister, Pam, also has Down syndrome, and Susan adores her.

I'm only four years older than Pam, and we played together, traded clothes, fought over the TV when we were little. We're sisters. I was never embarrassed by her. She's pretty and affectionate and all my friends accepted her too.

The first time I ever felt any stress about having Pam for a sister was in seventh grade in science class. This was back in 1969, the Dark Ages as far as Down syndrome was con-cerned. The science teacher started talking about Mongolian idiocy, and he said these children had a life expectancy of twelve because so many of them were born with holes in their hearts. Many died in infancy.

I felt my face get very hot and I had to fight back tears because Pam was seven at the time. I knew she had a life expectancy of more than twelve and that she didn't have a hole in her heart, but it was so scary to me to hear that my sister was part of a group that my science teacher would talk about in class.

One of the kids came up to me later and said, "Isn't your sister one of those Mongoloids?" And I said, "No," and brushed him off and walked away. It was terrible.

Sometimes feelings of embarrassment and resentment felt in childhood and early adolescence turn into love and pride when a sibling matures. Louis Perwien wrote an article in *Exceptional Parent* about his confused feelings about his brother Artie, who has mental retardation, when Louis was thirteen.

"There are times when I wouldn't mind having a different brother," he wrote. "Like when I have friends over and he walks by my room wearing nothing but his diaper. Or when we are in a restaurant and he starts screeching for no apparent reason. I can feel people staring, and I know they're thinking, 'What's wrong with that kid?' I know they just don't understand, but I still get upset.

"When I was younger, I was ashamed of Artie. I never had friends over–I was afraid they would see him. When I drew pictures of my family, Artie was always missing. At one point, nobody even knew I had a brother. But as we have grown, Artie has become my favorite sibling."

I talked to Louis recently–he's fifteen now–and asked him why he thinks his attitude toward Artie changed.

"I think I matured," Louis said. "Artie grew a little more in his level of skill and I grew in how much I could accept. It wasn't anything miraculous. I just came to accept him. I think my friends like Artie best of my brothers and sisters. He's a nice guy. You can't dislike him. He loves you unconditionally.

"I used to resent the fact that Artie got all these privileges and extra attention. Then, I came to a realization that it is because of his differences that he needs this extra attention and I understand that now."

As Louis wrote in this article: "I love Artie more than you can believe. And even though he doesn't say it, I know the feeling is mutual. I can see it in his eyes when we play a game and in his smile when I sing with him. I can hear it in his laughter when I talk to him."

Amy is so proud of her brother Paul, who has spina bifida, that she sent me a poem he wrote:

> I am a ten-year-old boy in a wheelchair,
> I wonder if there will be a cure for Spina Bifida,
> I hear my mom calling me to walk to her,
> I see my mom urging me on to walk,
> I am a ten-year-old boy in a wheelchair.
>
> I pretend to walk,
> I felt the urge to walk,
> I can feel my mom touching my leg,
> I worry about my disease,
> I cry at my disease,
> I am a ten-year-old boy in a wheelchair.
>
> I understand my disease,
> I say there will be a cure,

I dream there will be a cure,
I try to stay positive,
I hope there will be a cure,
I am understanding about my disease
I am a ten year-old-boy in a wheelchair.
in a wheelchair.

> by Paul Shaughnessy

Amy is eighteen and a freshman in college. Paul is eleven, and to Amy, he is just like any other little brother—sometimes annoying, sometimes lovable. When Amy talks about him, I know times have changed dramatically from the time I was a teenager, embarrassed and resentful of my brother:

My brother is *extremely* outgoing. He loves to call my friends on the telephone. When they come over, he sits in the room and talks to them—sometimes too much. It doesn't matter much that he's in a wheelchair.

It does take an extra fifteen minutes to get out of the house because of Paul's wheelchair, but you just make allowances for that. It was a thrill when we went to Disney World because we didn't have to wait in line because of the wheelchair.

My mom went back to school to become a nurse when I was fourteen, but she was always home after school. She was there more than I wanted her to be when I was a teenager. She made dinner every night. I never felt deprived.

My dad has done tremendous things with Paul. He used to work for the Louisville Sluggers, and he took Paul to meet all the Red Sox. He takes him to baseball games and to the golf course.

I asked Amy if she had to do a lot of baby-sitting for Paul. She said she did, but she didn't mind because she took him every place with her and just asked her friends to come over when she had to stay home with him.

"I definitely feel bad for him," Amy says. "Everything is a challenge. Just getting dressed in the morning is hard. I feel bad that he will encounter even more troubles when he turns eighteen. I hope he can deal with it. He's had twelve operations. The last one he was in a body cast for seven months. It was horrible. I stayed home with him a lot because he couldn't get out of bed. I don't remember ever being angry with him. How could I be mad at him?"

Would she like to go to a support group for other siblings of people with disabilities?

"I don't think I would need to go to reassure myself," says this confident, secure young woman. "But I would love to help anyone who needed help."

She has volunteered at the Special Olympics and at the camp where Paul goes in the summer.

What will happen in the future? Her parents will try to help Paul live on his own, be independent someday. And Amy will always be a part of his life. To her, anything else would be unthinkable.

6

WHO ARE YOU?

*a*ccording to researchers B. D. Blumberg, M. J. Lewis, and E. J. Susman, the most important tasks of adolescence are

- Establishing your own identity
- Achieving independence
- Preparing for the future
- Developing mature relationships with peers
- Developing a positive self-image and body image

As with everything else in your life, these tasks are all affected by having a sibling with a disability. Communication is the key to every one of them, starting with your parents.

ASKING TO BE INCLUDED IN FAMILY DISCUSSIONS

My mother was not the kind of person who could sit down with me and say, "Is there something bothering you? Let's talk about it." Our conversations consisted mostly of things she wanted me to do and my saying I didn't want to do them. I wish my mother had included me in her plans for Jack. I wish she could have asked for my help. Adolescence is a time when you often feel useless, and adults may treat you as if you are too young to understand the complicated, serious problems of a child in the family with a disability. We're not, though. Most of us had to grow up too fast, too soon, and we are often closer to the person with the disability than our parents are.

Sandra, a family counselor, recognized the signs of mental illness in her brother long before her parents were willing to accept it. When she was a teenager, she tried to persuade her mother that her brother needed help.

> My bedroom was right next to my brother's and I could see that he was in trouble. My parents were busy–there were five kids in the family–and they didn't want to see my brother's behavior as serious or chronic. They certainly didn't want to see it as a mental illness. They blamed it on other things, but I knew there was something really wrong.
>
> My brother often acted in socially inappropriate ways so that I was embarrassed when my friends were around. He also threatened to kill me. I was very frightened of him. It wasn't until ten years later that he was diagnosed as a paranoid schiz-ophrenic, but until he had a serious breakdown, my parents didn't want to recognize how ill he was.
>
> I remember telling my mother about my brother threat-ening to kill me many times, and I was really afraid he would do it. A couple of years ago, I brought this up with my mom and her version is that he only threatened me once. I realize now that I don't have to give up my story because my mother's version is different. She doesn't really have to give up hers either.
>
> It's not the goal of my life to get her to see things my way. That's very helpful for siblings to understand because they really do start questioning reality sometimes when no-body else in the family has had the same experience or the same memory. It's important for them to know that every-body's story is true for him.

Parents don't mean to ignore their other siblings when one child is seriously injured in an accident or struck down by a serious, disabling illness. They probably think they are shielding the other children from the devastating effects of the experience when they leave them out of the discussions.

Alan can tell you it left him feeling hopeless, alone, and desperate to find out what was happening. Alan was fourteen when his twin brother Craig was hit by a drunk driver and paralyzed from the waist down.

It was the one morning of my life that I decided not to get up and go to swim practice with my brother. He left on his bike and a few minutes later we heard a loud crash. My parents were out the door in a flash. When my dad came back to get his clothes to go to the hospital with my brother, he said to me, "Don't leave." He told me he didn't know if Craig was going to live. He told me not to go down there because there was blood on the road.

So I stayed there all alone. I didn't know how badly he was hurt or what was going on. After an hour or so I walked up the road and picked up some of the bike parts, the rim and the tire. Later a neighbor drove me to the hospital. During the eight-and-a-half hours he was in surgery I vowed never to be in a situation like that again where I couldn't do anything.

Alan is in medical school now considering a residency in emergency medicine.

Don Meyer, founder of Sibshops, says that adolescents are often left out of consultations with professionals. "Brothers and sisters seldom accompany their parents to clinic visits or individualized family service planning, individualized education program, or transition planning meetings, and if they do, their opinions, thoughts, and questions are unlikely to be sought. Left 'out of the loop' or relegated to waiting rooms, siblings report feeling ignored or isolated."

Ahadi fought against being left out. She was determined to be included in all consultations that affected her sister:

When I was in high school, I would go to the Pupil and Parent Team Teaching (PPTT) and the Individualized Educational Plan (IEP) meetings with my mother and ask Tia's teachers to show me how to help my sister at home. For special needs children, there is a statute called the Individuals with Disabilities Act (IDEA) enacted as the Education for All Handicapped Children Act in 1975 and renamed in 1990, which states that each child in special education must have an individualized educational plan, reviewed each year. During the year, the parent or the schools will call a PPTT meeting in order to discuss the child's progress. The teachers try to be positive, but at the same time, they have to be realistic about the child's abilities.

I was as much Tia's advocate as my mother, because by that time my mother was exhausted and she just couldn't fight as much as she did at one time. She would start to cry because she wanted to see a bright future for Tia. PPTT situations often seem to be very negative because they tell you what the child still needs to learn. It can be overwhelming for a parent to continually hear that her child can't read at this level.

Ahadi worked with children with special needs at the disabilities clinic at Yale University, when she was a graduate student there and an advocate at PPTT and IEP meetings for other children.

If your parents leave you out of planning for your sibling, ask to be included, as Ahadi did. No one knows your sibling as well as you do. Thomas Powell suggests ways that you can become more involved in the daily life of your brother or sister with special needs:

- Attend school meetings
- Discuss future plans for your siblings with your parents
- Offer your ideas on treatment and service needs
- Visit with professionals working with your sibling
- Learn how to teach your sibling new skills
- Find out how to advocate for your sibling

It is especially important that you be part of any discussions about your brother's or sister's future because you will probably play a major role in that future.

"It's appropriate for adolescent siblings to ask what the parents' expectations are about long-term care of the disabled sibling, their own responsibilities, and how the parents' plans jibe with their own," psychologist Sandra Harris says. "They need to be aware of their own feelings about the sibling and to talk to their parents, a therapist, or other siblings in a support group about those feelings."

Adolescence is not too early to explore the possibilities available for your sibling's future. You often have access to information through the Internet that your parents don't have and your input can be invaluable. The anonymous sibling of a sister with mental retardation emphasizes the importance of bringing this subject up with your par-

ents in an article in the *News Digest* of the National Information Center
for Children and Youth with Handicaps:

> Moms and dads don't usually sit down with their kids and
> say, "Okay, folks, I want to let you know the details of our
> finances now and our financial prospects for the future." This
> topic is difficult for parents and children alike. But you must
> attend to this in some way if family members are going to be
> prepared to take over the care of, or responsibility for, a per-
> son with disabilities.
>
> The difficulty with planning for the future is that it forces
> family members to deal with the inevitability of death. Sitting
> down and actually discussing these details can be very dis-
> turbing to everyone concerned.
>
> I strongly recommend that siblings without disabilities, as
> well as persons with disabilities, be involved in planning for
> the future as soon as they are old enough to understand the
> issues. Thus these financial and future planning discussions
> will most likely begin during early adolescence. The teenage
> years are a terrible time to have to cope with mortality. How-
> ever, I can promise you that sitting down and getting these
> issues out into the open will be much easier in the long run
> for everyone.
>
> I've had many sleepless nights, starting when I was a teen-
> ager, working through these problems by myself, afraid and
> overwhelmed before my family started discussing the issues
> more openly with me.

One good way to get information is to subscribe to SibNet (http://
www.chmc.org/departmt/sibsupp/) on the Internet. SibNet is an open
exchange of ideas by siblings of those with disabilities, started by Don
Meyer, founder of Sibshops. The subscription is free, and you will find
up-to-date information about planning for the future that you won't
find anywhere else.

In our house, nobody ever talked to me about Jack's future, or
indeed anything concerning my brother. I felt like the least important
person in the family. When my father came home on weekends, he
spent Saturday and Sunday on the golf course. He would spread out
large pieces of paper, labeled "Top Secret" and study them when he
wasn't playing golf. I found out later he was working on radar. At the

end of the war, he was sent with some other engineers to the islands in the South Pacific to investigate the equipment the Japanese had abandoned in foxholes as they retreated before the American forces. It must have been the most exciting time of his life. I wish he could have talked to me about it. I adored him. I remember secretly being glad when he got angry at my mother. Something else for me to feel guilty about.

My mother had lots of what were called "sick headaches" in those days, which allowed her to escape from her life for a few hours. She would lie in bed with a cold cloth on her head and I tip-toed around and stayed out of her way. She was in her early forties then, a pretty, lively, strong, energetic woman. What did she do with her worries, her fears, her feelings of inadequacy because she wasn't as well educated as my father?

Think of all the misery in this world because people can't talk to each other. If I could have talked to my mother about my guilt and anger about Jackie. If she could have talked to me about her worries that she wasn't giving me what I needed. If my father could have conveyed the excitement of his work to me. If we could have talked to a therapist about our hidden feelings. All those "ifs." Talking to each other or to a professional might have added some joy, some peace, some grace, to our lives.

I wish I could have talked to a counselor to get some idea of who I was besides the sister of a person with mental retardation, the high school student, the daughter of my parents, the child with no friends. Adolescence is a time of struggle for self-worth and self-identity, and I needed help.

THE SEARCH FOR IDENTITY

Psychologists tell us how tenuous our sense of self is when we have a sibling with a disability. We may develop the same symptoms they have, figuring in some subconscious way that if we become like the brother or sister, we will get the same attention and love that they do. The sister of a child with epilepsy might imitate the petit mal seizures. The brother of a child who needs braces to walk may suddenly start to limp. The child sees that the sibling with the disability gets extra attention because of his illness and may unconsciously try to get attention the same way. As Dr. Rolland says, "Healthy children sometimes feel excluded from the family and different because they do not have physical symptoms. In response, they develop somatic complaints as a way to get attention. Frequently this is not a conscious process, and may be resistant to change."

Tracy learned early that "sick gets attention." She was two when her sister was born with physical and mental disabilities. Her earliest memory is of her sister coming home from the hospital in a cast after surgery.

I learned from a very young age that being sick paid off—not success. When I was little, I would get stomachaches, I broke a lot of bones. When I was eleven I started drinking and taking drugs. By the time I was seventeen, I was a full-blown addict. Alcohol and coke. I got sick and I got a lot of attention.

I'm sober now, but that "sick gets attention" is still there. In some small way it's inbred in me. Just last week my sister got fired from her job while our parents were away. It was like a retaliation: "If you go away, I'm going to be bad." She just stopped going to work and they fired her. When my parents came home they drove immediately to her apartment to see her. I hadn't seen my parents in several weeks and at the age of twenty-six, I'm upset about the fact that they run to see her first, not me. So what do I do? I play Frisbee the next day and rip the hell out of my leg. That may just have been an accident, but the fact that I told them about it was just repeating an old pattern. It was very interesting because it was like I had a choice of playing it up and being the sick child or not mentioning it. This goes back to me being two years old and realizing if I have a stomachache, I'll get attention from my parents. And that's how ingrained that is. Just to think that that has translated for twenty-four years.

I don't think children in normal families consider their siblings as part of who they are. If you have a normal sibling, they have their own identity and their own life and at a very early age, you recognize the differences. You don't need to help them along. There isn't the focus on helping the sick child. And as a sibling, that becomes part of who you are. Illness becomes part of you. That's not the common consciousness.

The main task of adolescence for those of us with a sibling with a disability, psychologist Frances Grossman tells us, is to "avoid identifying with them." Good luck. In "normal families," each child develops his own personality and is allowed to be a separate individual from his brothers and sisters. The teen with a sibling with a disability has a much harder time separating from his brother or sister because so much of the focus of the family has been on the sick child. There is always the sense that you will be responsible for this person your whole life because he or she cannot lead an independent life without help.

The task of separating from your parents is a major part of adolescence, and it is much more complicated when you have a sibling with a disability. You may choose a college closer to home than you would have otherwise because you feel guilty about leaving your parents alone with your sibling and all the work and worry. You may choose a career based on the kinds of jobs available in your hometown because you know your sibling will be your responsibility in the future, and as one college student said, "He is much happier living in a place he is familiar with." You may marry someone from your hometown to be closer to your sibling.

FEAR OF ABANDONMENT

For some of us, the fear of losing the love of our parents if we are not "good" becomes part of our identity. We are always afraid of being abandoned by those who love us. I knew my parents loved me, but I was always afraid they would stop loving me. Why? When they were angry at me or at the world, when their faces shut down, when they looked at me without smiling, I thought they didn't love me. I was never "bad" as a child, but I was terrified they wouldn't love me anymore if I did anything wrong. I have been married for forty-four years, but I still think my husband might leave me if I do something to make him angry. He loves me and would never leave me, but that irrational fear left over from my childhood is still there.

Several siblings I talked to told me they were afraid their parents would send them away if they weren't good, just as their sibling with a disability was sent away for unmanageable behavior. Fran, thirty-five, drank and abused drugs in her teens, largely to test her parents:

> I pushed to see how far I could mess up before my parents sent me away the way they had sent my sister to an institution. I spent a good chunk of my childhood trying to make things right. Of course, you can't. My deepest fear was that they would get rid of me too.
>
> When I told my mother recently about my fears she was amazed. "We would never have sent you away," she said. "How could you have thought that?" But kids do think things like that.

One of the happiest days of my life was the day my mother told me we were moving back to New Jersey. The war was almost over and my father's work in Washington was done. I would be back with my friends in a place where everyone knew Jackie and no one was afraid of him. I couldn't wait. We bought a house in Summit, New Jersey, and my parents paid a fee to my old school district so I could spend my senior year of high school with my friends.

I went wild—well, wild for a girl in the 1940s. I stopped studying, but did well in school anyway. I cared only about boys, Frank Sinatra, Tommy Dorsey, and Glenn Miller. I danced, was silly, started to smoke, skipped school when a boyfriend came home from the Naval Academy, stayed out late, giggled on the phone for hours with my best friend Catherine, and just generally made up for my lost years in Baltimore. My friends had no fears about coming to my house. They greeted Jackie, talked to him, joked with him, and I was almost happy.

PEER PRESSURE

We always hear about the crucial part peer pressure plays in our lives, especially when we are adolescents. "Peer pressure," as we all know, is just jargon for wanting to fit in, wanting to be like everyone else, wanting to be popular, and if you are like me, you didn't have a clue about how to do this when you were a teenager. It's all trial and error—mostly error. For every happy, well-adjusted, mature class president, there are a hundred miserable, insecure high school students.

Acceptance by your peers, popularity, whatever you want to call it, is doubly important when you have a sibling with a disability and at least twice as elusive. Dr. Seligman warns that healthy siblings who are rejected by their peers and ignored by their parents are definitely at risk for adjustment problems. So how do you figure out the whole peer situation? Dr. Thomas Powell gives us a few suggestions:

- Teach your friends and others. Remember that many people naturally have questions about people with disabilities and want to learn how they can help. By watching you and your interactions with your brother or sister, they will learn.

- Be an advocate for people with disabilities. Let others know that your brother or a sister is first and foremost a person, who just happens to have a disability.

- If your friends tease a person with a disability or say something thoughtless, don't join in; it will only make you feel guilty later.

- Keep your sense of humor. Look at the bright side. As in all families, funny things happen. Take time to laugh, smile often, and be happy.

- Keep a positive outlook. While it may be easier to make a list of someone's shortcomings, everyone has strengths. Keep a balanced perspective by reminding yourself and your friends about your brother's or sister's good points.

I wish I had felt comfortable enough about having a brother with a disability that I could have explained my feelings to my classmates. I could have used a short course in helping them understand what it was like to have a brother like Jackie. If I hadn't tried to avoid the subject of a brother with mental retardation, I could have educated them and helped myself at the same time. What *do* you say to people you want to be your friends? How do you explain embarrassing behavior? How do you make it clear that you're okay even if your sibling has a few physical or mental problems?

Julie struggles with this problem all the time. Her twin sister Janna has cerebral palsy and Julie says, "I felt really badly at first because she couldn't walk, and I wanted so much for her to be like me. So I do everything I can to help her be like me. I have a boyfriend. Janna has a boyfriend. I don't want her to feel differently.

"The hardest thing is to convince my girlfriends. I try so hard to show them that Janna—she's fifteen—likes to go to the movies and she likes to come with us. She's just a fifteen-year-old, and by the way, she can't walk. My friends understand and that's how sometimes I can decide whether they are my friends or not. If they can accept my sister, good. If they can't, then it's their loss."

Sara Brown, whose brother has mental retardation, has some suggestions in her book, *Parents on the Team*:

> When you talk to your friends, it's a good idea to teach them the things you've learned. If they see that you know more about your brother's or sister's handicap than they do, they may begin to ask questions because of their desire to learn and help.
>
> Some children will tease you about your special brother or sister because they don't understand. If they hear you using the words "mental retardation" or "brain damaged" to describe your brother or sister in a realistic manner, they will no longer enjoy using these words to get on your back. If you don't get "hairy" about it, they will soon learn to understand, as you have done.

If a high school classmate refers to someone who has done something stupid as a "retard" and you have a brother with mental retardation, you shrivel up inside, but you also want to make sure that person will never use that word again. How do you do it without getting into a fight? What words do you use to make it clear that mental retardation is not something to ridicule? Sandy, an enterprising high school student gives a speech every year to her classmates about her brother who has mental retardation and other people with disabilities. "When people have the facts, they are more understanding," she says. "It always makes me feel better to do that."

I do remember one boyfriend in New Jersey who had not known Jackie before we moved away. I liked this boy a lot. One day he came over with a friend and they were shooting baskets in the backyard. Jackie came out and wanted to play, too. My boyfriend imitated the halting way he walked and I was mortified. I was ashamed of Jackie instead of being ashamed of that boy. I feel guilty to this day because of it. My mother must have been watching from the house because she came out, her face grim, and without a word took Jackie back inside with her. I assumed she was mad at me and my boyfriend, but if we could ever have talked about anything, she might have said, "I'm sorry you were embarrassed. I know it's hard for you having a brother like Jackie, and I wish there was some way I could help." I probably would have said, "I feel terrible that I'm ashamed of Jackie sometimes, but it's not his fault, it's not your fault, and it's not my fault either. It's just the way things are."

I wish Gwen had been one of my friends at that time. She would have given me good advice. Gwen, whose brother has autism, remembers not wanting to bring home the boys she was dating. "I was really nervous that I wouldn't be accepted by guys," she says. "Who would ever want to marry me because of the baggage I come with? I didn't want them to see Simon. Then I realized that I could make some choices about men. I could decide whether to accept them or not instead of the other way around. My boyfriend now completely accepts my brother and likes him, and I realize it was my own insecurity that made me embarrassed."

Insecurity doesn't begin to describe the precarious state I was in when I was a teenager. I needed a good therapist to help me understand that I was a good person living under circumstances most people don't have to deal with. That I was a stronger, more compassionate person because of it, and later on those qualities would be of great help to me. If I could have known that then, it would have saved me hours of grief and guilt.

The next part of the book is about becoming an adult, but sometimes I think I'm still working on that.

PART 3

Adulthood

7

SOMEONE TO TALK TÓ

*W*hen I was seventeen, I left that house of tension and worry. I fled to Wheaton, a small women's college on a lovely, secluded campus in southeastern Massachusetts. I didn't know at the time that I wanted to get away from my brother. I just knew I had to escape the tense, angry, atmosphere in that house— my mother's nagging, my father's silence, my brother's retardation.

Going to Wheaton was like leaving the black-and-white part of *The Wizard of Oz* and going to the color part. I was surrounded by "normal" people, smart people, happy people. I loved it there. My room-mate, Ann, was the sister I always longed for. We could talk the night away about boys and parents and life. We could study or not study (usually not). We could go to the basement and smoke, play poker or bridge, talk to other normal people, laugh and joke and obsess about clothes, hair, boys, men's colleges, and food. We could drink beer (illegally) at Bill's, eat English muffins with peanut butter and jelly at Marty's. We sent our laundry home and it was returned with brownies and cookies and jars of peanut butter, tucked among the shirts and underwear and pajamas.

But I can't remember ever talking to anyone about my feelings about Jackie. It was as if I willed him out of existence. If people asked me if I had a brother or sister, I would say, "Yes, I have a brother, but he's retarded and he has cerebral palsy." No one knew what to say after that, so we moved on to another subject. One of my best friends told me recently that she had no idea I had a brother with mental retardation until she visited me in New Jersey after we had graduated from college, shared an apartment in New York, married, and were pregnant with our first children. She had no idea. I'm sure I didn't keep it a secret, but how else could she not have known?

I don't know why, but outside of support groups, many siblings rarely talk about their brothers or sisters with special needs. It's not so much that we hide the fact that we have a sibling with a disability. We just don't discuss it with most people, and psychologists tell us that's not healthy. We need to talk to someone–a therapist, a best friend, other siblings in a support group, siblings on the Internet.

I thought perhaps it was my generation that had trouble talking about our brothers and sisters with a disability, but I found that it's also true of many men and women in their twenties, thirties, and forties. The reluctance to talk about our negative feelings is only natural since most of us are taught as children that we must love and help those less fortunate than ourselves. In "normal" families, when siblings get mad at each other they say, "I hate you," or "I wish you'd go away and never come back," or "Mom and Dad aren't your real parents– you're adopted." But you can't say things like that to someone who may die by the age of twenty or whose retardation is not his fault.

DEALING WITH ANGER

As I said before, I'm terrified of anger–my own and other people's. It's very hard for me to get angry. I tend to keep it all inside. Talking to people while I was writing this book, I found that most of us healthy siblings have trouble with anger. Nobody is very good at handling it, but the brothers and sisters of people with disabilities perhaps have the most difficulty with it because we've had to suppress a lot of anger when we were children.

"Anger is the bane of my existence," says Lucy, whose sister has Angelman syndrome. "Until recently, I didn't deal with it at all. I took it out on myself. I was terrified of getting angry, so I never expressed it as a child. I was the perfect Stepford child who got straight As, never got in trouble in school, never did drugs or drank or smoked. There was a lot of safety in that.

"That was how I got attention in our family–by being good. When

I brought home a good report card I was showered with praise. When I washed the dishes after dinner, my parents hugged me. I got the attention I needed by being super good, for never showing my anger. I never acted out. It would have been much healthier for me if I had. I was bulimic in college and had a serious depression. I'm working on it with a therapist, but I still have a lot of trouble with anger."

What happens when you suppress your negative feelings? Psychologists tell us it can cause problems in our relationships with other people (as we will see in the next chapter); it can lead to depression, as in Lucy's case, and even suicide attempts; it certainly keeps us from having a loving relationship with our sibling with the disability; it can make us express our anger in inappropriate ways, such as bulimia or anorexia, because we have never learned to deal with it constructively; it can make it harder for us to establish our own identities because we either identify too strongly with our sibling or block out the very existence of a brother or sister with a disability; and it can keep us from dealing with the jealousy that arises in normal sibling rivalry and leaves us with debilitating guilt. Find someone to talk to, therapists tell us.

Terrell Dougan writes in *We Have Been There* that she always kept her anger at her sister with mental retardation closed inside because her rage always made her feel so guilty. Then one day she exploded:

> I realized this habit of mine the day she was expelled (for her tantrums) from the group home I had worked so hard to establish. Our parents were out of the country at the time, and it fell to me to help her move out and back home again. We climbed into my car and I let loose with a tantrum the likes of which Irene herself has never produced. I yelled at her about her behavior and how she had to learn to control herself. I found myself shaking with rage and screaming.
>
> Two things happened. I realized that for the first time in my life I had given myself permission to be angry with her (I suppose that my mind had to wait until my parents were clear across the ocean!), and at that moment she was reaping thirty-odd years of pent-up rage—not just today's grievance. And—this is the kicker—I stopped in mid-sentence screaming and looked at her. She was observing this wild fit I was having,

absolutely amazed that I too was capable of it, and we started to laugh. We concluded that perhaps she needs to cool it a bit, but perhaps I, too, should have had the right to a few more tantrums.

My parents are not to blame for my guilt. Perhaps no matter what they did, you see, I would have decided to feel guilty about any angry feelings toward Irene. So I think all you can do as a parent is to give permission for the anger to show itself when it's there. The rest is up to the sibling, and no matter how you try to take the blame for everything, you just can't engineer your children's lives and feelings.

All we can do is share our experiences in life with our family members, affirm their rights to love and hate and fun and anger and frustration and growth and pain, and then relax. Let the good times roll. And they will, quite often. If we let them.

TALK TO SOMEONE

Janet was finally able to talk about her feelings, good and bad, about her sister with mental retardation when she was thirty years old. She had placed her sister in a group home and there were regular meetings of siblings and parents:

That was the first time I had an experience like that. I felt very safe talking about my sister. Comfortable. We had the same concerns and I could talk to them about her and they could understand what I was saying. As wonderful as my husband is, there's nobody who really knows how I feel or cares about my concerns the way other siblings do. They've been there.

I can talk to them about getting mad at Ellie for no reason when she comes to visit me. She's fine, but some days I look at her and get crazy. I get upset because she won't bring her coffee cup to the kitchen and I know she does that in her group home, or she asks for soda when she can get it herself. These people understand all this. I can tell them it makes me sick to my stomach to have to help her with a depilatory for her facial hair. None of my other friends would want to hear this.

I can ask their advice about allowing Ellie to travel on two buses to work at McDonald's because she's tired of working at a sheltered workshop and wants to be more independent. I know she's trained to go on the bus, but if there was a change in the schedule, she wouldn't know what to do. I don't want people staring at her while she's cleaning tables. She'll just be another freak to them.

I can ask the people in the group how to set up a trust for her that won't deprive her of medical care. We talk about all the things that bother me, and it's a great help.

Claire too found a support group that helped her when her brother was hospitalized with schizophrenia when she was in her twenties. She had just moved to California from the East Coast and a friend told her about a women's group that met in her city:

One night someone asked about my family, and three hours later we were all in tears, not just because of my own story, but because seven out of the eight women in that group had immediate family members who had schizophrenia, manic depression, or some kind of mental illness. They were from all walks of life, all ages, all personalities. The therapist's brother, who had schizophrenia, committed suicide when he was a teenager. But none of these women had talked about their mentally ill family members in the group before I brought up my brother that night. I could tell them how guilty I felt about moving 3,000 miles away from him and they understood. We connected.

I told them about the first time I realized there was something really wrong with my brother who had been quiet and rather shy until he was eighteen, but showed no sign of mental illness until he went away to college. It was on my wedding day. I remember Peter coming over and standing on the train of my wedding gown, not realizing what he was doing. That incident made me finally accept the fact that my brother wasn't all there. I still have the dress. I've been married and divorced, and his footprints are still on the back of the dress.

I told the women in that group that when I smoked pot—which I don't do anymore because it makes me paranoid—but when I did smoke pot, I realized what it must be like to be inside my brother's head. It's as if you're somebody else. Part of your mind says, "What are you doing? You'll get arrested." And the rational part of your mind says, "Oh, that's crazy. Your neighbors aren't going to call the police because they smell the pot." Irrational thoughts pop in and out of your mind. Oddly enough, that helped give me insight into my brother. Imagine having all these irrational thoughts tenfold, a hundredfold, all the time. Or not being able to sleep. Pacing back and forth. In a strange way it helped me to empathize with his situation. Those other women knew exactly what I was talking about.

They all identified with my fear that I could become mentally ill too. I told them about the time I had incredible PMS and totaled my car. I cried for a day and a half and thought, "Oh my God, I'm going into a depression. It's going to happen to me. I'm all alone. My boyfriend won't understand." I pulled myself out of it, but I got so frightened.

And they knew what I meant when I said that my brother's illess robbed me of both my parents. My mother lives 3,000 miles away and she can't come and see me very often because my brother needs her. I need her, too. The group understood my strong feeling that Peter was somehow to blame for my father's death. I think my father lost his will to live when he realized his son would never be well. He got cancer at a time when my brother had to be hospitalized. I know there's a connection. The mind is very powerful.

That group helped me to accept the fact that my brother may never get better. I'll never lose hope, but if I could have accepted his limitations more quickly, I would have saved myself a lot of pain.

Alicia, whose brother is also mentally ill, went to a therapist to help her deal with her guilt. "Guilt is my constant companion," she says. "I'm seeing a therapist and am trying to let go of it. But I still feel guilty if five weeks go by and I haven't called my brother. If I go to the city where he lives to visit friends, I feel guilty if I don't see him. But at least I no longer feel guilty about not being able to cure him. His illness is not my responsibility. Thousands of dollars later, I learned this."

Marylee Westbrook, who has two brothers with mental illness, has led support groups for the siblings of people with mental illness in Los Angeles for the last twelve years. She helps those in her groups cope with the rage and guilt they feel. "The guilt is overriding because you keep thinking you can do something," she told me. "When the brother or sister asks you for something, you think it's just a little thing. But they ask over and over and will totally invade your life. You feel guilty saying no, but on the other hand, you know if you do one thing, they will cling to you and want more. You feel like you're betraying your sibling by not standing by him, but the other half of you knows that you have to live your own life."

Marylee describes the dynamics in a family with mental illness, or indeed any disability. She says:

> There becomes a high tolerance for inappropriate behavior. You change your standards for what is normal. Behavior that is quite abusive or chaotic seems all right to you. In a healthy family, there is a focus on the person with a problem and then you come back to center. In families with a mental illness, everything just stays focused around the person with the problem. Everybody else leads a sort of shadow life.
>
> There is such stigma and shame attached to mental illness that most people don't want to admit a sibling is ill. They're afraid other people will think they are ill too.
>
> The hardest part is the frustration of dealing with somebody so self-absorbed you can't get through to them. No matter what you say to them, whether it's pitying or angry, you feel frustrated because you're not able to get the other person to understand what you're saying, or trying to do for him. If you have a sibling with mental retardation, you know that the person can't really understand what you're saying. But with a mentally ill person, his verbal skills are very high. He doesn't lose his IQ with the illness, but he loses his mental maturity. So you see someone who is very verbal, who seems to understand, who is an adult quite bright in some ways, yet no matter what you say to him, he either can't get it or he twists it around to mean something else.
>
> It is very hard for most family members because they keep getting seduced by what this person is saying. They look for the normal in the person and they hear what they want to hear.

Many siblings will tell you they feel as if they've lost the person they knew. There's someone who looks like the other person but definitely is a different individual from the one they knew their whole life. Here is this big brother or sister they looked up to and then all of a sudden, the healthy sibling becomes the older person and has to deal with it. In some families, the one who develops mental illness in his late teens or early twenties is the shining example who went to the best schools and had a brilliant future.

Some people even feel their family would be better off if the ill person were dead because then at least you could mourn. You can't complete the mourning because you've lost the person, but you haven't. It's an ongoing open wound for- ever and ever. Plus you see the person suffering and see the things you can't do for them. Siblings understand the person is ill, but they don't understand why they can't just do a few basic things—like live in a nice clean place.

Many times siblings are left out of the information loop about the mental illness because the psychiatrist or psycholo- gist treating their brother or sister cannot legally tell them anything. If a sibling has cancer or anything else, the family would be told, but not when there is mental illness.

What does Marylee tell these siblings to help them cope with an impossible situation?

The first thing I say is, "You need to get educated about what's real about the illness. Instead of thinking the person will start to be normal again, find out about the illness as you would about cancer, diabetes, or mental retardation."

The second thing I tell them is that *they* are gong to have to change, not the ill person. If they think they can change the person with the illness, it just isn't going to happen. You have to learn to give up some things you want to do for the person. Step back. Do less. It's very difficult because part of you thinks, "If I just do one more thing, that will fix it." You have to keep reminding yourself that it's just the opposite. You have to do less to allow your sibling to develop some sense of his own illness. What you try to do is become less than 80 percent of anybody's support system.

Some people cannot talk about their siblings in a group or anywhere else. Allison, who is thirty-eight, hates talking about her brother with mental retardation. She shies away from the subject and avoids other people whose siblings are similarly afflicted. "I'm doing this weird dance," she says. "I deal with it practically, but I'm in willful denial most of the time. I met a woman recently who has a mentally retarded brother too, and she wanted to have lunch and talk about our brothers. She had never had the chance to talk to anyone about it before and she was bubbling over with her feelings about him. But I avoided her because the last thing I wanted was to talk about Jim. I don't need to be sad."

SIBNET

If you are like Allison and don't want to talk about your sibling in a support group, you might feel more comfortable venting your feelings on the Internet anonymously. Just call up SibNet on your computer and vent away. SibNet, as I mentioned in the last chapter, is an interactive Web site created by Don Meyer to give siblings a place to let loose with their feelings about their brothers and sisters with a disability. It's an exchange of messages posted by siblings all over the country, and there are no rules or taboos.

Lucy, who has a sister with Angelman syndrome, an illness that robs children of speech, is one of the subscribers (it's free) and her experience as she explained it to me, is typical:

> SibNet is great because you just go. You don't have to worry about perfect form or spelling or grammar, and that's when the good stuff comes out. When I first found it, I thought "Wow! Here's a forum that's never existed before for siblings to talk to other siblings who understand completely what they've been going through." You don't have to explain your-self because they know.
>
> For me, that was a tremendous part of my healing when I was going through a serious depression in college. On SibNet, I met people whose emotions were as raw as mine, but nobody expected you to apologize for saying that you wished your sister was dead. Nobody judged you for saying you resented the fact that you were going to be responsible for her when your parents died. All feelings were acceptable

because they had them, too. It was safe to express them in a heightened way, which I had never been able to do before.

My first few months on SibNet were spent venting the anger that I never got to express any other way. "I hate this. I hate that." Then once I was able to get through all of that, I started remembering the good stuff about my sister–how close we were, how much fun we had together, how much I loved her. I let go of the hurt of losing her when she went off to boarding school at the age of nine.

Psychotherapist Julie Tallard Johnson often helps siblings find ways to deal with a disability in the family. She says:

My favorite quote is, "If you always do what you always did, you'll always get what you always got." Sometimes it's just putting a little dent in somebody's way of looking at things. You've always been relating to your sibling this way. Try something different. Families get stuck in how they respond to each other. I encourage them to start changing patterns. Everything is related to everything else. Just change one small behavior pattern and see what happens.

In every family there are silent agreements, and it's important to break some of them. If you've never discussed one member's alcoholism, or a mental illness, or the fact that all the time, attention, and money seems to be focused on the person with the disability, bring it up. Even if it doesn't change anything, you'll feel more at peace.

The Dalai Lama says, "My friend the enemy." So in our lives, who do we label the enemy? It's not always the disability. Sometimes it's the system, sometimes our parents, a teacher. You don't have to agree with them or like them. Just turn the enemy into your friend.

One of the most important things is that the whole focus of the family can't be on the disability. There's more to that person than his disability. There's life beyond the crisis. In families where there is a disability, everyone is supposed to sacrifice everything for the ill person. That's not right. Of course we have to go the extra mile for that person, but we're not supposed to literally keep giving up pieces of ourselves.

FRIENDS

If you find a friend who also has a sibling with a disability, you are lucky. Friends can often be the best therapy when you are trying to work out a problem that seems to have no solution. Danielle, whose brother has autism, discovered a kindred spirit when she went to London to study the way people learn languages. She had dinner with a colleague one night who told her that she had a brother with Down syndrome. The two women became friends and Danielle says, "It was the first time in my life I met another sibling by chance, not through a sibling support group. We talked about growing up with siblings with disabilities—the difficult part and the good part. But it was much better than a support group because we had so many other things in common. We came to the conclusion that we were studying the way babies learn languages because our siblings had problems learning to talk. I can tell her anything and she understands."

Siblings of people with disabilities make very compassionate friends. Fran's closest friend was mistakenly diagnosed as having mental retardation as a child because of an undetected hearing impairment, and Fran, whose sister has Down syndrome, is a tremendous help to her. Indeed, they are a help to each other.

"She had a horrible time as a child," Fran says. "She had to fight with her teachers to include her in regular classrooms because they were convinced she couldn't do the work. She had to beg them to give her a chance. Now she is trying to get into a master's program and is going through the whole thing again. I have complete and total empathy for her, as she does for me."

Alicia's best friend is a Japanese-American woman. "On the surface, she is not the kind of person you'd think I'd be friends with. She's not an intellectual, likes to go shopping, goes to psychics. We work out at the gym together. But I found out after we became friends, that her father was interned in a camp during the war and her mother was at Hiroshima. There must have been an undercurrent there that I responded to."

For me, the friends I made at Wheaton were lifesavers. For four years I lived a carefree, almost normal existence, surrounded by friends

I'm still close to today. I majored in English literature and minored in French. I wrote a story about Shakespeare that won a prize. One of my teachers wrote words of encouragement on my first, primitive novel. Wheaton was a golden oasis between my life with my family and the start of my real life when I graduated in 1950.

When I went home for holidays and vacations, I remember wanting to make Jackie laugh. My mother was too serious to do it, my father too remote. But I could take him to a movie I knew would make him laugh–any of the slapstick comedies would do it. My father built a television set in 1949 when the programs were primitive and unintentionally funny many times. Jack loved Milton Berle, and while I thought myself too sophisticated for his broad hu-mor, I laughed with Jack when we watched him stumble across the stage in high heels.

I know we could make each other laugh now too. The last time I was with him in Florida, we were eating dinner and watching the birds fly over the ocean. "There's a lot of pelicans out there," he said. Sur-prised, I said, "How did you know they were pelicans, Jack?" "I just took a wild guess," he said, and we both laughed. That's just the kind of thing our father would have said.

I miss the brother I don't have. We could have compared teachers, laughed about school, been allies against our parents. He could have helped me with geometry and I could have helped him with writing assignments. We would have a whole history of triumphs and tragedies that would keep us close today. Just a phrase or a look would be enough to cement our bond. We could have fought and punched each other without my having to feel guilty and bad.

After graduating from college, I had a period of grace before my real life started, the chance to do something I had wanted to do all my life. I went to Paris, lived with a French family and studied at the Sorbonne and the Ecole des Sciences Politiques for a year. Jackie couldn't have been farther away than if I lived on the moon.

Paris in 1950 was a student's dream. Taxiing from the station to the Left Bank, I felt I *belonged* there, that my heart was really French. None of us in the cab spoke as we passed the Louvre, saw the Eiffel Tower against the blue September sky, crossed one of the bridges to

Montparnasse, my home for the next year. It was as if someone waved a wand and made the pictures we had seen in books come alive. The maids carrying baguettes home for dinner, the men on bicycles puffing Gauloises out of the sides of their mouths, a glass of red wine on a small table at a corner café, the Metro stations. I felt I had come home.

Everything was incredibly cheap in this period just after the war. You could get a three-course meal at Waja's, a Left Bank restaurant, for fifty cents. There were no ugly tall apartment buildings. You could actually see the rooftops of Paris. My roommate Joan and I lived in the salon of an apartment owned by a French couple on the Boulevard Montparnasse, right across from the Select Café and down the street from Hemingway's Dome and the Coupole. The walls were covered in rose silk, the mantelpiece was white marble, and I slept in a Madame Récamier bed. Doors led to a balcony that overlooked the boulevard, where we could watch high-priced poules bargaining with customers below. Hilda brought us hot chocolate and croissants every morning. Madame served us coq au vin or blanquette de veau, followed by snowy-white wheels of chèvre. Once in a while she would leave the apartment in the afternoon, dressed in black, wearing high heels and a tiny hat with a sequined veil, to go to "Versailles," she would say with a wink.

My friends were artists, writers, actors, directors, publishers of art books, expatriates who didn't really do anything. We could sit all afternoon with a cup of coffee and talk about how materialistic Americans were and how we knew what really mattered in life. It was heaven.

There was only one reminder of my brother: Rosie. Rosie was another American student, and her brother was mentally retarded too. She was beautiful—tall and dark. Men followed her down the boulevard, begging for her phone number, but she always put up a barrier when they tried to get close. When I asked her why, she said, "Because I have to go home and take care of my brother. I can't ask a man to take on that burden." She meant it too. When she returned to the States after the year was up, she lived with her parents and helped them take care of Frank.

I called her recently and asked her if she was glad she did that.

"No," she said forcefully. "I would never let my mother take my life away from me if I had it to do over again. I remember going out to dinner with some friends and my mother one night. They suggested I might like to meet a man who had just moved to our town. Before I could say anything, my mother said, 'No, she wouldn't want to do that.' And I let her. I let her keep me in that house helping her take care of my brother until both of them were dead. Now it's too late."

I asked Rosie why we never talked about our brothers when we were in Paris. "Maybe we just wanted to forget them for a while," she said. But you never can forget. They're always there in the back of your mind all your life. Whenever you think life is letting up a little, and you can relax and enjoy it, smack! you are reminded that your life is different.

Which brings us to one of the most difficult pieces of the puzzle of growing up with a sibling with a disability: how it affects your relationships.

8

YOUR RELATIONSHIPS

*M*y mother never asked me to choose between my brother and marriage, and I'm forever grateful to her for that. But I certainly knew my choice of men was limited by having a brother with mental retardation. Who would want me? I came with a built-in problem that most men would back away from. Men are not famous for rushing into marriage and I couldn't imagine their wanting to take on a retarded brother-in-law. My usual method of dealing with this was to wait until a man was really interested in me before telling him about Jack. Most decent men would say, "I love you. We'll work it out." One man I almost married said, "It's as if Jack belongs to your mother—he isn't part of you. It wouldn't affect our life together." But I was having too much fun to even think of marriage then. I figured I had until I was twenty-five before I was considered too old to marry.

But the world now is an entirely different place from the way it was when I was dating in the early 1950s. I wanted to find out if it was still difficult to establish a relationship when you have a sibling with a disability. Is it easier now because the world is more accepting of those with disabilities? I wanted to know what kind of person other siblings like me were attracted to. When they looked for a partner, did they seek someone who would help take care of that brother or sister someday, as I did? Did they tell that person about their sibling with a disability right away, later when the relationship looked like it might be serious, or just before introducing the brother or sister? How did they handle it? I talked to many siblings about their relationships and got a wide variety of answers, but all agreed their sibling with a disability definitely affected their choices.

Family counselor Julie Tallard Johnson, author of *Hidden Victims, Hidden Healers*, tells us that we siblings are often either "caretakers" or "escape artists," and, as you can imagine, this definitely affects our choice of a partner. Caretakers put others' wants and needs before their own. They see their role in life as a rescuer. "They are either dissatisfied with their relationships because they are usually giving more than they receive or are unable to maintain intimate relationships," Julie writes. "They find it difficult to end destructive relationships, empathizing with the problems of the abuser. If you constantly try to please others, denying your own needs, you may very well end up in an abusive relationship."

CARETAKERS

Julie, who is also a sibling of a brother with schizophrenia as well as a family counselor, told me she used to have her radar out for men who needed to be taken care of:

> I was always in charge of the relationship. Can you imagine whom I would attract? I had to have someone who knows what suffering is about, but what I really deserved was someone who had an understanding and compassion for suffering but was healed. I ended up getting men who hadn't healed, who weren't working on what they needed to work on.
>
> I was such a caretaker. I would provide all the goodies in the relationship. It took me a while to see all this. What you should do is try to meet people whose original wound can be healed. If you can heal somebody, you feel, "Oh, I can finally help someone," because when you are the sibling of a person with a disability, you can't do that. I spent a lot of energy trying to get my brother help on every level—spiritual, religious, physical, social. I tried a lot of things and they didn't work. So, like other siblings in my position, I looked for someone who had similar issues.
>
> I finally married the man who was my first boyfriend in

high school after being parted for fifteen years. He had solved a lot of his own problems and is one of the finest human beings I've ever encountered. I am very happy with him and we just had our first child.

Unfortunately, many siblings who are caretakers think they can fix whatever is wrong with their partners. Anne has always been drawn to men who needed fixing because she grew up with a brother with mental retardation. I met her one evening at a party where we were watching the Golden Globe Awards and making fun of them. Even so I was moved, as I always am, when a clip of *Rain Man* was shown. Dustin Hoffman captured the walk, the dull look in the eyes, the stance, the way people with retardation talk, so perfectly that I felt like I was watching Jack. My brother, of course, is not a mathematical savant, but in so many ways he was the man in that movie.

Across the room I noticed a man watching that scene and his face crumpled as if he were trying not to cry. A thin, intense woman reached out her hand and touched his arm. I knew that one of them must be a sibling of someone with mental retardation.

Sure enough, later I was talking to the woman, Anne, and her fiancé, and when I told her about my book, she said, "My brother has mental retardation. I was four when he was born. At first the doctors didn't know there was anything wrong with him. My mother knew. She didn't give him a name at first. When people in kindergarten asked me what my brother's name was I had to say 'He doesn't have one.' Then when the news of his retardation spread through my school like wildfire, I felt incredible shame. I was afraid people would think I was retarded too.

"I'm still full of anger. When stupid, little things go wrong in my life, I rail at the sky. 'I have a retarded brother,' I say angrily. 'I don't need a lot of aggravation on top of that.'

"My parents sent my brother away when I was eight. That's where all the trouble began. I felt I had abandoned my brother and that has colored all my relationships, especially with men. I tend to connect with people who are hurt in some way. Like my brother. I always wanted to fix him, and that's my approach to other people. I have repeated the same mistakes endlessly. Now I know you can't fix people."

Anne is engaged to a man who obviously needs no fixing. "Cal is wonderful with my brother. We went on a hike last weekend and Cal made a walking stick for him and said to him, 'You're the leader.' It was something my brother had always wanted to hear."

Alicia, whose younger brother was mentally ill all through her childhood and had a complete breakdown when he was nineteen, is sure that she married her former husband because she thought she could fix him. It took many years of therapy for her to understand this:

> My parents were obsessed with my brother's illness, and I always felt neglected, overlooked. I've never really had a satisfying relationship with a man. All the men I have chosen have been injured in some way. The man I was in love with in college was brilliant, but he was an alcoholic. At thirty-seven, I finally married a man whose sister had bi-polar illness. The marriage was disastrous. I almost died. He wasn't physically abusive but he was emotionally abusive. He had a total breakdown. Just like my brother when he was nineteen. I kept trying to fix him. Then I realized "*Hello!* He doesn't want to be fixed. Fix yourself."
>
> His breakdown forced me to face a lot of the problems I had papered over for years—especially the way I dealt with my parents. When I first split up with my husband, I didn't even tell them because I didn't think I could confide in them. I thought they would say, "Oh we spent all this money on the wedding and he was a jerk and you never should have married him." Finally I told them.
>
> I tried to make them understand the pain and anguish of all this and that I needed them to help me. They started talking about my brother again. I couldn't believe it. I said to them, "You know what? I'm the needy family member right now and if you can't be there for me, then we're not going to talk."
>
> That was a big thing for me. I was one of those people who are always taking care of other people instead of myself. We had some very angry phone conversations, but I have to tell you, they got it. They understood that I needed them and that was the opening door to expressing our feelings. I think

a lot of people carry all these destructive feelings around with them all their lives. I'm glad I got help because my parents and I are extremely close now.

Janet knows her sister Ellie had something to do with her choice of men. She was a caretaker during her first marriage, but as she learned to value herself more, she made a wiser choice the second time. She says:

> I still don't understand the connection, though I've talked about it with my therapist a million times, but I always had the most screwed-up relationships with men. It has to have something to do with my mother, but there's definitely a connection with my sister.
>
> You know something funny—I could always tell a lot about a man by the way he acted with my sister. There was one guy who wouldn't even go near her—as if he would catch it if he touched her. Appearance was very important to him. Can you imagine what it would have been like going to a restaurant with him and my sister?
>
> But I'll tell you something ironic. My first marriage was to a man who only had one arm. Because of my upbringing with my sister, I didn't really think about his disability. It didn't detract from him at all. He was very good looking. I was never put off by people's disabilities. I was twenty-four and I was dying to get out of the house. Maybe I needed to set up a situation that was like the one I grew up in. Anyway, we ended up getting divorced. My second husband works with people with disabilities and he's wonderful with my sister.

ESCAPE ARTISTS

If you are an escape artist, Julie Tallard Johnson writes, you have "learned to deal with the stresses in your life through escape and isolation." You are comfortable being detached and uninvolved. Your life becomes a "cycle between inviting and avoiding crises." There are many ways of escaping. You can use alcohol or drugs to numb your feelings. You can isolate yourself from others and look for a mate who will join you in that isolation. To the outside world, you falsely appear happy, healthy, and secure, but inside you worry that "if others found out the secret of who you really are, they wouldn't accept you."

Some siblings of people with disabilities choose marriage as their escape route from an impossible situation at home. Angela did that. As I have related, she grew up in a home with two brothers with mental retardation and a mother who was an alcoholic. She had a breakdown in college when she was nineteen.

"To keep from returning home, I got married and became pregnant right away," she says. "I know I married him because he was the only way out for me. He had a lot of emotional problems. I felt I had abandoned my brothers, and I've always felt guilty about that."

"We were married for seven years and then I divorced him. That was tough because I was raised as a Catholic and the divorce meant breaking with my family even further. Now I'm married to a wonderful man. We've been married for ten years."

Beth, whose sister has spina bifida, is an escape artist who decided to elope instead of having a traditional wedding, but convinced herself she chose her flight as protection for her sister. "I wanted to shelter my sister from my being the center of attention as a bride in a white gown with bridesmaids and the whole deal, while everybody pitied her," she says. "My whole life I've tried to protect her from things I've done, to downplay my own enjoyment. If I went to a concert or a dance, I would come home and say, 'Oh it was no big deal.' I didn't want her to think she had missed anything."

But as a result of her protection of her sister, they are not very close now. Beth never felt she could share either the fun or the dis-appointments in her life, and their relationship is mostly a superficial one. She has managed to escape a close bond with her sister.

Lucy escaped intimacy in a different way. She wondered why she had trouble telling men what she was feeling, why she had trouble getting close to the men she liked. Then during a serious bout of depression during college, she went to a therapist and found out why:

I grew up with a younger sister with Angelman syndrome. My sister couldn't speak except for three words: Mom, Dad, and

Sister. She communicated in sign language and body language. I was only three years older than she was and we were to-gether all the time. I could understand her when my parents couldn't. We formed a very strong bond, almost like twins. Many twins develop their own kind of unspoken mental te-lepathy, and my sister and I learned to communicate without speaking.

I'm very comfortable with silence. I don't need to fill it up with words. When I was growing up, there was so much going on within that silence. That's how I learned to com-municate with my sister. I tend to observe more than partici-pate. In order to have a relationship with her, I had to become very observant of what she did, her body language and facial expressions. That carried over when I was in junior high school. I was not terribly comfortable in conversations. People tell me my face is very expressive, especially my eyes, and I worry that people can tell exactly what I'm thinking. So I tend to be guarded.

Because of that, I have a very difficult time opening up to people in romantic situations. I can be open with friends, but in intimate relationships, it's very hard for me. I often expect people to know what I'm thinking without having to express it. I forget that's not how most people function, that you have to say what you are thinking. I have to remind myself that if you want somebody to understand your feelings, you have to tell them.

USING SIBLINGS AS A LITMUS TEST

Many people with siblings with a disability told me they often used their sibling as a kind of litmus test to see how a date would react when meeting the brother or sister. Angela remembers riding on a school bus with her brother, who is mentally retarded. "He always wanted to be one of the guys. He went to the back of the bus where the older guys were sitting and they started to teach him some swear words. I got up and sat down next to Bill. I knew that would calm things down.

"A few years later I dated one of those guys who had been sitting in the back of the bus. He had grown and was fine with my brother by this time. I told him about this incident and said, 'I almost didn't go out with you because of that.' He felt terrible about it and apologized. But it was very important to me that a man respect and be nice to my brother."

Frank obviously loves his sister Amy, who has Down syndrome, very much, and almost married someone just to provide a home for Amy when his parents considered sending her to a group home. "I've avoided marriage for a long time–I'm forty-one–but I considered it briefly just so I could take care of her. My parents decided not to send her to the group home, but when I do get married, I will have to find someone who will be willing to have Amy come and live with us when my parents are no longer here.

"All my relationships with women, serious or not, include Amy in some way or another. It's important to me to help my sister feel independent. Sometimes I ask a girlfriend to take Amy to a movie without me. We go to a Cineplex and I see one movie while my girlfriend and Amy watch another. It's not that big a deal, but it makes a big difference to Amy. Her life is so constrained. She can't go to the store by herself or do much on her own, so this at least gives her the illusion that she is going somewhere on her own with a nonfamily member that we trust. She sees the rest of us in the family having friends and I want that for her too."

Alex, a thirty-six-year-old pediatrician, feels the same way about his brother Tom, who has mental retardation. Tom's feelings are very important to Alex. The two men are a year apart in age and have always been very close. Alex is thinking about getting married, and Tom is always part of his selection process:

> I don't know if it's conscious or subconscious but it's kind of an unwritten rule with me that it's a two-for-one deal. If a woman isn't able to relate to my brother Tom, I couldn't tolerate being with her. He's such a part of me. I'm not drawn to that kind of person to begin with.
>
> The last woman I was seriously involved with was wonderful with Tommy, and I think that was one of the reasons I was so much in love with her. I remember once we were walking in the city, hanging out with Tom, and I was holding

her hand. Then, without saying anything, she just kind of nudged me and I looked over and saw that Tommy was holding her other hand. That's such a sweet memory.

Richard found a wife who accepted his brother's deformed arms and deafness. He remembers taking his brother back to school one weekend. "I drove the car about a quarter of a mile or so. I stopped the car and I started crying and could not stop. The whole thing: It was just too much.

"My wife said to me something like, 'You know that this is a very good thing that is happening for him; he is fortunate to have such a good experience.' We drove another quarter of a mile and she started crying. Sometimes it is very hard to see this as good."

It came as no surprise to me to find out that many people with siblings with a disability marry someone who had something in their background that made them more patient, more understanding, more tolerant of people with a difference. Sometimes it was a brother or sister who had died young or their parents had divorced or they had gone through some especially difficult period in their childhoods that gave them that extra dimension I find in the siblings of people with disabilities.

Glenn was instantly attracted to a woman he met skiing, but it wasn't until years later that he made the connection between his brother's mental retardation and his wife having a sister who was born with a congenital heart condition that took her life when she was thirteen.

"We had lots of mutual interests," he says, "and it only occurred to me recently that one of the reasons we felt drawn to each other was the part of our personalities that was formed by having a sibling with a serious disability, even though the disabilities were so different."

WHEN DO YOU BRING IT UP?

Some siblings wait until they are sure a relationship is on solid ground before bringing up the existence of their brother or sister with a disability. Lydia did that.

"When my junior-year boyfriend came home with me for spring break," she writes, "I waited until we were safely airborne, and he couldn't turn back, before telling him about Phil."

Gloria remembers the deep humiliation she felt when she brought her fiancé home to meet her family:

> I was engaged and I hadn't told my fiancé that I had a retarded brother. We went to the house and everyone was out. I was so relieved. I went inside to get something, and my fiancé waited outside. When I came out of the house—oh, I was so embarrassed—my family's car pulled up and my twenty-one-year-old brother got out wearing rubber pants and a diaper. I could have died.
>
> Because I hadn't told my fiancé, I had to say, "Oh, by the way, my brother is retarded." My brother was happy, and I was glad my family included him in their outings, but I was so angry at them for letting him run around in a diaper and rubber pants so everyone could see.

Elizabeth sums up the feelings of most siblings of people with disabilities. "My parents say, 'You will never have to worry about your brother.' But of course I will always have to worry about him, make sure he's all right. Whoever I marry will not only have to love me but they will have to love my brother too. They will have to help me decide how to take care of him."

CHOOSING FRIENDS

Psychologists tell us our choice of friends is also affected by having a sibling with a disability. Because I grew up feeling like an outsider, I choose friends who are interesting, a little different, slightly neurotic—like me. They are writers and poets, artists and editors, photographers and musicians.

One of my best friends grew up with two deaf parents—she is compassionate, funny, loving, generous, and infinitely patient. Another friend lost her mother when she was thirteen—and she seeks to fill that emptiness today with an exploration of the new spirituality, a kind of mystical journey I find fascinating. Still another friend of mine lived in an ashram, married and divorced two men, found the love of her life and adopted a little boy who fills her days with sunshine and song. All of these women satisfy some need in me to reject what is ordinary, bland, conservative, boring. Other people I talked to said the same thing.

Gwen, whose younger brother has autism, remembers talking to a close friend in college whose mother was very ill, and discussing a fellow classmate, "She's not like us because she hasn't been through adversity."

Peggy, whose brothers are mentally ill, said at first that all her closest friends were functioning members of mainstream life, but as she thought about it, she realized they all had something in their background that gave them an awareness and sensitivity to things other people don't have.

"One of my friends was dumped by her parents and brought up by her grandparents," she says. "For many years she wasn't sure whether her parents were going to come back and get her or not. Her grandmother would always say, 'You're just staying here until they come for you.' Another friend is an incest survivor. But the bond between us is that we are people who want to talk about our feelings."

Anne, a psychotherapist, whose brother has schizophrenia, looks for friends who are "eccentric, the way my brother Jimmy is eccentric. I like people who march to another beat. They have a depth that other people don't have. Growing up with my brother I was always trying to figure out what was going on inside his head and trying to understand how he saw the world, from the moment I was conscious that he was different. It strengthened my skills at being empathetic and listening to people."

Allison who has a sister with Down syndrome says, "I have this theory that there isn't any family that doesn't have something hidden away. Once you peel back that layer, as soon as you get close enough to somebody, you'll find that out about them. As I think about my friends, two of them have brothers who committed suicide. God, that's weird, isn't it?"

Although Gwen, who is now twenty-four, has friends she cherishes, friends who accept her brother with autism, she didn't really appreciate how little help or understanding she got in high school from her classmates until she met her current boyfriend.

"Tim adores Simon," she says. "He is fascinated by him and includes him in our relationship. I didn't realize until he came along how little attention any of my friends ever paid to Simon. They never talked to me about how tough it must be or offer help. No one in our church group or anywhere else ever said, 'Can I take Simon for a day?' or 'How can I help you?' "

It's hard not to be angry at people who are insensitive, but sometimes the anger isn't really at the friend. It may be the residue of the resentment you felt as a child because of your brother or sister with a disability.

Alicia learned early to suppress her anger. Like me, she holds it in and then explodes at something very minor:

> If somebody leaves the cap off the toothpaste, I become Norman Bates ready to kill.
>
> One of the major problems about keeping anger inside is that people often treated me shabbily and I allowed it to happen. One incident with a friend helped me try to change the way I handle anger. I got really mad at her and then I apologized. But she said to me, "You know, your apologies mean nothing, Alicia. Your anger is so out of proportion to what happened, it's frightening and I never know when you're going to erupt again. I can't be friends with you."
>
> I was stunned. I've always wanted to tell her what a tremendous gift that was. It really made me think. I vowed from that moment forward to develop other ways to deal with my anger. I try to tell people about things that bother me before it builds up into a rage. I say, "Look there are some issues I want to discuss with you," and then I try to present them in a rational, logical way. It's hard though. Anger will always be a problem for me.

Who would have thought that anger can sometimes be a plus in relationships? Not Gwen, who, like Alicia has always had a problem with anger. She has discovered an interesting fact about the men she knows at work and in her social life. "Men really seem to like it when I get angry," she says with a laugh. "Especially when I'm mad at somebody else. They tell me I'm attractive when I'm angry–it excites them. I never would have believed there could be anything good about anger."

RELATIVES

Friends are sometimes a lot more help than relatives when things get rough. Gerri Zatlow says her relatives deserted her and her mother because they could not cope with her brother's autism.

"I wouldn't cross the street to say hello to them," she says bitterly. "But my friends have given me the support my relatives didn't give me. I once heard a good friend say she was going to my house for an autistic Thanksgiving. 'What's that?' asked the other person. My friend said, 'That's where some of the turkey winds up on the plate and some winds up on the floor.' And when I heard this, I felt good because she *got* it. It didn't shock her, it didn't repulse her."

It's often a lot harder for grandparents and aunts and uncles to accept the birth of a child with a disability into the family than it is for friends. As I mentioned earlier, my father's mother often implied that it was my mother's fault that Jack was born with mental retar-dation. She never really thought my mother was good enough for my father–not smart enough, not educated enough–and to her, my brother's birth proved it. My mother couldn't even give her son a healthy child.

According to psychologist Milton Seligman who has done research on the extended families of children with disabilities, grandparents can often mean the difference between a good adjustment in a family and a difficult one. "Grandparents aren't always accepting of their grand-children with disabilities," he told me. "They might be embarrassed. There may be some shame involved. They may even feel some guilt in terms of having passed along a gene that may have led to the disabil-ities. Some grandparents, for reasons that have nothing to do with the disability, are just really unsupportive and not involved in the family. But the nuclear family, especially in the beginning, when the child's illness is first diagnosed, need a lot of support, especially from their own parents. It's not always there."

In his book *Ordinary Families, Special Children*, Dr. Seligman says that more research is being done on the importance of the extended family to the parents and siblings of people with disabilities. He cites one study by Hornby and Ashworth in which "a quarter of the grand-parents were considered to have added to the parents' burdens and almost a third of the parents expressed a wish for more support from grandparents."

"But there are also a lot of positive aspects when grandparents do give their support," Dr. Seligman told me, "in terms of emotional sup-port, concrete support, even baby-sitting. Some grandparents are well known in their communities and can help the parents get the services they need."

Ahadi had a beloved Aunt Betty to help her through her child-hood with a sister with epilepsy. "Tia would go and have her own vacation time with Aunt Betty, but when I went there, it wasn't al-ways with Tia so I was finally able to have some attention of my own," she says on a videotape about the siblings of people with epi-lepsy. "I was finally able to be with someone who was very concerned with my needs and was interested in listening to what was going on in my life."

Ahadi's mother passed along all the information she learned from the doctors to her sister. "Whoever is sharing the caregiving should have all the information," she says.

Aunt Betty thinks it would be a good idea to have workshops for other family members to advise and educate them.

Obviously, figuring out how to have healthy relationships with friends, partners and members of your extended family is one of the most important tasks of your life unless you plan to escape entirely into a house in the woods or a monastery. If you don't have an open, honest rapport with your parents, then a therapist, counselor, or sup-port group can help you understand the positive effects a sibling with a disability has on your relationships. Compassion, tolerance, and ap-preciation of differences in other people will result in a stronger bond with your partner, as long as you don't sacrifice your own needs to those of the other person.

My own marriage has changed over the years. I was very much a people-pleasing caretaker at first, partly because most women were like that in the 1950s. When I learned to stand up for myself, our marriage improved and I changed into what Julie Tallard Johnson calls a "care-giver"–the healthy version of the caretaker. "Caregivers take care of themselves first even while they provide support and nurturing to others . . . They are able to end relationships that are a threat to their psychological, spiritual, or physical well-being."

Good relationships are important in a career too, of course. Some-one once said success in a career depends 85 percent on relationships and 15 percent on skills. Your choice of a career can be dramatically influenced by having a sibling with a disability.

9

YOUR CAREER

J wanted to stay in Paris when my year was up. I found a typing job at *Time* magazine and an apartment in Pigalle, right next to the police station. I don't know what Pigalle is like now, but in those days it was full of hookers and criminals as well as artists and entertainers. My mother came to Paris for a couple of months, and was not at all sure I should stay. She cried over hot chocolate and croissants, she cried in hotels in Italy, Switzerland, and England. She cried at the Select and she cried in my bedroom on the Boulevard Montparnasse. She was sure I would end up pregnant and poor, preyed upon by thieves and predatory men. I was a good girl. I loved my mother. I came home.

Back in New Jersey in that house in Summit, I knew I had to get out. At twenty-two, I was too old to be living with my parents. Too old for my mother to be telling me what time to come in at night. Too young to be talking about cars and gardens and golf. And Jackie was there all the time, reminding me once again that our family was different. By this time, my mother finally admitted to herself that Jack could never lead a normal life. The last entry in her diary, written when Jack was twenty-one, is heartbreaking: "The doctors were certainly right about one parent not being able to cope with a child with cerebral palsy, the other members of the family, and all the family responsibilities," she wrote. "I was too much of an optimist."

I wish she were still alive so I could tell her that without that optimism, that courage, that energy, that determination, Jackie would never have made it–nor would I.

My friend Ann was now living in an apartment in New York with two other Wheaton classmates and she asked me to join them. I found a job with a management consulting firm giving psychological tests to business executives and moved to the city. I wanted to be a writer, but the personnel director at *Time* said, "We don't hire women writers." Period. That was it. This was long before my consciousness was raised, and I just accepted the fact that I couldn't get a job at *Time* as a writer because I was a woman. So a headhunter found me the job as assistant to a psychologist, and I took it.

HELPING OTHERS

I had no desire, ever, to become a social worker or a special education teacher, but many siblings of people with disabilities do choose a career in the helping professions. One study by D. W. Cleveland and N. Miller in 1977 found that "older female siblings were found to enter the helping professions more often than other siblings. Only sisters of retarded children were most influenced by the retarded child in their career and family decisions."

In 1991 S. L. Burton and A. L. Parks, while conducting a study of siblings of people with disabilities, noticed that twice as many of their subjects who were college students majored in one of the helping professions, but a study in 1993 by V. Konstam and colleagues found that *his* college students were no more likely to choose one of the helping professions than the siblings of people without disabilities. So once again, we have conflicting results that make it difficult to reach a definite conclusion about our career choices. In my own very unscientific survey of the siblings I talked to for this book, almost a third went into one of the helping professions and many of the others participate in some kind of volunteer work that reflects their compassion for the less fortunate, or they use their careers as lawyers or film producers to help others. Many would have been high achievers anyway, but an illness or injury to a brother or sister can be a powerful force in the healthy sibling's life.

My favorite example of someone who has helped millions of people, perhaps as the result of a sister with a disability, is Helen Gurley

Brown. Mrs. Brown would probably have been a success even if her older sister Mary had not contracted polio when she was nineteen and Helen was fifteen, but the added incentive in her case was the need for money to help her mother take care of her sister. Her family desperately needed the money she could earn.

Helen was already an achiever—class valedictorian, president of the scholarship society, president of the World Friendship Society—but the added impetus of Mary's unexpected and devastating illness was perhaps the motivating force that turned *Cosmopolitan* into one of the most successful magazines in the world under her leadership. She says:

> I got out of high school and had to hit the deck running. My mother had been widowed five years earlier when my father died in an accident in Little Rock, and there weren't a lot of jobs for women in those days. She devoted so much time, energy, love, devotion, and guts to taking care of my sister and me. Sometimes she would lie down on the bed and just turn her face to the wall and sob. I would lie down beside her and hold her, just trying to absorb some of the grief.
>
> There was no money for college. I had to start working immediately. I barely had any skills. I went to business school long enough to learn shorthand and typing. My other choices in those days were becoming a nurse, which didn't appeal to me, a librarian, or working in a department store. My sister had been a secretary and it seemed the best thing for me to do.

Helen Gurley Brown climbed steadily to the top and is famous for her kindness to writers and the people who work for her. I think Helen has that extra dimension because of her love for her sister.

Ahadi, whose name means "promise" in Swahili, is another good example of those siblings who choose to spend their lives helping others because they grew up with someone with a disability. She earned a law degree and a Ph.D. in political science at Yale and spent a summer in South Africa studying their legal system. She wants to use her two degrees in a unique way—to help others, like many other healthy siblings. But Ahadi has taken the compassion and problem-solving skills she learned growing up with her sister Tia, who has epilepsy, to a new level. She says:

> I'm interested in African legal systems and seeing how people with disabilities are being integrated into African society, particularly in those countries that are now recreating themselves, such as South Africa and Mozambique. I want to help draft legislation to be sure that this population is protected from the start.
>
> Because of apartheid, there are many people with mental illness because of torture and incarceration in prisons. And in Mozambique there are so many people with disabilities because of the land mines. I don't think the new government can neglect or ignore a large population like this. I want to work in Africa and help analyze their developing legislation and policy in regard to disability. If possible, I would like to help to develop the necessary laws and policies to protect people with disabilities from discrimination and to help them integrate into the greater communities.

I was impressed over and over again by the useful lives so many siblings of people with disabilities choose. One of the best examples is a thirty-six-year-old police officer, Liz, who uses the sign language skills she learned when her younger brother was born deaf to help other deaf people in the community where she works. She told me about one dramatic incident where her skill and compassion saved a man's life:

> One morning I was sent to another precinct where a man who is deaf was threatening to jump off the ledge of a building. The rescue squad tried giving him notes to read, but he refused them. That's when they sent for me because they knew my brother was deaf and that I knew sign language. I was nervous and scared. I just knew there was a deaf man on the roof and he wanted to talk to someone.
>
> When I got to the roof, I saw him pacing back and forth. I couldn't get his attention at first so I banged on a pipe near him with my Mickey Mouse ring and the vibrations made him look at me. He could see the concern on my face and he

responded right away when I started to sign. He told me his girlfriend had died and she was the only person in his life he had to talk to. I told him I was very sorry and that there was help for him, that he shouldn't take his life. I talked to him for a long time and promised him he wouldn't be handcuffed and that I would go to the hospital with him and talk to the doctors and nurses for him. Finally he stepped back over the ledge. I put my arm around him and went to the hospital with him. I made sure he was all right before I left.

I'm often called to help other deaf people—a rape victim, a man who was robbed, anyone who needed an interpreter. Sometimes they come back to the precinct just to talk to me. Being deaf is probably the loneliest of all the disabilities.

This caregiving runs in her family. Her younger sister is studying speech pathology and plans to teach deaf people when she gets her degree.

Remember Lucy? She's the one with the sister with Angelman syndrome, and because her sister cannot talk, Lucy learned to communicate with body language and facial expressions from the time she was a small child. She is so good at expressing her emotions with nonverbal techniques she was a natural for a career as an actress, but after a while she realized it wasn't fulfilling enough. She says:

> Everyone told me my strong point was my eyes—that they really beamed out from the stage. Actually, I wasn't that great an actress, but I found myself enjoying stage management. It put me in control, and I liked that. I'm sure this all relates back to my sister somehow. Anyway, it turned out I was quite successful at it. After all, it was all about creative problem solving and dealing with people's crazy personalities—what else had I been doing all my life?
>
> Then, after I went into therapy and started unfreezing, after that outer shell of ice began to melt, I wasn't satisfied anymore. It was unfulfilling, kind of a two-dimensional way of life. I didn't think I was doing any good for anybody. I felt like my heart wasn't really allowed to soar, to allow me to make a difference. That's what I wanted to do.
>
> I read Joseph Campbell's books about this time and one line particularly stuck with me. "We must let go of the life

we have planned so as to accept the one that is waiting for us," he wrote. My heart told me to give up stage management and get a degree in social work, and that's what I'm doing now.

Lucy is not sure if she will work in the field of disabilities because she wants to see what else is out there, but it's clear that her sister's influence will be felt in any kind of work she does.

Gwen is an older sister and the only sibling of a young man with autism. "I've always wanted to set things straight," she says. "I train teachers and kids in negotiation techniques. I want to help them navigate through the world. The root of so much controversy and inefficiency in the world is that people don't communicate. Helping people through difficult conversations and situations gives them more freedom to do their jobs better. Eventually I'd like to go into politics."

Ellen, whose twin lost his sight because of retinitis pigmentosa when they were growing up, became an elementary schoolteacher. She says:

> Because of my brother, I developed a unit on disabilities for my third grade class. We did a lot of role playing. I got them to make peanut butter sandwiches with blindfolds on. I asked guest speakers to come and talk to them—a woman in a wheelchair, a man who was deaf. I wanted to help them understand what it's like to have a disability so they will be more compassionate.
>
> It's hard because little children are sometimes afraid. I remember the first time my own son saw a woman in a wheelchair. He edged up close to me and held on to my leg. The woman said, "It's nothing to be afraid of. It's just a wheelchair." But I remember thinking, "He just didn't know. He had never seen a wheelchair before and this big thing coming at him was frightening for him." Children have to be taught to feel comfortable with people with disabilities.

They should also learn that people with disabilities can be lawyers, doctors, accountants, actors, and scientists. It would be wonderful if teachers would invite people with disabilities to tell children about their work, not just their disabilities. A businessman in a wheelchair could talk about his job so the children could see that not all people in this field are able-bodied. A blind writer could speak about technical advances, such as a talking computer that allows her to edit manuscripts. Too often people with disabilities are defined by their injury or illness when that is just one aspect of their personalities.

Even those who enter seemingly nonrelated professions, such as law, engineering, writing, and producing movies, often choose projects that will benefit those less fortunate than they are. One student with a brother with autism, while a business major in college, helped organize a group on campus to support a soup kitchen in the town. A woman whose brother is mentally ill edits an environmental magazine "to save the planet a little bit." The sibling of a sister seriously injured in an automobile accident is studying for a doctorate in the psychology of law, with a focus on children with an environmental disability.

Amanda Bennett, the Atlanta Bureau Chief for *The Wall Street Journal*, and a member of a Pulitzer Prize–winning team of science writers, says she was encouraged to become a writer because a piece she wrote about her sister Catherine, who has Down syndrome, was published in a local newspaper when she was eleven. "I wrote about what a delightful child she was. She was cute and funny and fun to be around. I said it made me feel very special to have her as a sister.

"Later, when I was working as a journalist, I lived in different places, and wherever I was, Catherine would come and spend a week with me. I would take her to work with me. She would come to my office in Toronto and type letters to her friends while I worked and then we'd go out to lunch. Even though I didn't go into one of the helping professions, my sister had a big influence on my choice of a career."

Unlike Amanda, many healthy siblings I talked to denied that their brother or sister with a disability had anything whatever to do with their choice of a career. One woman who is the sister of someone with brain damage became a psychologist, and she is doing research on Alzheimer's disease.

"I became a psychologist almost by happenstance," she says. "I really wanted to be a vet. I not only didn't want to work with wounded people, I didn't want to work with people at all." Nevertheless, her life's work is the study of those with brain disorders–like her sister.

My friend Florence saw no connection between her children's choice of careers and her sister's retardation until I asked her what her children did. She told me that her oldest daughter works with people with mental illness and her son married a woman who is helping a Down syndrome child integrate into public school.

Florence's sister died when she was only fourteen, so her children didn't know her, but I think there is a connection. I believe that something happens while you're growing up with a brother or sister who is disabled in some way that gives you an extra layer of sensitivity, compassion, and understanding that most people don't have. Perhaps Florence's children drew that from their mother while she was reading to them or playing with them or putting them to bed. Somehow they wanted to help people when they grew up.

When I asked Gerri Zatlow, who spends her life obtaining funding for group homes for people with autism and directing an organization called Siblings for Significant Change, if a lot of siblings of people with disabilities go into the helping professions because of guilt, she said, "How about familiarity? How about we're good at mothering, good at taking care of people? It doesn't have to be guilt.

"In junior high school I went on a class trip to Willowbrook and I came home thinking, 'This is not what I want for my brother. He'd be better off dead than living like an animal.' So now I spend my time working to establish group homes for Douglas and others like him.

"Having a sibling with a disability doesn't mean that we stopped living our lives or that we started living entirely new lives. We live *different* lives. And that's what people have to understand. We have to make different choices than we would have if we hadn't had a sibling with a disability."

WHEN A HELPING PROFESSION IS NOT THE RIGHT CHOICE

Developmental psychologist Bryna Siegel thinks it is not always healthy to choose a career in the helping professions if you have grown up with a brother or sister with a disability.

"These are people who grew up thinking 'Hey, this is something I can be good at–taking care of those who can't take care of themselves,'" she told me. "It's as if they have gotten stuck at some phase of their development. They are often very productive, very creative members of the helping professions, but at some point they may look around and say, 'I think I became a special education teacher because of my brother and never really considered anything else.' That's not such a good thing. They might have been great painters or pianists or something else."

Dr. Stuart Silverstein, a pediatrician and co-author with Dr. Siegel of a book about the siblings of people with disabilities called *What About Me*, told me, "Just be sure your decision is made by free choice. You owe it to yourself to do some soul searching and maybe even talk to a therapist to find out your real motivation. Do you really like doing this or are you trying to please somebody else?" Dr. Silverstein, incidentally, is the brother of someone with autism.

Bill is a twenty-one-year-old college student who feels he must tailor his choice of a career to the job opportunities that are available in his hometown because of his brother who has mental retardation. "My parents have talked to me about this," he says. "They talk about what's going to happen to my brother when they die. I know he'll be my responsibility and it really will affect my life. I'll have to come back to Columbus to live because he's comfortable in a program here and he won't be able to function anywhere else. It will affect my major–what I decide to do with my life–because there aren't that many jobs in Columbus. I'll have to study something that I can get a job in when I come here. Even if I go away, get a good job somewhere else, I know I'll have to come back here to live when my parents die, to take care of my brother."

If siblings of people with disabilities go into a helping profession out of guilt, it probably won't work out. Janet, whose sister is mentally retarded, tried working with a special education class in a public school. "They were emotionally disturbed children. One was autistic, one was born brain damaged because his mother was a heroin addict. They were all seriously disabled. After two years of teaching them, I said, 'Good-bye. This is not for me. I do not want to be around this every day.'"

Marsha, the younger sister of a woman with spina bifida, thought she wanted to go into nursing when she was in high school. "I volunteered a lot at the hospital, but I just really hated dealing with sick people. I'd rather work by myself. I'm a horticulture major in college and I work in a plant nursery. I love it. I do really well in science, but rather than study medicine, I do horticulture. I may not make a million dollars, but I love what I'm doing."

When I was in my early twenties, I volunteered to work with young adults with cerebral palsy, in some kind of attempt to feel useful, or to please my mother. Every Saturday I took a subway up to the Bronx and played cards and games with people, some in wheelchairs, some who had difficulty walking and talking, all of whom had no social life except for this Saturday at the youth center. I connected with them. I had no trouble talking to them, no matter how hard they were to understand. I learned this growing up with Jack. But after a while, I realized that I didn't like spending my Saturdays that way. I might as well be home with Jack. I assumed that since I grew up with a brother with this disability, I would be the best person to help others who were like him. Not so–at least in my case. Every time I looked at someone like that, I saw my brother and my ambivalent, if not hostile, feelings about him came back in a rush. So I stopped going, and I felt guilty about that too. I was a champion at finding ways to feel guilty.

Julia Ellifritt, whose younger sister has Down syndrome, struggled with similar feelings. She did volunteer work with those with mental retardation and studied to be a social worker in college. But she was very unhappy and couldn't figure out why at first.

"I began to realize," she wrote in an article in *Exceptional Parent,* "that I had been doing all kinds of work with the mentally retarded partly to assuage my negative feelings for my sister. I felt that in God's eyes I was making amends–that good works made up for bad thoughts. That was a scary thought. I knew I would never be able to help anyone as a professional unless I could deal with my own feelings. I knew then that I could not do it alone. With the help of an excellent therapist, I began a healing process that was very painful, but very much overdue. I am learning how to deal with my negative feelings. I realize that I can learn from Bonnie who has a gentle spirit, pure unconditional love, and selfless giving. I am on my way to becoming more like her."

Julia is now doing hospice work in a hospital and enjoys it. For a long time she thought there was something wrong with going into one of the "helping professions," that she was neurotically driven to taking care of others because she grew up with a sister with Down syndrome. Then, she told me, something happened to change her mind:

> One day I went to a lecture by a psychologist named Dale Larson. It was one of those lightbulb experiences for me. He said that often people who are labeled "codependents" are just responding to their environments and to do anything else but act as a caring person under those circumstances would be wrong. I realized that when I helped Bonnie get dressed in the morning and made breakfast for her, it wasn't because I was a codependent but because she was mentally retarded. My mother was busy with three children and I wanted to help. There was nothing wrong with that. Not to respond in such a situation would be the bad behavior, not the other way around.
>
> Helping other people is a wonderful way to spend your life. Maybe some of us go into the helping professions for the wrong reasons, but it's not a bad way to spend every day. I know my limitations. I can't work with those with retardation because I can't be objective. If I counseled parents of a Down syndrome child, I would be more concerned for the other children in the family than the child with the disability. But I love doing hospice care.

In Greenberg, Seltzer, and Krauss's study comparing the siblings of those with mental retardation and those with mental illness, both groups were influenced by their disabled siblings in the choice of a career, although for different reasons.

A typical response of those whose siblings had mental retardation was, "I'm in sales and have to deal with all sorts of people with different personalities. To be a good salesperson, you have to adapt your personality to theirs. Living with my sister has given me the patience for this, as well as adaptability." One man was really good at task analysis, breaking a problem into smaller pieces because he knew what it took to teach his brother how to use his phone or how to talk.

Those whose siblings were mentally ill typically said things like, "If my brother is viewed as a failure by society's standards, it motivates me to be as successful as I possibly can. My brother's 'failures' push me to want to be successful in my career."

Claire is a dramatic example of a sibling whose whole life changed when her brother developed a serious mental illness in his twenties. After seeing what he went through, she was determined to do something about the plight of those who are mentally ill, so she packed her bags, moved to Hollywood, and became a film producer. Claire is thirty-eight now and knows her brother will be her responsibility after her mother dies:

I will be alone in the world with him. I will have to take care of him. That's my driving force. If my brother hadn't become ill, I would have been content just writing magazine articles and making very little money, marrying, and popping out babies. Going through this jolt made me look at myself.

A lot of people say to me, "It's not healthy to work so hard just because you know you're going to have to support your brother someday." But it's not just financial support. I'm driven to be well enough and secure enough to support him emotionally, to be there for him, because I see the toll it's taken on my mother.

After my brother's experience, I realized that people don't understand what mental illness is about, that it's a physical illness, like cancer or diabetes—a disease a person can't help. People are not crazy by choice. However, the average person doesn't know that. When he sees someone walking along the street ranting and raving, he might think it's just a "crazy home-less person," when that person might be anything from an accountant to an advertising executive battling mental illness.

There are some public people who have been able to use their celebrity status to downplay their bouts with mental illness. Look at Margot Kidder. Lucky for her, she has a good publicist who has been able to put a positive spin on her public displays of mania. Mental illness has no societal or monetary barriers.

You don't hear people say he *is* cancer or he *is* diabetes, but you do hear them say he *is* schizophrenic or he *is* manic depressive. People suffering from these disorders are no more the disorders than those stricken with more socially acceptable diseases. But for some reason, they *are* the illness. That's what defines them.

My goal is to produce a film that will help alleviate the stigma of mental illness. I wanted to help people understand what mental illness *really* is. I toyed with the idea of calling the movie, *There Are No Telethons for the Mentally Ill,* but then I pictured the look on the studio executive's face upon my uttering those words.

There's certainly nothing wrong with spending your life helping other people. Just be sure that you have explored other options too, so that you don't feel trapped in a field you chose for the wrong reasons. Compassion and understanding are as much a part of you when you have grown up with a brother or sister with a disability as the color of your eyes, but you don't necessarily have to make a career out of it.

When you have your career plans sorted out, a partner to spend your life with, and a good therapist to help with those minor adjustment problems, you have another big question to ask that is most certainly influenced by growing up with a brother or sister with a disability: Should you have children? Do you want them? All of us grapple with this one at some time or other.

DO YOU WANT CHILDREN?

J wouldn't exactly call the work I did after college a career. It was more like a holding pattern until I got married and had children—my *real* career. That's the way it was for most women in the 1950s. A job was just a way to earn money to pay the rent and buy clothes.

Every night after work, I went to the bar in the building where I worked with my friends. I drank until I had a pleasant buzz on and then went back to the apartment. I needed to feel numb. I needed not to think. I'm not exactly sure what it was I didn't want to think about, but I'm pretty sure it was a mixture of wanting children, but not meeting any men I wanted to marry; worrying that if I did find someone, he wouldn't want to marry me because of Jackie; working at a job that was not what I really wanted to do; and feeling I had no control over my life. And part of the need to anesthetize myself every night must have been the fear of the anger lurking inside me waiting to explode.

I went out with a lot of men, but none of them were right. I guess I was looking for someone like my father—solid, hard-working, brilliant, responsible, and above all else, funny. He had to be able to make me laugh, he had to surprise me. It wouldn't hurt if he was good-looking.

Just after my twenty-fourth birthday, I found Earl. He was a lawyer working at a Wall Street firm when I met him. He loved all the things I did—travel, music, the theater, the Brooklyn Dodgers, good restaurants, and reading, reading, reading. We both wanted to read every book in the library and see every country in the world before we were through, and in our forty-four years together, we've almost done it. He was an iconoclast and a Democrat. There had been very few of those in my father's house, and I converted. I changed from an Eisenhower Republican to an Adlai Stevenson Democrat. Earl would say things I always wanted to say but felt too inhibited. He was funny, very smart, and he loved me.

I told him about Jackie on our second date. It didn't seem to bother him. He asked me to marry him on our third date, and on our sixth date, after we were engaged, I said, "You know, I'll have to take care of Jackie when my parents die."

He looked startled. This had never occurred to him, and since a lawyer's job is to think of everything that might go wrong, he said, "I'm not sure I'm prepared to do that."

I took off the ring he had given me and handed it to him. "Then I can't marry you," I said. I had been dreading this moment all my life.

"Wait a minute," he said. "There has to be a way to work this out. I love you."

We went to see a counselor who pointed out that no one has any idea of what will happen tomorrow, much less in ten or twenty years. No one knew how long Jackie would live. My father would provide for Jackie financially. It was not something that should keep us from marrying. The counselor allayed our fears and we were married five months after we met, just under the wire of my twenty-fifth birthday.

I always wanted children. I could not imagine life without them. Because I was convinced that Jack's mental retardation was not genetic, I was not afraid of passing his disability on to my own children. But it's different when the retardation is not the result of a birth injury.

PRENATAL TESTS TO DETECT DISABILITIES

If you are the sibling of someone with a disability, you will certainly want to take advantage of the modern techniques that can detect a problem in your genetic background or that of your spouse. As I'm sure you know, genetic counseling before becoming pregnant will give you information about your risk of having a child with a disability. A "pedigree analysis" of your sibling's disability will tell you whether the disability was a random occurrence or whether it is likely to be re-peated in future generations.

Genetic screening gives you even more information to help you decide whether to have a child or not and can even be done after the birth of a baby so that treatment can alleviate the effects of a disease like phenylketonuria, which requires a special diet to prevent mental retardation. Other diseases such as Tay-Sachs (usually carried by those of Eastern European Jewish ancestry) or sickle-cell anemia (found pri-marily in African-Americans) can be discovered prenatally.

There are several tests available now that can find four hundred disorders in a developing fetus. In addition to amniocentesis, which can detect Down syndrome or neural tube closure disorders like spina bifida, there is a blood and/or amniotic fluid test called alpha-fetoprotein screening (AFP) which can also indicate spina bifida, Turner's syndrome, or an abnormality in which a fetus has incomplete sex chromosomes if the AFP level is very high, or Down syndrome if the AFP is low. (If the level is only slightly high, it means the age of the child was miscalculated.)

Ultrasound can also detect problems in the fetus, as well as a newer technique called chorionic villus sampling, in which the cells of the chorionic membrane of the fetus are analyzed. Other techniques are fetoscopy, and percutaneous umbilical blood samples, which can find physical disorders. Sophisticated surgical procedures can even cor-rect an abnormality in the fetus.

The tests cannot detect all disabilities, of course, but they can give you more information to go on. Some people want to know everything that is available to make an informed decision. Others would rather not know.

SHOULD I HAVE CHILDREN?

There seem to be several reactions by people who have siblings with disabilities: some are afraid to have children because they would never want to go through what their parents had to go through; some feel they are better able to take care of a child with a disability because they have been through it with their siblings and know how to do it;

but most are somewhere in between, unable to make up their minds about this crucial issue.

Julia Ellifritt wasn't sure whether she would have children after she married or not. "I was afraid at first that my sister's Down syndrome could be inherited because my mother had her when she was only twenty-one," she told me. "But my parents were tested and there was no genetic component. Then I thought, 'God is going to pay me back for having a horrible attitude toward my sister, and I'll have a child who has retardation.' At one point, I even thought it would be a good idea to have a child with a disability. It would give me a second chance to get it right since I messed up the first go-round with my sister. That's not healthy."

Julia is thirty-six years old now and has decided to adopt a baby from China.

The decision about whether to have children or not is probably hardest for women because they must decide before they run out of time.

Janet is thirty-seven years old and is still debating this issue. "I know it's because of my sister who has mental retardation," she says. "Ninety percent of me never had a strong urge to have children– repulsed is too strong a word–but I've never wanted children. My brother has one daughter, but he had to be convinced to have one. My sister-in-law had amniocentesis, and before they knew the results, my brother said to her, 'There will not be a handicapped child in this house.' He was absolutely determined not to repeat the experience our parents had with my sister. My sister-in-law didn't understand it, but I told her, 'You can't imagine what it's like. To go through it again is unthinkable.' When their child was born, there was something special about her birth because she was normal. That meant we were normal too. We didn't always give birth to abnormal children."

Lydia, whose brother Phil has cerebral palsy, writes in *Glamour*, "Though much of my conflict with Phil is in the past, our relationship is strongly influencing my life right now–in my decision to have, or not have, a child. I'm thirty-three and have been married for almost five years, but I still feel ambivalent–in part, I'm sure, because I know that I could not ever raise a handicapped child. Feeling responsible for my brother for most of my life has nearly depleted my supply of self-lessness."

Some people refuse even to consider the possibility that there could be anything wrong with their children. One of my friends whose sister has Down syndrome said, "I told myself this couldn't happen to me because it already happened once in our family. Of course that doesn't make any sense, but I convinced myself of that."

Other women, whose brothers or sisters were disabled as a result of a brain injury, still hesitate to have children. If you've lived with it growing up, you can't help but think about it. When you've been through it, you know what it's like and there's a real fear that it could happen to you just as it happened to your mother.

Even with abortion as an alternative, many women, even those with siblings with severe disabilities, do not feel they can consider this option. Donna's sister has Down syndrome, which can be detected by tests when the mother is carrying the child. Would she have an abortion if she discovered that she too was carrying a child with Down syndrome?

"Never!" she says vehemently. "I wouldn't have missed knowing my sister for anything. She's one of the bright spots in my life. If I found out that my baby had Down syndrome, I would know exactly how to take care of her, to make her life better, to help her achieve her full potential. I can't imagine having an abortion."

But many other women and their husbands would not hesitate to terminate a pregnancy, no matter how much they loved their brother or sister with a disability.

"I know that growing up with a brother with autism made me a stronger person. I can cope with anything," says Kevin, a physician. "But I'm petrified of having a child with a disability. My wife is pregnant and is having tests now to make sure the child is all right. If there is anything wrong with that baby, I would abort it in a New York second. It sounds selfish, but I want no part of it. I realize now how much I missed while growing up with a brother with autism, and I want to be involved in my child's life the way my parents couldn't be."

Susan, whose sister has Down syndrome, remembers her mother

saying to her when Susan was pregnant with her first child, "I just want to let you know that things have worked out very well for us. We love your sister very much. I wouldn't have done it any other way if I'd known ahead of time. But it was a different world then—abortion wasn't a possibility. If you find out there is something wrong, my suggestion is to terminate the pregnancy."

"I thought that was wonderful of her," Susan says. "She would never have considered an abortion for herself. But I would absolutely have one. In this world, I'm afraid for normal children. Even though I knew my sister's retardation wasn't the hereditary type, I was still scared. My mother had my sister when she was only thirty-one and she had no idea she could have a Down syndrome child at that age. I wouldn't dream of having a child at any age without amnio first."

Diane and her husband do not agree on this subject. "Because he has never been exposed to people who are retarded and who are disabled in some way, he seems to feel, especially about people like Cathy, that they would be better off not having been born because they are so severely retarded," she says. "You know, if you can do something about it, if you know they are going to be born this way, why let them be born? He feels that their life is being lived for no reason at all. It is difficult for him to understand it because he has never been around her. He cannot see that her joy in life is playing with people, listening to music, or being well. Her joys are simply not what our joys are."

Those with siblings with mental illness often express their determination not to have children. In Greenberg, Seltzer, and Krauss's study comparing the siblings of those with mental retardation to those with mental illness, a typical response from the siblings of those with mental illness was, "I have a tremendous fear of having children with mental illness, due to my genetics. I am totally against having my own children due to this fear."

Claire is thirty-eight and living with someone she loves very much. She wants to have children but is afraid to do so because her brother developed schizophrenia in his twenties. "There's always going to be something in the back of my head wondering if my child could be like my brother. I think it's so unfair to bring a life into this world that's nothing but a tortured soul. My brother has very few pleasures. He doesn't have relationships. He leads a very simple life. He eats and sleeps and goes to a program. This is a man with a brilliant mind who plays the piano like a virtuoso.

"I once asked my mother, 'If you had it to do over again, would you still have children?' She looked at me and started to cry. 'I don't know,' she said, 'I can't bear to think that I brought a tormented human being into the world—but I'm happy I had you.'

"There was no mental illness in my family, but in looking back, I see certain patterns. I have a cousin who has not been labeled mentally ill, but it's clear to me that his behavior is that of someone with a mental problem."

Julie Tallard Johnson was afraid of having a baby for a long time. But at the age of forty-one she had her first baby after coming to terms with her fear. "I found out it was a fear of differences. The fear that I might give birth to an imperfect child. A lot of the suffering of people with disabilities is due to the way we treat them. It's very hard to be blind or to be mentally ill, but the suffering is not all because of the disability."

There is no satisfactory answer to this difficult question, but at least you can make a more informed decision than women in the past because of the new technology.

Whether you decide to have children or not, someday you will be faced with another, equally difficult dilemma: Who will take care of your sibling with the disability when your parents can no longer do so?

WHO WILL TAKE CARE

OF YOUR SIBLING?

*O*n our wedding day, I wore an exquisite satin dress made by my mother. It had a tulle panel in the front appliquéd with tiny mother-of-pearl leaves. Our wedding was perfect, but it wasn't until I started writing this book that I realized something that seems astonishing to me now. Jack wasn't at our wedding. Where was he? All alone in our house while I walked down the aisle and exchanged vows with my husband? Watching television while we celebrated at the reception with our friends? Why wasn't he there? I'm sure my mother wanted to save me from embarrassment. Did I ask that he not be there? I hope not, but I honestly don't remember.

My feelings about him are so hopelessly jumbled. He's my little brother and when he looks in my eyes and smiles, when he laughs after I remind him of something that happened while Mother and Dad were alive and we all lived in that house in Summit, I love him very much. When he holds tight to my hand in a crowd, I want to protect him from the world. But when I'm away from him, I just want to forget him and live a "normal" life—whatever that is.

Earl and I lived in New York in the fifties after we were married and had a better than "normal" life. I worked for a book publisher, and we ate in French restaurants for three dollars and fifty cents, went to the theater for three dollars, gobbled up books at the local library, and read almost every night, sitting side by side on the sofa, and comparing notes on what we read. Because my cooking was limited to hot dogs with cheese, tuna casseroles, and lamb chops, we went to my parents' house for dinner on Sundays. Jackie was there, but since he ate early, he wasn't at the dinner table with us. Come to think of it, I don't remember Jackie at the table on Thanksgiving or Christmas or any holiday. I don't remember celebrating his birthdays either. Instead he was there, playing with his train set, watching television, smiling or twisting his hands in anguish when thoughts tormented him. I don't know what caused him such agony, but he would shake his head and grimace in anger or fear. He does that now, and I try to hear what he is saying to himself, but it's always something incomprehensible to me. I just put my arms around him and say, "Are you okay, Jack?" and he snaps back to reality.

We left the city after our second daughter was born, to live in Hartsdale, a Westchester County suburb north of New York City. Earl started the Criminal Division of Legal Aid for the county, building up a respected staff of lawyers who represented those committing felonies in the forty-six courts of the county. I worked with the League of Women Voters and the National Council on Crime and Delinquency, wrote for small magazines, and worked as a portrait photographer.

My mother was wonderful about taking our children for weekends and vacations so we could get away by ourselves once in a while. I thought my daughters had no idea Jackie was different from other people when they went to my parents' house. They seemed to accept him. They hugged him and climbed on his lap and played trains with him. They watched television in the den with him, and my younger daughter still remembers eating peanut butter and crackers while watching I Love Lucy. But recently, thirty-five years later, she told me she was afraid of him. She said she definitely knew that he was different from other people, but she never said anything to me. I, of course, never talked to her about it. How could I not have known that my children might have been a little anxious around a person with retardation? Why didn't I reassure them? Even so, my daughters care about Jack now. They send him presents on his birthday, call him, visit him when they are in Florida. Even when we don't see him, Jack is a presence in all our lives.

One of the things that made it easy to pretend that I didn't have a brother with mental retardation was my mother's determination to protect me from having to take responsibility for him. She never said, "When we die, you'll have to take care of Jack," or "I need some help with Jack. Could you stay with him this weekend?" She never expected me to change my life for one minute to look after Jack. But she often said to me, "Mary, I don't want Jack to go to a state institution." There was such panic and fear in her eyes that I promised her no matter what, he would never be sent to one. She had visited state institutions and had seen people like her son living in filth, naked, abandoned, abused, drugged. I had seen the television documentary on Willowbrook. I tried to reassure her that I would never allow him to go to one of those places, but I don't think she believed me completely.

Because of that fear, she and my father saved every penny and set up a trust fund for my brother so he could live at the Duvall Home in Deland, Florida, where he has been for the past thirty years. It is run by kind, humane, compassionate people who truly care about the adults with mental retardation who live there.

Many siblings are not so lucky as I was. They are left with the financial, as well as emotional, responsibility for their siblings who have a disability. It's often very difficult for siblings to persuade their parents that some provision should be made for the disabled sibling while the parents are still alive. As a result, there can be chaos when the person with the disability is suddenly left alone, without money, without a home, without people he knows to take care of him.

TALKING TO YOUR PARENTS ABOUT THE FUTURE

Thomas Fish, Director of the Nisonger Center at Ohio State University, told me, "When it comes to planning the future for disabled people, it's often an either/or kind of proposition. It's either 'You will take care of your brother and promise me you will for the rest of your life,' or 'You won't have to take care of him because you shouldn't have the responsibility. I don't want you to have it.' More often than not, the normal siblings are not asked to participate in planning the future."

In M. E. McCullough's 1981 study of the siblings of people with mental retardation and physical disabilities, it was clear that parents and the nondisabled siblings made assumptions about the future of the disabled child without ever talking to each other about it.

"Sixty percent of the parents said they had not made plans, while 60 percent of the siblings thought plans had been made. Sixty-eight percent of the siblings thought their parents had made financial arrangements for the disabled sibling's future care, while sixty-eight percent of the parents indicated they had not made financial arrangements."

It's a subject nobody wants to talk about because it is uncomfortable for most people to discuss their parents' death. But in families with a child with a disability, it is absolutely vital that they do so.

Because administrators of group homes for people with mental retardation or autism and other people who provide services for families are so accustomed to talking to parents, they often ignore the adult siblings of the person with the disability. Siblings have a lot to say. They are often more aware of certain aspects of the sibling's care than the parents are.

There has been a gradual realization by psychologists and health care professionals that the healthy siblings are part of the family too, and should be included in plans to help the sibling with the disability. It's hard to understand why it took such a long time for people to grasp the fact that brothers and sisters often understand the sibling with a disability as well as or better than the parents. They play with them, help feed them, try to teach them to ride a bike or read. They can often understand the speech of a child who has trouble forming words better than other people. Siblings have a lot to contribute and all they ask is to be included, to be appreciated, to be listened to.

In Krauss and Seltzer's study of the siblings of those with mental retardation, the researchers asked for comments that would be helpful to service providers. This comment from one healthy sibling sums up the way they are generally treated: "Listen to the retarded person's siblings. They know what they're talking about. They grew up with the retarded person. It's much different from reading about it or learning it from a college course. You will never totally understand what it's like to live with a retarded person unless you do it. Service providers should all spend time in a group home or even several days with a family and their retarded child. That way they have first-hand experience."

Don Meyer emphasizes the importance of consulting siblings in planning for the future of a person with a disability. "Increasingly, adults with disabilities ... are living and working in their communities," he writes in the National Association of Sibling Programs newsletter. "As their parents age and die, their nondisabled brothers and sisters will be involved in their lives in significant ways. Because of the move-ment toward community life for people with disabilities and the scar-city of needed resources (e.g., residential options and employment opportunities) for adults with disabilities, siblings' roles will likely be greater than in previous generations. Many adult, nondisabled siblings will struggle with seemingly incompatible loyalties they feel toward their brothers and sisters and loyalties they have toward their own families.

"Adult brothers and sisters are an extraordinarily overlooked population, receiving little attention from agencies serving people with special needs. This is despite the fact that siblings generally have the longest-lasting relationship in the family. Most of the forty-three mil-lion people with disabilities in the United States have brothers and sisters."

FIND THE RIGHT LAWYER

One thing you can do, or strongly suggest that your parents do, is consult a lawyer who specializes in setting up guardianships, con-servatorships, and supplemental income trusts for those with a disa-bility. If your parents make an appointment to see the lawyer, insist that you be included in the discussions of your sibling's future. You will probably be the one who has to take care of your brother or sister, so you should be sure you understand and have a say in the planning.

Not all lawyers are qualified to give advice on estate planning for someone with a disability. Don't just pick someone out of the yellow pages who writes wills. Call up the organization that represents your sibling's disability—The ARC (formerly known as the Association of

Retarded Citizens), the National Alliance for the Mentally Ill (NAMI), The National Parent Network on Disabilities, etc.–and ask for the name of a legal expert in this field. Better still, click on SibNet on the Internet and ask other siblings in your state for names of attorneys who have done a good job for them.

When you are sure that you have the right lawyer, discuss what kind of arrangement is best for your sibling. The lawyer might suggest that you become your brother's or sister's guardian, either for financial or personal affairs or both. You can set up a limited guardianship that would allow you to make decisions in certain areas of your sibling's life, if you wish to help your brother or sister be as independent as possible.

As your sibling's guardian, you might be consulted on medical treatment. You might find homemakers and health care services if your sibling needs them. You might decide how his funds will be spent if he or she is not capable of this. Today, with more respect for the independence of all individuals, you should talk to your sibling about the decisions made for him and, depending on his ability to understand, listen to his wishes and desires.

If you and your parents agree that you are the best person to be your sibling's guardian, your lawyer will obtain court approval after evaluations and interviews to establish your competency to act as a guardian. If you do not want to be his guardian, you can help your parents select a friend, another relative, or a public agency to do so.

Ask your lawyer if a conservatorship is a better arrangement for your sibling than a guardianship in your state. A conservator is appointed by the court to manage your parents' estate, and if there are several siblings in your family, one person could be the conservator, another the guardian.

If your parents can set up a trust fund for your sibling that provides for all his needs, including medical, you are lucky. Many people are not as fortunate and some join a "pool trust" in which many parents (or siblings) invest together. The money paid out later to the sibling with the disability depends on the amount they paid in. Again, organizations like The Arc and NAMI can help you set up a pool trust.

If your sibling is eligible for Supplemental Security Income and Medicaid because he has only $2,000 in assets and cannot earn more than $500 a month, your lawyer can help your parents set up a supplemental income trust. This is a trust that is put in someone else's name and provides income for quality-of-life expenses like recreation, clothing, and such not covered by SSI. It's important that money not be left directly to your sibling or he will lose his government funding.

You can help your parents write a letter of intent that will spell out what you want for your sibling with the disability–living arrangements, health care professionals, hobbies, skills, likes, dislikes, and anything that you want other people to know about your brother or sister. Financial planners and lawyers who specialize in these cases usually have forms that include suggestions for letters of intent.

LIVING ARRANGEMENTS

Aside from financial arrangements for your sibling, you can help your parents decide where he should live. With you? With another sibling? In a group home? In a supervised apartment? With a boyfriend or girlfriend? You must be part of this decision, of course, because one day you will most likely be in charge.

Graham and Anita's parents are still alive and responsible for Pammy, their daughter with Down syndrome, but Graham as a specialist in early childhood education and Anita as a lawyer who specializes in cases concerning those with a disability, are both very much involved in Pammy's life and worried about their sister's choice of a boyfriend and her decision to move in with him. They feel he has robbed her of much of her independence because she defers to him on her choice of clothes, jobs, food, behavior, and worst of all, her attitude toward her family has sometimes been one of open hostility.

"That's the part that's hardest on my parents," Anita says. "Pammy insists that they accept her boyfriend in their home and she says she hates them when they suggest she come to see them without him. My parents don't like him because they think he is exploiting her and encouraging her to behave in self-destructive ways that will make her unhappy. The whole family is divided about whether we should re-spect our sister's wish to live her own life or whether we should rescue her from what many of us consider a bad situation."

Those siblings who are not as independent as Pammy may do better in group homes and supervised apartments. Healthy siblings of-ten urge their parents to place their brothers and sisters who are higher functioning, like Down syndrome adults, or those with physical disabilities like epilepsy or spina bifida in these facilities. They usually have more confidence in their siblings' ability to be independent than their parents do. They try to help them find creative solutions to housing, such as combining their resources with other people to buy a home for those with special needs. They arrange for someone to supervise the group home—a college student for instance, who can live there free, but who is required to drive or cook dinner or help in some way.

You have to be creative. The waiting lists for group homes grow longer and longer every year. At least 60,000 people are on waiting lists for government-funded residential programs. About 80 percent of the seven million Americans with mental retardation live at home, a growing number of them in the care of aging parents.

Celine Fortin, public relations director of The Arc of New Jersey says, "Our waiting list for residential services, either in institutions or in the community, has grown to over 4,700 individuals, and the list is growing by two persons a day.

. "One of the reasons the waiting list is growing so rapidly is that the baby boomers are getting older and so are their parents, so the healthy siblings are beginning to assume responsibility for their broth-ers and sisters with disabilities. They are mostly two-worker families, and now they suddenly have a brother or sister with a disability who has always been taken care of at home but whose parents can no longer keep them. These siblings are dependent on two incomes so one of them can't just quit and stay home with the person with the disability. When they come to us and ask us what to do, we tell them to get on the waiting list as quickly as possible. The average waiting time is five to six years in the urgent category and ten to fifteen years if the placement is nonurgent."

In an emergency you can turn to agencies like Lifetime Assistance Networks and Plan New Jersey, which step into crisis situations and find foster homes for people with disabilities who are left alone suddenly. They can also act as guardians, visit disabled people to make sure their needs are being met, and administer trust funds.

"For instance," Catherine McHugh, acting executive director of Plan New Jersey, says, "If we were the guardian and a person needed a change in living arrangements, we would advocate for that, using the resources that are available, and make a lot of noise to make sure the changes that need to be made are made."

There is no getting around it. When parents die, our brother or sister is *our* responsibility, whether we want it or not. People with disabilities, especially those with mental retardation, often live much longer now because of better care and advances in medicine. When I was growing up, my mother used to say, "We really don't expect Jack to live beyond the age of thirty." I believed that. My brother is sixty-seven now and there is no reason he won't live into his eighties or nineties too. He's healthy, strong, and well taken care of.

"It's psychologically very difficult to deal with the future of a retarded child," Marty Krauss told me. "Parents want their children in a residential setting, but the waiting list is so long they get discouraged. Unless there is a crisis, it's very unlikely that the son or daughter will move into a residential setting. Some just assume that one of the other brothers or sisters will take over. They know they want their children to be in a nice, residential home, but they haven't taken any steps to make that happen. It's a huge issue."

In Marty Krauss and Marsha Seltzer's study of 140 siblings of brothers and sisters with mental retardation, they found that 64 percent of the siblings they talked to planned to live apart from their siblings, though making sure they are provided for by others, and 36 percent planned to live with their brother or sister with mental retardation.

WHO WILL TAKE CARE OF THE SIBLING WITH THE DISABILITY?

When it comes to which sibling will take care of the brother or sister with a disability when the parents die, it often turns out to be an older sister. Krauss and Seltzer found that more than 75 percent of those siblings who planned to live with their siblings with disabilities were women. And it was usually a sister residing with a sister, rather than a brother.

But this situation is changing. Men of this generation seem to be more nurturing of their own children and probably are more likely to take on the responsibility of a sibling with a disability than was true a generation or two ago.

Alex is thirty-six and lives in another state from his brother with mental retardation. They have always been close because they are only a year apart in age and they both love sports. "It's generally assumed, just because there is such a rapport between Tom and me that I'll be the responsible person. I don't think we've ever talked about it in such concrete terms though. My sister is five years older than Tom and has a harder time identifying with him than I do."

Gwen feels the weight of being the only sibling in a family where there is a child with a disability. Her brother has autism and she has talked to her mother about Simon's future. Both agree he will go into a group home, but it's not that easy for Gwen. "Nothing has come to my attention that sounds even remotely like the place that I want for Simon," she says. "This is the heartbreaking part. He has such an enriched environment now. He is a musical savant and can play anything he hears on the piano. I am really committed to finding a place for him that is enriching. But I will find just the right home for him. He's the most important responsibility I have. My mom had a heart attack recently and I went to a lawyer and became Simon's guardian."

PERSUADING PARENTS TO LET GO

It's often a sibling who realizes that it's time for a brother or sister with a disability to leave home, but the parents—most often the mother—cannot bring themselves to do it. "Many siblings have higher expectations for their brothers' and sisters' independence than their parents do," Dr. Krauss told me. "Some of them say, 'I know my brother could do more, but my mom does everything for him. She won't let him make his own bed.'

"They wish their parents would let their siblings go into a group home where they would have a social life and learn to take care of themselves. The big problem in most homes is the lack of social activity for the sibling with the disability. They don't have a social life unless the parents arrange it. The healthy siblings want their brothers and sisters to have more friends too."

Allison's sister has Down syndrome. She is bright, talented and able to live on her own at the age of thirty. But Allison tells me her mother cannot accept the idea of her daughter living on her own:

> I think my mother is using Dee as an excuse not to get on with her own life. She's a professional mother and the rest of us managed to escape that orbit, but Dee couldn't. So she continues to help my mother fulfill the role of being a mother instead of doing something else, which my mother should have done a long time ago. She's a brilliant woman. She let my sister become her life's work. Dee is the baby she didn't have to lose.
>
> The first ten or fifteen years, it didn't seem so obvious. She was being a mother to all of us. But now that she's older, she can't let go. I feel sad that my parents don't travel as much as they should. They won't travel without her. I think my father would just as soon send Dee off to us and travel for a week with my mother.
>
> When I suggest that they place Dee in a group home, my mother says, "You can't tell me to send my child away, to send her to a home. You're telling me to throw her away." I think she's still reacting to the doctors who told her to put my sister in an institution when she was born.

For a while, Dee actually was in a group home, but it was so difficult for her mother, who tortured herself thinking about her daughter not getting the care and loving attention she got at home, that she soon took her out of there.

"I think that Dee would be a lot happier living on her own, but my mother can't let go of her," Allison says. "Now that she's older, my sister is kind of snappish, and she always used to be cheerful and sunny. She'll say, 'I'll do my own thing. Don't you tell me what to do.' I think a lot of that is because she wants to be on her own."

Another sibling told me, "My mother once said that she had always wanted a baby that would be a doll for her whole life, and she got her wish. My sister was tiny, the size of a baby, and she couldn't walk or talk or function in any way."

There are many ways to deal with the future of a disabled sibling. Colleen says, "I told my parents, 'I love my brother, but I don't want to be his parent. He cannot come and live with me.' They said, 'You're letting the family down. He'll be out on the street.' But that's not what I meant at all. There are other options, other arrangements that can be made. I just cannot have him live with me."

MENTAL ILLNESS

If it is difficult finding a loving home for a sibling with mental retardation or autism, it must be next to impossible to commit a brother or sister to a mental institution when his or her illness becomes unmanageable. When you have loved a sibling through childhood and adolescence and known him as a healthy person, it must be devastating to face the situation that he needs more help than you can give him.

Claire had to help her parents find a place for her brother with schizophrenia when she was in her mid-twenties. They persuaded her brother to sign himself into a private hospital, which cost them $30,000 a month. They assumed the doctors there would be able to help him. That was not the case:

> We went to see Peter every night. My parents would cry when they left there. The hospital released him after four months, but he never should have come home. He was still very ill.
>
> I watched my family fall apart from my brother's illness. It was devastating. My parents' whole lives were about their children—raising them so they could grow old together, retire,

and travel. All their savings went into Peter's hospitalizations. I'm sure my father's death from cancer was related to his disease over his son. My mother had to go back to work because they spent the majority of their savings on Peter. I watched all my family's dreams disintegrate.

That experience with the doctors and the staff, the whole mental health system, either public or private, was something that changed my life. I had a new career goal after that–to do something to help people like my brother. I became a documentary film producer and am looking for the right script to show the anguish families go through when someone they love has a mental illness.

There is a big difference between the way siblings of those with mental illness feel about taking care of their brothers and sisters and the way siblings of those with other disabilities react. The Greenberg, Seltzer, and Krauss study comparing the siblings of those with mental retardation and those with a mental illness revealed a much different attitude. When it came to future plans, those with a sibling with mental retardation said typically, "We know that someday when my parents are no longer able to care for my brother, we will take over that responsibility."

Those whose siblings were mentally ill tended to say things like, "I do not plan on having Jim live with me. I could not handle the whole concept of living with someone who is mentally ill unless I knew he'd never stop taking his medicine."

Peggy tried to help her brother with schizophrenia when he was discharged from military service by inviting him to live with her:

He was so violent and angry, a friend finally said, "You have to get him into a hospital." I didn't think it was him. I just thought I wasn't helping him enough. A lot of people in their twenties have trouble getting on with their lives. It wasn't like he was babbling in a corner. I couldn't tell if it was a real mental illness or just confusion. But he got worse and worse.

For the last eight years he has lived in an alley down the street from me. Every time I see him I just want to shake him and say, "I can pay your rent or you can live with me." But when I push it, he runs. He won't move inside because he thinks the government is after him and he doesn't want them to have his address.

At least I know where he is. Not seeing him would be easier in a way because I wouldn't be constantly reminded of him. The guilt and frustration of seeing him every week is hard. When it rains or is windy, I worry about him, feel guilty that he's out there and that I can't do anything about it. At least we talk. He comes over to see me once in a while.

Even that makes me feel guilty because I know if I allow him to sit down, he'll talk for the next two or three hours without stopping and I won't be able to do anything else. So when he stops by, I tell him I have a headache or am stressed out and can't get in a conversation with him. I know he's dying to talk. He wants to spew out all these manic things on his mind. He could talk for the next twenty-four hours. I know what I have to do, but it feels mean.

The whole thing is, I don't really have a brother. I have this person that I have to be a parent or a teacher or some kind of guard over, and it's not the role I want with my brother. Then there will be a moment every now and then when he'll be quite nice. It's like a pearl, that moment. I put it in my heart and treasure it because there may not be another one for a year.

By the time my parents were in their sixties and Jack was in his thirties, they decided it would be a good idea to find a place for him to live while they were still alive, so he would be settled and comfortable when they died. They didn't want me to have the worry of finding a place for him during a crisis, and I'm grateful to them for that.

I helped them investigate possible residences for Jack. At that time, there were very few places for adults with mental retardation. Most of the homes available were for children. I thought I had located a good place in northern Westchester, not too far from where I lived. It was run by a former marine and was spotless and seemed ideal. It wasn't. Family visits were not allowed without advance notice. When my brother developed an infection on his hand, I called and said I wanted to come and see Jack that day. "If you come here, be prepared to take him home with you," he said, so I did. I packed his things and brought him back to my parents' home.

After a couple of other false starts—this is not an easy thing to do—my parents found the Duvall Home, where he still lives today. The Duvalls had an adult child with mental retardation, and because they couldn't find a place where they wanted him to live, they started a home for people like him. Jack was one of the lucky ones who went to live there.

Today there are many adults, young and very old, male and female, living in clean, comfortable, attractive rooms, either in the main building or in group homes. The attendants are kind, caring, loving people who work hard to take care of people with serious disabilities and physical problems.

Even though she realized it was best for my brother, it must have been terribly painful for my mother to put him in a home. I will never forget the look on my mother's face when she left my brother at Duvall for the first time. Jackie didn't want my mother to go, but he was such a sweet-natured person, he wouldn't make a fuss. He stood by the car, holding on to the door, looking at my mother, hoping she would say, "Come on, Jack, hop in." But she couldn't. He went back inside and my father drove away. My mother turned her face to the side and cried quietly for a long time. Now that I'm a mother of a child with a disability, I know how agonizing it must have been for my mother to even think about letting Jack live somewhere else. It must have broken her heart every time she had to leave him there. She had taken care of him for thirty-seven years. Would he be all right? Would he get the proper food? Would they be kind to him? Would he like the other people living there? Would he be miserable away from my mother? What would happen if someone abused him? I don't know how she stood it. If she hadn't thought it would be much harder for him to have to make that move when she was dead, I'm sure she wouldn't even have considered it.

After Jack went to Florida, it was even easier for me to forget that I had a brother with cerebral palsy and mental retardation. I didn't have to visit him—he was too far away. I could push him far, far back into the part of my brain that stored all the unpleasant parts of my life.

My younger daughter developed diabetes about the time Jack went to Duvall, so I persuaded myself I didn't have time to worry about Jackie. I had worries enough at home, and I began to feel as if I were living my mother's life. I had a child with a disease that could kill her, but I was determined to live a "normal" life. I denied the seriousness of the diabetes, learned to give insulin injections, and deemphasized the illness in our home and with friends. I didn't want her to be like the other patients I saw in the doctor's office who dwelled on their symptoms and were obsessed with being sick. I persuaded myself my daughter had an illness, but she wasn't really sick. Just as my mother kept hoping that my brother wasn't really retarded. When my daughter had insulin reactions, I learned how to bring her out of them and my older daughter learned that too. But as soon as the reaction was over and Kyle was all right, we acted as if this were a minor inconvenience.

When you have grown up with a sibling with a disability and then have a disabled child of your own, it's hard to understand it. Why should it happen again? Wasn't once enough? Are you doomed to live your parents' life all over again? Don't ever tell me that having a child with a disability is just as easy as having any other child. Don't tell me that a positive attitude and a prayer will take away all the pain and sorrow, because I know better.

I certainly felt many times that I was reliving my mother's life when my younger daughter became blind, had a kidney transplant, and then had her leg amputated as a result of the complications of diabetes. The difference is, of course, that knowing my daughter has been one of the most rewarding parts of my life and the world would be a poorer place without her. Though I am haunted by the fear that she may die before I do, I am lucky to have her as my daughter and friend.

As we all know, life is not fair. But, as I've learned from the people who spoke to me for this book, you just have to live the best life you can in the middle of very difficult circumstances.

My older daughter Karen must have learned about the unfairness of life when she was a child. I didn't realize it, but there had to be times when she resented the fact that I wasn't there for her when she needed me. I had to spend so much time with her sister in the hospital when her blood sugar went out of control. I talked to Karen about it when I began this book, and she seems to have come to terms with her feelings.

"When I had children of my own," she told me, "I realized that the worst thing that can happen is having one of your children sick, and Kyle's illness was so serious, I can understand now how worried you must have been, how difficult it must have been for you. I used to think you spoiled her when I was a child, but I don't now."

I'm grateful that she feels this way, and I talked to many siblings while I was writing this book who accept the fact of their brother or sister's disability with grace and kindness.

When I was in my forties, I started to write books. Old as I was, I still yearned for my parents' praise and approval. My first book was a kind of benign feminist book about the changes that had taken place in our society since the publication of Betty Friedan's *The Feminine Mystique*. It got a good review in *The New York Times Sunday Book Review,* and I took a copy of the book to my parents, to whom I had dedicated it. My father looked at it and handed it to my mother without saying a word. She flipped through the pages (illustrated with photographs by me), smiled, and said, "How nice, dear," and put it on the table next to her.

My mother's next sentence is one I'll always remember. "Jackie bowled one hundred last week."

"How nice, Mom," I said.

I wrote five more books after that and gave up expecting either of my parents to understand how important they were to me. When my mother was ninety-three, she began to tidy up her life in preparation for her death. She threw out or gave away most of her possessions and just kept the essentials. One day I noticed that my books were no longer on the shelf. I asked her about them. "Oh, I gave them to Karen, dear," she said. "I didn't want anything to happen to them."

I felt like she had given away my children, but as my father used to tell me, there's no use getting mad at someone who doesn't mean to hurt you. I guess he was right, but I still wish she had kept my books.

As we grew older, my life grew fuller and my mother's and father's grew emptier as their friends died and their bodies kept them from doing some of the things they had done when they were younger. Still, my father played golf almost every day until he died at the age of eighty-seven. My mother went to Florida to see Jackie as often as she could, and I went with her sometimes to help her.

I wanted to spend as little time at Duvall as possible, but my mother would spend an hour talking to Vicky, Jack's room mother, about his clothes and what he needed. She would go through his small closet and chest of drawers, counting the underwear, his pajamas, checking his sport shirts to make sure they were in good condition, looking at his pants, his belts, his shoes, his socks, his blanket. She must have given me five little notebooks from time to time listing all the clothes Jack would need throughout the year. Now that my mother is no longer alive, Vicky checks on his clothes for me and counts everything that comes back from the laundry.

Vicky Sheppard is a remarkable woman from Peru who married an American, had two sons, and came to live in the United States. She found a job as a housemother at the Duvall Home and has been wonderful to Jack. She brings him to her home at Christmas and Thanksgiving. She takes him to movies and out to lunch. She drove him to the doctor when he needed a series of radiation treatments and she stayed near him when he had to go to the hospital. Vicky cares about all the people she takes care of. She washes them, shaves them, makes their beds, looks after them, lifts them in and out of wheelchairs, cleans up after them, loves them. I don't know what I would do without her. Jack loves her very much.

When I wasn't actually in Florida with my mother visiting Jack, I continued my old habit of forgetting about him. And my life changed dramatically in my fifties. We moved to Pennsylvania, far from my friends in New Jersey and my beloved New York. While we were there, my younger daughter Kyle began to lose her eyesight because of diabetic retinopathy. She was at Boston University, and I would meet her in New York, where she received laser treatments and then I would drive her back to Boston.

I don't know how to convey to you how terrible it was to watch her slowly, slowly, lose her sight. She had to leave college and come back home to stay with us. She would lie in bed every day, waiting for the last glimmer of light to go. I rubbed her back, tried to make her laugh, played Scrabble with her while she could still see a little bit. I sent for Braille instruction books and we learned it together. While we waited in the doctor's office I would spell out messages to her on the back of her hand in Braille dots. I would tell her what the people in the waiting room looked like. I wanted to see her smile.

Then one day when I went to wake her, she said, "I can't see your face anymore." I went downstairs and howled and raged at God for doing that to my daughter. How could He do that? Wasn't it enough that my brother was maimed when he was born? Why would You do this to me? Leave me alone! I sobbed and cried, thinking no one could hear me. But Kyle heard me. She had crept to the stairs and she heard me wailing in despair. She went back to her room, picked up the phone, and found out where to get help. My daughter learned to walk with a cane, organized her life, found an apartment in Boston, went back to school, and finished getting her degree.

Letting her go was one of the hardest things I ever had to do. I wanted to keep her safe at home with me. I wanted to protect her from walking in front of a car, from falling down subway steps, from bumping into poles and cabinet doors and other people. But then I would have stopped her from living. She got a job with a state senator after she graduated from college, then went to Harvard and got a master's degree in public administration and traveled to England, Ireland, Germany, and Ukraine to write reports on health care in those countries. To say that I'm proud of her doesn't begin to tell you how I feel. She lives on her own in Boston, and seeing her lights up my life.

When I drove Kyle to Boston after she became blind and left her alone in her apartment, I felt my mother's grief after leaving Jackie at Duvall that first time. At least I knew Kyle could pick up a phone and ask for help when she needed it. Jackie couldn't even do that.

When we moved back to New Jersey from Pennsylvania, it was with the same sense of relief and joy that I had felt years before when we left Baltimore to come back to Summit. I was with my friends again—supportive, loving women who are a vital part of my life. I wrote a book on death and dying for teenagers and then started to write about successful women for *Cosmopolitan* because of the books I had published about women in various professions.

Helen Gurley Brown encouraged me by writing about me in several of her columns. She is a generous, kind woman who told me to "keep on doing what I was doing." While I was writing this book, she talked to me at length about her sister Mary, how much she loves her, what an important part she has played in Helen's life. We compared notes on guilt, the need to achieve, the power of a sibling with a disability to affect our lives.

"She had an enormous impact on me," Helen says. "I am the person I am today because of my sister's illness and my love for her that made me work very hard to succeed.

"I have never resented one hour or one minute of the things I have done for her. I have no regrets ever, ever, ever. There we were, two sisters breathing the same air, sleeping in the same bedroom, eating the same food, associating with the same people, and she went off one morning and got polio, and it didn't happen to me. I owe her everything. She made me a better person."

I wish I had had the same feelings for Jack. I was still ignoring him for the most part, aside from a Christmas present here or a birthday card there. My mother called him, but after my father died, she couldn't go down to see him except when I was free to take her, and that wasn't often. I think, finally, at ninety-three, my mother just decided to die. All her closest friends were dead, she felt that Jackie was in a safe place, she knew that I was all right and her grandchildren were doing well. It was my mother who gave Kyle the money to get her master's degree at Harvard. When Kyle walked across the platform

on a beautiful day in May and accepted her diploma, the whole audience cheering and shouting, "Way to go, Kyle!" my mother felt she
had helped her granddaughter achieve something wonderful. She must
have decided it was time for her to go. A few months later, she had
a heart attack and died.

IT FEELS LIKE LOVE

*a*fter my mother died, my relationship to Jackie changed, and I wrote this piece about it for *The New York Times Magazine:*

Hands reach out to touch me, pull me, grab me as I walk into the home for retarded adults where my brother has lived for the last twenty years. "What's your name?" they ask. "Where's your mother?" Like children. But they are adults. Retarded adults, from their twenties to their seventies. I just want to do what I came to do and get away as fast as I can.

I hate coming here. It reminds me of shopping trips with my mother and brother when I was a little girl. I felt embarrassed by my brother who walked with short, shuffling steps, clung to Mother's hand, smiled and looked at Mom when someone spoke to him. I felt as if everyone was staring at us. I was ashamed of him and ashamed of myself. I knew I should love him, should help my mother, should be a good girl. I tried, but I never learned to love him.

I reminded myself that my brother was brain damaged by a careless doctor. I tortured myself wondering what he could have been if the accident hadn't happened. An engineer like my father, a lawyer like my husband? Just a few minutes more oxygen and the spark of intelligence would be there in his eyes. Instead there's a worried, frightened struggle to understand. He knows enough to realize that he's missing the point—an embarrassment that he's not as smart as other people.

Now it is my job to tell him that our mother is dead. And somehow I must learn to take her place.

"Jackie's waiting for you," the supervisor says.

My brother comes toward me, then backs away as I try to kiss him. "How's Mother?" he asks.

"Let's go in your room, Jack," I say.

He is taller than I. His face would be handsome if the light of intelligence were reflected there. His hair, like mine, is still a dark blond with only a few gray hairs at the age of fifty-seven. I am two years older. He turns toward me, smiling, not wanting to hear what I have to tell him.

"Jack," I say, taking his hand, "Mom died last week of a heart attack."

He brushes away his tears with the back of his hand. Who taught him it was wrong to cry? I put my arms around him, but he stiffens.

"What will happen to her car?" he asks. He fastens on details when he can't fully grasp the meaning of something.

"I'll take care of it for her, Jackie," I say, hugging him. He's like a little boy, I think. My little boy now.

"I'll make sure you're okay, honey," I say. "I'll come and see you. I'll write to you."

He is quiet for a minute. I can't tell what he is thinking. I don't know him at all. I had gone to college, married, had children and had seen him only occasionally after my parents put him in the home in Florida when Jack was thirty-seven. Busy raising my children, I often forgot to send him birthday cards and Christmas presents. I didn't visit or call him. I would say, "I don't feel anything for my brother," but of course I felt a lot—a lot of resentment and anger.

I take him out to lunch and try to think of things to talk about. He looks down at his ice cream and says softly, "It's a shame about Mother dying."

My God, I think, he's the retarded one, but I'm the one pretending she hasn't died, not talking about her.

"Yes, it is a shame, Jack," I say. "But you know, we were lucky to have her for ninety-three years. She loved us so much."

"I knew she was either ninety-two or ninety-three, but I couldn't remember which one," he says.

Numbers are like a lifeline to Jack. He could often recall birthdays, street addresses, and ages when I had forgotten them.

"It was good of you to remember that, Jack," I say.

He smiles. I feel a rush of love for him that overwhelms me, surprises me. I hold his hand as we walk to the car. The embarrassment is gone. I'm my mother now.

Three months later I take a week off from my job as an editor in New York to come to Florida to take Jack to the beach for a week. This time I don't dread the trip as much as I did before. I want to find out how much he understands, how much he feels, if he's happy.

Our motel room has a large picture window facing the ocean. The sight of the white caps, the wide beach, the sea gulls soothes me. It will be okay, I tell myself. I can do this.

Jack clicks on a *Golden Girls* rerun on TV. I'm surprised to hear him laugh out loud when Rose says she wants her head to be frozen after she dies. I didn't expect him to laugh at the same things I did. I don't know why.

He surprises me all the time. He reads the names "New Mexico," "Oklahoma," "Mississippi" on the pieces of a jigsaw puzzle of the United States I brought him and figures out where to place them. I had taught him to read when we were children playing school, but I had no idea he could read that well now.

One of the strongest lessons I learned from Jack is not to be so afraid of my father. We are watching TV one day in the motel room and I am sitting in back of Jack and can see his face in the mirror. I turn on an old Tyrone Power costume epic, and after I while I hear Jack whisper, "This is the worst stuff!" I laugh because he sounds so much like my father and his face is just like my father's when he was angry. I realize my father's anger had nothing to do with me. He was just an angry, tense, troubled man.

One night Jackie and I go for a walk on the beach.

"Do you know what my daughter Kyle gave me after Mother died?" I ask. "A star. There's a company that names stars for people who die, and Mother's is near the Big Dipper. See, it's right up there."

He tries hard not to cry, but I am not as successful. Mother took full responsibility for teaching Jack, encouraging him to take care of himself, worrying about him every day of her life. She was the one who traveled the bad roads from New York to Boston in the 1930s to see the doctors at Children's Hospital. She bathed, dressed, and later shaved him every morning until he went away. Dad retreated into golf and Scotch and left Jackie to my mother.

I asked her one day if she minded, and she said, "Sometimes I would just like to get up in the morning and not have to take care of Jackie all day. I would like some time off."

But she didn't complain. She just did what she had to do. And it was rough. People used to say to her, "Jack was given to you for a reason." And I, watching her struggle to care for him, to do her best for me, to manage her marriage with a brilliant, difficult man, used to think, "Oh, sure. He was given to her to make certain that she suffered enough, to make me feel guilty that I can't love him." I wondered what kind of a God would decide we needed a retarded child to prove a point.

"Does my dad have a star too?" Jack asks.

Again, I am caught off guard.

Why, he loves Dad, I think. He loves that angry, cold man who ignored him when he was growing up. He must have wanted to be like him. I know so little about this boy.

We go to Disney World and he clings to my hand, and I realize he is afraid of losing me. People stare at us as we eat in a Western saloon, where they play "Home on the Range," but when I look up to confront them, I realize their expressions are kind, concerned.

"Remember, Jack," I say, "Dad used to play the piano and sing that song when they had parties."

He laughs and remembers with me.

We go back to the motel tired and hot. I fill the bathtub with warm water. His room mother told me he needs help with his bath. I'm not sure how to do this without embarrassing him, but he doesn't seem to mind. I scrub his back and arms and hand him the washcloth to bathe his genitals.

"Do you mind my helping you with your bath, Jack?" I ask.

"No," he says. If you've lived in a home for retarded people for twenty years, you probably don't have much privacy.

Bathing him, feeding him, looking after him brings back the years of taking care of my own children.

At night I tuck him in and say, "I love you, Jack," and realize I mean it, at least for this moment.

After my article appeared, other siblings of people with disabilities wrote to me from all over the country and England to tell me they were grateful that I had written about my feelings for Jack. They said they felt the same way and had never been able to tell anyone about it. A producer optioned my story for a TV movie, and a script was sold to NBC with Steven Weber from *Wings* eager to play my brother.

When I went to Florida that winter, soon after the script was sold, I took Jackie to Epcot. We were sitting in a French café, and I said, "Jack we're going to be in a TV movie." "What channel?" he asked. "NBC," I told him. "What time?" he asked, as excited as I was. I told him I didn't know, but would tell him the minute I knew.

Even though the movie still hasn't been made, the best part is that I have helped Jack to feel a little more important than he had ever felt before. The people at Duvall teased him about a handsome television star like Steven Weber playing him in a movie. Later, when a photographer took Jack's picture for an article I wrote for *Good Housekeeping*, the staff told him how great he looked and made him feel like a star. I hope he will be able to understand enough so that he will know how important he has been in my life–in good ways, I mean. It was difficult growing up with a brother who wasn't like other brothers, but I think it made me stronger, better able to handle my own daughter's disability and the other vicissitudes of life that happen to everyone.

There are many ways of reacting to a brother or sister with a disability, of course. Some people are embittered by the experience. Some are so compassionate that they are filled with loving feelings for their sibling all their lives. Most of us are somewhere in between.

LOVE AND PRIDE

If I have emphasized the difficulties of growing up with a sibling with a disability, I didn't mean to exclude the love and pride most of us feel for our brothers and sisters. We know that their lives are much harder than ours, and when they compete in the Special Olympics, hold down a job at McDonald's, or bag groceries at the supermarket, we burst with pride because we know the Herculean effort they put forth.

Gwen says her brother Simon, who has autism, is a "Yes!" kind of person. "The reason he has thrived and talked when doctors said he would never speak, the reason he has a job and functions in this world is because my mother had such high expectations for him and she never gave up.

"When you talk to him, he will say, 'Yes! I did good work today. Yes! I am wonderful. Yes! we are a family. I am so good and so right!' How can you feel bad with a brother like that?"

Alan is fiercely proud of his twin brother who was paralyzed from the waist down when he was hit by a drunken driver. He was only fourteen, but he determined while he was still in the hospital that he would be in the wheelchair Olympics and he achieved that goal.

"He had such a positive attitude from the very beginning that we all wanted to help him," Alan says. "I learned everything I could about his disability and I did as much as I could for him in the early days. He wanted to do everything for himself. He's done incredible things. He holds the U.S. record in the marathon and the mile. He just finished his graduate work in sociology and went to Central America to do his thesis on disabilities. I would do anything for him because I admire him so much."

When Danielle was applying to college, she wrote an essay about her brother with mental retardation and all her feelings of love and pride came pouring out.

"I love talking to my brother on the phone," she wrote. "Whenever I'm feeling sad, he always cheers me up. No matter how upset I am, I know I can call Jimmy and talking to him will put things into perspective. He makes me feel better in an uncontrived way. Although my family helps him and gives to him in a conventional sense, our relationship is perfectly balanced in all that he gives us, and I've been lucky."

Danielle graduated from college and is now studying the way infants learn language. She thinks her brother gave her a lot.

"The experiences with Jimmy growing up and feelings I felt because of him are happy memories," she says. "I feel that I have benefited enormously by having a disabled brother, both in trivial matters—like a guaranteed grin to brighten my day—as well as more important matters such as my development as an individual and my attitude toward life in general. Jimmy has made my family stronger. It is so easy to make him happy. He gives us an escape into his world. He is the naive child who can brighten the day without trying."

When you talk to Alex about his brother Tom who has mild mental retardation, you can feel the love and pride he feels for his sibling. Alex is only a year older than Tom, and in spite of the disability, the two are buddies:

> The last time I saw Tom, we had a boys' day out. I picked him up at the home where he lives and headed for a restaurant for lunch. I didn't really know my way around the area and pretty soon I was totally lost. I was debating in my mind whether to disclose this to him because I didn't want to get him anxious or upset. But finally I thought, "What the heck. I'll confide in him."
>
> "Tommy," I said, "I have to tell you I don't know where we are, and it might take me a while to figure out where we're going." I'll never forget his answer for the rest of my life.
>
> "Don't worry, Alex," he said. "You're with me. You're safe."
>
> And I was. He knew exactly where we were, and he directed me to the restaurant.

When Allison, a journalist and editor, talks about her sister Dee, who has Down syndrome, it is obvious how much she loves her and how proud she is of her:

> She makes me feel special. Dee is pretty and smart, extraordinarily gifted artistically, and a wonderful dancer. She won a

prize for designing a program for our symphony orchestra one year. She designs textiles, makes pottery.

When she was born thirty-four years ago, the doctors told my parents to put her in a mental institution and tell their other children that she had died. My mother, who was usually kind of retiring, said, "Damn you! I'm not going to do that!" It was the first time she ever stood up to anybody. And I think she continued to stand up to people because of Dee. She always said when we were growing up, "I can't do much for myself, but I can do anything for Dee."

Because my parents wouldn't let anyone tell them what to do with their kid, it gave me a sense of making up my own mind about things and not worrying about what other people thought. I used to take Dee to work with me, and I found people generally took their cues from me. If I was open and bright and said, 'I'd like you to meet my sister Dee,' people would respond in a friendly and positive way.

Many brothers and sisters of people with disabilities learn to appreciate the qualities of their siblings, but none, perhaps, expressed their pride and love more movingly than Jim Watson in an article in *Reader's Digest*. Jim's brother Page has autism, mental retardation, and is deaf. When Jim and his family took Page to the nursing home where their grandmother lay dying, they were sure that Page would not understand what was happening. When Grandma was well, she never stopped talking and Page could not talk at all:

> In his silent fortress Page was unaware of the impenetrable wall of words Grandma built around herself. She kissed him and smiled at him and, more important, accepted him just as he was. She never showed disappointment that he was not "normal," but rather regarded him with fascination, patience and warmth.

When the family arrived at the nursing home, no one could think of anything to say. "The strokes had left Grandma trembling and unresponsive," Jim wrote. After struggling to speak, the brothers and sisters fell silent:

> Page was standing quietly next to the window, his face brilliant red, tears streaming from his eyes. Just then, he pushed

through the group and made his way to the bed. He leaned over Grandma's withered figure and took her cheeks gently in his hands. Head bowed, he stood there for an eternity, cradling her face and soaking her gown with his tears. Those of us with healthy ears were deaf to the volumes being spoken in that wonderful, wordless exchange.

I felt a rush of warmth deep inside me. It surged upward like an inexorable flood, filling my eyes until the room melted in a wash of colors and liquid shapes. As the picture blurred, my perception snapped into brilliant focus. How wrong I had been about Page. Far better than the rest of us, he knew the true meaning of our visit. He knew it perfectly because he grasped it not with his head but with his heart. Like a child unrestrained by propriety or ego, he had the freedom, courage, and honesty to reach out in pain to Grandma. This was love, simple and pure.

I saw that Page's condition, for all the grief it brings, is in one sense a remarkable and precious gift. For among the many things my brother was born without is the capacity for insincerity. He cannot show what he does not feel, nor can he suppress urgent emotion. Inside him is a clear channel straight to the center of his soul. As I stood next to him, consumed by his expression of unselfish love, I stopped wondering why Page could not be more like me. At that moment, I wanted to be more like him...

That afternoon by Grandma's deathbed, when none of us knew what to say, my speechless brother had said it all.

Peggy, whose mentally ill brother has been homeless for the last eight years, says, "There is a part of me that feels guilt and shame and another part that is quite proud of him and would love other people to know how much he has done. I'd like people to know what a hero my brother is."

I'm proud of Jack, too, for living uncomplainingly in a world he often doesn't understand but puts up with cheerfully and bravely. He's lost the mother he adored, and lived with people not always as gentle as he is. And when I talk to him, I ask, "Are you okay, Jack? Do you need anything?" And he always says, "I'm fine, Mary. I could use a little candy." We're both chocoholics, so I send him a box of chocolate creams in the next mail.

I can't say that I look forward to my trips to Florida, but I don't dread them the way I did that first time. I feel more comfortable with Jack and I hope he feels easier with me, too. I keep trying.

I know what interests my brother now. He loves to hear about my daughters and about his grandnephews. He puts their pictures carefully in the photo album that his room mother bought him. He still loves cars, trains, and airplanes, and I buy them for him every time I'm in Toys 'R' Us getting things for my grandsons. He likes books that make noises, especially the ones based on Disney movies.

He can listen for hours to my reminiscences about our parents. He wants me to tell him about our father riding a horse in Haiti when he was in the marines at the end of World War I. He eats up tales of old family friends like Uncle Leon and Aunt Dorothy who used to trim the Christmas tree with Mom and Dad every year. He remembers every car my father ever bought, and he loves the Tulip Street house in Summit that he lived in for twenty-five years.

He likes Jim Carrey and Arnold Schwarzenegger movies. We watch reruns of *The Golden Girls* and *The Odd Couple* together and eat chocolate cream pie, ice cream, potato chips, and nuts, which I tell myself I bought for Jack.

I am trying to feel love for him, but after a lifetime of wishing he weren't my brother, I still have a long way to go. Whenever I think of Jackie, even now when I've had therapy, when I know it's not my fault that I resent Jack, when I understand that I'm doing my best, when I've written articles and a book about my relationship with him, I still feel guilty. Guilty that I don't call him more often. Guilty that I don't send him more letters, presents, photographs. Guilty that I can't carry on a conversation with him. Guilty that I don't love him enough. Guilty that I've never loved him enough. Guilty that I let my mother bear the full burden of caring for him. Guilty that I don't visit him in Florida more often. Guilty that only luck kept me from being the one who was brain damaged at birth.

Fortunately, attitudes toward people with a disability have changed enormously since I was a child, and that makes it easier for their siblings. Because of the openness in our society now and a willingness to talk about our feelings, there is a healthier atmosphere in many families where a child suffers from a disability. When I was little, having a child who was not perfect was often considered shameful, something to be hidden. My mother never felt like that, but she was the exception in those days.

It's much better now since the Education Act of 1975 mandated that children with a disability be included in regular classrooms whenever possible; and the Americans with Disabilities Act has helped to end job discrimination against adults with disabilities. The Special Olympics introduced us to these special people too. People still stare, but often their faces are kind, concerned, rather than fearful because they are more accustomed to seeing people with disabilities in their lives. They go to school with them, work with them, see them in public, talk to them in church or temple. In the case of people with disabilities, familiarity breeds respect. As a sibling of someone with a disability, you know better than anyone that a person in a wheelchair, a man or woman walking with a white cane, or someone using sign language all have something valuable to give us. Other people need to find out what they are missing.

Today we are free to talk about our most intimate feelings, encouraged to share guilt, anger, embarrassment, and resentment, without being condemned for such emotions. We are more likely to be included in consultations on the future of our siblings. Our ambivalent feelings as children are more likely to be considered by parents who know it is sometimes difficult for us. When we are included in family discussions and encouraged to give our opinions in family planning, we can make a major contribution to the well-being of our household.

Because of people like Donald Meyer, who encouraged siblings to speak out through his Sibling Support Project; Debra Lobato, who set up sibling support groups in spite of a great deal of opposition from her colleagues; Stanley Klein, who published stories by siblings in *Exceptional Parent* magazine; new research by Thomas Powell, Milton Seligman, Bryna Siegel, Stuart Silverstein, Alexandra Quittner, Myra Bluebond-Langner, Marty Krauss and her colleagues, and Julie Tallard Johnson, there is much greater recognition of the importance of siblings in the lives and well-being of their brothers and sisters with disabilities.

Lobato suggests that attitudes toward people who have a disability started to change in the 1970s along with the civil rights movement. "People felt entitled to information, to fairness," she says. "And because the Kennedys were open about their daughter, Rosemary, people didn't hide their children with mental retardation at home as much as they once did. They wanted their children to have an education."

Evelyn Hausslein, associate director of the Federation for Children with Special Needs, helps to set up training and information programs around the country to teach parents what rights their children with disabilities are entitled to. She too credits the Kennedys and other public figures for taking some of the stigma away from having a child with a disability.

"We made great progress in the disability field when Hubert Humphrey showed off his grandchild with Down syndrome and when the Kennedys started the Special Olympics. When Dick Thornburgh, whose son suffered brain damage in an automobile accident, was attorney general of the United States, he and his wife Ginny were strong advocates for the Americans with Disabilities Act, which mandated acceptance of people with disabilities in our schools, the workplace, and our social lives."

Ginny Thornburgh continues her advocacy today for the National Organization on Disability, where she directs a program on religion and disability. She advises congregations of all faiths on ways to welcome people with disabilities into places of worship.

"A ramp is not enough," Ginny says, and she works to help people in congregations all over the country to recognize the talents of people with disabilities.

Evelyn Hausslein credits The Association for Persons with Severe Handicaps (TASH) for the inclusion movement for young children. "These are people who pushed for the integration of children with severe disabilities into public schools. The idea was if you can get these children into the schools, then you can certainly include children with lesser disabilities. These people were way ahead of the game. That's where younger parents turn to make sure their kids are really part of mainstream society.

"Today there are services from the time a child is diagnosed. Parents are told of resources in the hospital before they take the baby home. They get connected with agencies that can help. By federal law, states are required to write a plan to help direct parents to resources."

Some states have provided individual plans that include the needs of the whole family, not just the child with the disability. In Minnesota and Michigan, for example, money is provided to buy support services and it can be spent in any way that is most helpful to that particular family—respite care, nursing help, a wheelchair, a van, a ramp.

"One family said, 'What we need is money to repaper our hall-way,'" Evelyn says. "They said, 'Our son picks the wallpaper off and it depresses us to live in a house like this. If we can wallpaper the hall once a year, that will make all the difference in the life of our family.' It honors that family integrity to say, 'What is it that you need to cope with your daughter or son? We'll help you.'"

Marty Krauss thinks the present movement of inclusion of children with disabilities in mainstream society can be traced back to the Head Start days in the 1960s when there was a mandate for family involve-ment. Parents were part of the advisory councils to the Head Start programs. That led to early intervention for children from birth to three years old who had disabilities. It was clear that the family's needs couldn't be avoided, that they needed more information, more services. So special teams started working with parent groups to help mothers learn how to prepare their children for special education classes.

Whatever caused the changes in our society that make it easier for us siblings, it seems clear that everybody benefits from our brothers and sisters being out in the world.

And, of course, the most important factor here is how the parents react to a child with a disability. When they are able to put a positive spin on the family situation, to find help for themselves and their siblings, to approach the problems as difficult but manageable, then the other children in the family adopt that attitude too.

Jessica must have wonderful parents. She is only nine years old but she really has it together. Jessica wrote in *Views From Our Shoes*, "I think parents, teachers, and doctors should have more understanding for siblings, because they go through difficult experiences with their brother or sister." Then she gives her advice to other children who have a sibling with a disability, and it is filled with more common sense and practicality than a lot of learned textbooks on this subject:

It's tough sometimes, but you get through it.

They might act up in ways you don't understand when you are little.

If they hurt you, don't get mad because they don't know any better.

If they do certain things that annoy you, try to ignore them or go into another room.

If they're angry, try to stay out of their way.

It seems to be true that the siblings of people with disabilities have a sensitivity to the suffering of others, a tolerance for the differences in human beings, a compassion for the underdogs of the world, an understanding that we all have a burden to bear. These siblings are often achievers, problem solvers, engaged in the helping professions, living up to "Do unto others as you would have them do unto you." But as one sibling of a sister with mental retardation said, "There should be an easier way."

A couple of years go, Vicky called to tell me that Jack's derma-tologist had found a cancerous spot on Jack's face and he would have to have a series of radiation treatments. "Will it hurt?" I asked. "No, Mary," she said. "The doctor said it might feel a little warm. But don't worry–I'll be with him." Jack went through the six weeks of twice-a-day treatments like the brave old Kennard that he is. Never a word of complaint. Vicky had to encourage him to ask for pain medication when he needed it. I wrote him every day, sent him puzzles, books, candy, cars, pictures of his grandnephews–anything I could think of that would cheer him up and let him know that I loved him.

And I do love him now, you know. Sometimes I have thought my life would be easier if he died, but when he had cancer, I didn't want anything to happen to him. I didn't want him to suffer. I didn't want him to be gone from my life. Isn't that strange after all I've written about the difficulties of having a brother with mental retardation? He's my brother, after all is said and done, and I admire him for his sweet-ness, his courage, his never, ever complaining about anything.

Sometimes I imagine meeting him wherever we go when we die, and he's not retarded anymore. He tells me what it was like to live a life where he understands that he isn't like other people and wanting desperately to be like me, like our father, like my husband. He tells me that he forgives me for not being a good sister to him many times, and he thanks me for writing a book that will help other people.

I hope that reading this book has helped you understand your own feelings about your siblings with a disability a little bit better and given you some resources you might not have known about before. Unlike me, you don't have to deal with it all by yourself. You can go to a support group, talk to a psychologist, tell your parents how you feel. If you need information about anything in this book, or if you just want to talk to me, E-mail me at mmchugh655@aol.com. We're already friends just because we're siblings of people with disabilities.

NOTES

INTRODUCTION

6 *"There is a difference..."*: Anonymous, "I Never Figured You Were Disabled," *News Digest*, National Information Center for Children and Youth with Handicaps, no. 11 (1988), p. 6.

9 *The study of siblings...*: Frances Grossman, *Brothers and Sisters of Retarded Children* (Syracuse: Syracuse University Press, 1972), p. 176.

PART I: CHILDHOOD

1: YOUR NEEDS

18 *Debra Lobato, a developmental...*: Debra Lobato, *Brothers, Sisters, and Special Needs* (Baltimore: Paul H. Brookes, 1990), p. 177.

21 *In an interesting study conducted in 1994...*: Alexandra L. Quittner and Lisa C. Opipari, "Differential Treatment of Siblings: Interview and Diary Analyses Comparing Two Family Contexts," *Child Development* 65 (1994), pp. 800–14.

23 *One study by S. V. Coleman found...*: S. V. Coleman, *The Siblings of the Retarded Child* (Doctoral dissertation, California School of Professional Psychology, San Diego, 1990).

24 *Lydia's mother was explicit...*: Lydia Ross [a pseudonym], "I Could Not Love My Brother," *Glamour* (May 1991), p. 152.

29 *Dr. Elisabeth Kübler-Ross's five stages of grief...*: Elisabeth Kübler-Ross, *On Death and Dying* (New York: Macmillan, 1974).

2: YOUR PARENTS' MARRIAGE

32 *One researcher, D. Baumrind, identifies three types of parenting...* D. Baumrind, "Child Care Practices," *Genetic Psychology Monographs* 75, 1967, pp. 43–83.

34 *"I feel that in the beginning..."* Groves B. Smith, M.D., "Cerebral Damage in Children," paper read at 93rd annual meeting of The American Psychiatric Association, Pittsburgh, May 10, 1937.

36   *Marital unhappiness leads to . . .* : Zolinda Stoneman & Phyllis Waldman Berman, *The Effects of Mental Retardation, Disability, and Illness in Sibling Relationships* (Baltimore: Paul H. Brookes, 1993), p. 21.

39   *"more apt to become more isolated . . ."*: Donald J. Meyer, "Fathers of Children with Handicaps," in *Families of Handicapped Children: Needs and Supports Across the Lifespan,* eds. R. R. Fewell and P. F. Vadasy (Austin: Pro-Ed,) 1986. p. 231.

42   *According to a study by . . .* : J. Markowitz, "Participation of Fathers in Early Childhood Education Programs." Unpublished manuscript, George Washington University, Washington, DC, 1983.

3: Your Feelings and How to Cope With Them

46   *"The whole situation is profoundly unfair . . ."*: Helen Featherstone, *A Difference in the Family: Life with a Disabled Child* (New York: BasicBooks, 1980), p. 162.

47   *"I would come in and . . ."*: *The Rest of the Family*, videotape produced by the Epilepsy Foundation of America, Landover, MD, 1991.

49   " *'Lemme see,' my brother said . . ."*: Lydia Ross, op. cit., p. 152.

51   *"My family likes . . ."*: Sarah Lowry, in *Views from Our Shoes,* Donald Meyer, ed. (Bethesda, MD: Woodbine House, 1997), p. 39.

51   *"Inhibition of anger . . ."*: Stephen P. Bank and Michael D. Kahn, *The Sibling Bond* (New York: BasicBooks, 1982). p. 261.

52   *"We are all taught . . ."*: Ibid., p. 265.

52   *"I used to trick my brother . . ."*: Stanley D. Klein and Maxwell J. Schleifer, *It Isn't Fair* (Westport, CT: Bergin & Garvey, 1993), p. 11.

53   *"A recent study of people . . ."*: John S. Rolland, *Families, Illness, and Disability* (New York: BasicBooks, 1994), p. 218.

53   *"In instances where . . ."*: Milton Seligman and Rosalyn Benjamin Darling, *Ordinary Families, Special Children* (New York: Guilford Press, 1997), p. 168.

55   *"It is easier to . . ."*: Bank and Kahn, op. cit., p. 235.

55   *"We were having a very good . . ."*: Donald H. Shillingburg, "Sometimes It's Hard to Love." *Boy's Life* (December 1982), p. 24.

56   *"My friends would come . . ."*: Julia Ellifritt, "Life with My Sister," *Exceptional Parent* (December 1984), p. 17.

62   *"No, I didn't resent Martha . . ."*: Maryjane Westra, "An Open Letter to My Parents," *Sibling Information Network Newsletter,* vol. 8, no. 1 (1992), p. 4.

4: How Did You Get That Way?

68   *"Phil is a hulking . . ."*: Lydia Ross, op. cit., p. 152.

71–72 "It would be better . . ." *The Next Step.* Videotape produced by the Nisonger Center at Ohio State University, 1992. Funded by the Columbus Foundation.

72   *there is usually less stress . . .* : Marty Wyngaarden Krauss and Marsha Mailick Seltzer, "Current Well-Being and Future Plans of Older Caregiving Mothers." *Irish Journal of Psychology* 14 (1993), pp. 47–64.

75   *"the vast majority of siblings . . ."*: Jan S. Greenberg, Marsha Mailick Seltzer, Marty Wyngaarden Krauss, et al., "A Comparison of Coping Strategies of Aging Mothers of Adults with Mental Illness or Mental Retardation," *Psychology and Aging* 10 (1995), pp. 64–75.

75   *"The effects of mental illness..."*: Elizabeth Swados, *The Four of Us: The Story of a Family* (New York: Farrar, Straus & Giroux, 1991), p. 4.

76   *In Dr. Krauss's study...*: Greenberg, Seltzer, and Krauss, op. cit., pp. 64–75.

77   *"allows more sympathy..."*: Bank and Kahn, op. cit., pp. 234–35.

79   *"It wasn't a problem until..."*: Julia Ellifritt, op. cit., p. 16.

79   *A study done by S. M. McHale and W. C. Gamble...*: S. M. McHale and W. C. Gamble. "Sibling Relationships and Adjustment of Children with Disabled Brothers and Sisters," *Journal of Children in Contemporary Society* 19 (1987), pp. 131–158.

83   *"I'm four years younger..."*: *The Next Step* videotape, op. cit.

84   *"Usually seem to occur..."*: Donald J. Meyer and Patricia F. Vadasy, *Sibshops* (Baltimore: Paul H. Brookes, 1994), p. 18.

PART II: ADOLESCENCE

5: ADOLESCENT ANGST

92   *"This was my chance..."*: Ellifritt, op. cit., pp. 19–20.

94   *"The siblings of people who..."*: Greenberg, Seltzer, and Krauss, op. cit. pp. 64–75.

94   *"I was entering..."*: Margaret Moorman, *My Sister's Keeper* (New York: W.W. Norton, 1992), p. 42.

101   *"You're confused..."*: *The Rest of the Family* videotape, op. cit.

101   *"I can't stay..."*: *What About Me?* Videotape produced by Educational Productions, Beaverton, OR, for the Kennedy Institute, Baltimore, 1990.

101   *"It always hurt me..."*: Klein and Schleifer, op. cit., p. 14.

103   *"My brother broke away..."*: *What About Me?*, ibid.

104   *"When sibling guilt..."*: Rolland, op. cit., p. 218.

105   *"I kick myself..."*: *Keeping the Balance*. Videotape produced by the Department of Communications Media at the University of Calgary, Canada, 1992.

107   *"The majority of siblings..."*: Thomas H. Powell and Peggy Ahrenhold Gallagher, *Brothers and Sisters: A Special Part of Exceptional Families* (Baltimore: Paul H. Brookes, 1993), p. 117.

108   *"social services and..."*: ibid., pp. 118–19.

108   someone born before...Meyer and Vadasy, op. cit., p. 18.

111   *"I became a more accepting person..."*: Megan Patterson, op. cit. Meyer, ed., pp. 88–89.

112   *"There are times..."*: Louis Perwien, "My Brother Artie," *Exceptional Parent* (August 1996), p. 84.

6: WHO ARE YOU?

116   *"According to researchers..."*: B. D. Blumberg, M. J. Lewis, and E. J. Susman, "Adolescence: A Time of Transition" in *Chronic Illness and Disability Through the Life Span: Effects on Self and Family* (New York: Springer, 1984), pp. 133–49.

118   *"Brothers and sisters..."*: Meyer and Vadasy, op. cit., p. 38.

119   *Thomas Powell suggests ways...*: Powell and Gallagher, op. cit., pp. 225–26.

120   *"Moms and dads..."*: "Planning for the Future," *News Digest*, National Information Center for Children and Youth with Handicaps, no. 11 (1988) (reprinted 2/91), p. 6.

122   *"Healthy children..."*: Rolland, op. cit., p. 221.

123   *"avoid identifying..."*: Grossman, op. cit., p. 34.

125   *Dr. Seligman warns...*: Seligman and Darling, op. cit., p. 140.

125   *Dr. Thomas Powell gives us...*: Powell and Gallagher, op. cit., pp. 225–26.

126   *"I felt really badly..."*: *What About Me?* videotape.

126   "When you talk to...": S. L. Brown and M. S. Moersch, *Parents on the Team* (Ann Arbor: University of Michigan Press, 1978), p. 67.

PART III: ADULTHOOD

7: SOMEONE TO TALK TO

133   *"I realized this..."*: Terrell Dougan, "Let the Good Times Roll," in *We Have Been There*, Terrell Dougan, Lyn Isbell, Patricia Vyas, eds. (Nashville: Abingdon, 1979, 1983), pp. 119–22.

8: YOUR RELATIONSHIPS

146   *"They are either..."*: Julie Tallard Johnson, *Hidden Victims, Hidden Healers* (Edina, MN: PEMA Publications, 1994), p. 36.

149   *"learned to deal with..."*: ibid., p. 40.

150   *"if others found out..."*: ibid., p. 77.

153   *"I drove the car..."*: Klein and Schleifer, op. cit., p. 22.

154   *"When my junior-year boyfriend..."*: Lydia Ross, op. cit., p. 154.

154   *"I was engaged..."*: *The Next Step*, op. cit.

154   *"My parents say..."*: ibid.

158   *"a quarter of the..."*: G. Hornby and T. Ashworth, "Grandparents Support for Families Who Have Children with Disabilities: A Survey of Parents." *Journal of Child and Family Studies* 3, pp. 312–403.

158   *"Tia would go and..."*: *The Rest of the Family*, op. cit.

159   *"Caregivers take care of..."*: Julie Tallard Johnson, op. cit., p. 46.

9: YOUR CAREER

161   *"older female siblings..."*: D. W. Cleveland and N. Miller, "Attitudes and Life Commitments of Older Siblings of Mentally Retarded Adults," *Mental Retardation* 15 (1977), pp. 38–41.

161   *In 1991 S. L. Burton and A. L. Parks...*: S. L. Burton & A. L. Parks, "The Self-Esteem, Locus of Control, and Career Aspirations of College-Aged Siblings of Individuals with Disability," research study, 1991. Moscow, ID.: Idaho Center on Developmental Disabilities, The University of Idaho.

161   *a study in 1993 by V. Konstam...*: V. Konstam, M. Drainoni, G. Mitchell, R. Houser, D. Reddington, and D. Eaton, "Career Choices and Values of Siblings

with Individuals with Developmental Disabilities," *School Counselor* 40 (1993), pp. 287–92.

168   *"My parents have talked..."*: *The Next Step* videotape.

169   *"I began to realize..."*: Ellifritt, op. cit., pp. 20–21.

171   *"I'm in sales..."*: Greenberg, Seltzer, and Krauss, op. cit., p. 70.

10: DO YOU WANT CHILDREN?

175   *If you are the sibling*: The information on prenatal testing comes from Powell and Gallagher, op. cit., pp. 205–8.

176   *"Though much of my..."*: Ross, op. cit., p. 154.

178   *"Because he has never..."*: Klein and Schleifer, op. cit., p. 23.

178   *"I have a tremendous..."*: Greenberg, Seltzer, and Krauss, op. cit., p. 72.

11: WHO WILL TAKE CARE OF YOUR SIBLING?

183   *"Sixty percent of..."*: M. E. McCullough, "Parent and Sibling Definition of Situation Regarding Transgenerational Shift in Care of a Handicapped Child." (Doctoral dissertation, University of Minnesota, 1981.)

183   *"Listen to the..."*: Krauss and Seltzer, op. cit.

184   *"Increasingly, adults with..."*: Donald Meyer, *The National Association of Sibling Programs Newsletter*, no. 3 (Winter 1993).

188   *In Marty Krauss and...*: Krauss and Seltzer, op. cit.

189   *Krauss and Seltzer found...*: ibid.

191   *"I told my parents..."*: *The Next Step* videotape.

192   *"We know that..."*: Greenberg, Seltzer, and Strauss, op. cit.

12: IT FEELS LIKE LOVE

208   *"In his silent fortress..."*: James Watson, "The Day My Silent Brother Spoke," *Reader's Digest* (November 1992), pp. 105–6.

213   *"I think parents..."*: Jessica Kolber, in *Views from Our Shoes*, Meyer, ed., p. 28.

BIBLIOGRAPHY

Bank, Stephen P., and Michael D. Kahn. *The Sibling Bond*. New York: BasicBooks, 1982.

Baumrind, D. "Child Care Practices." *Genetic Psychology Monographs* 75, 1967.

Bluebond-Langner, Myra. *The Private Worlds of Dying Children*. Princeton, NJ: Princeton University Press, 1978.

————. *In the Shadow of Illness: Parents and Siblings of the Chronically Ill Child*. Princeton, NJ: Princeton University Press, 1996.

Blumberg, B. D., M. J. Lewis, and E. J. Susman. "Adolescence: A Time of Transition," in *Chronic Illness and Disability Through the Life Span: Effects on Self and Family*. New York: Springer, 1984.

Bonnell, Lois. *Psychological and Social Adjustment of Siblings of Children with Autism as Related to their Sex, Birth Order, and Family Size*. Ph.D. dissertation, 1990.

Brown, S. L., and M. S. Moersch. *Parents on the Team*. Ann Arbor: University of Michigan Press, 1978.

Burton, S. L., and A. L. Parks. "The Self-Esteem, Locus of Control, and Career Aspirations of College-Aged Siblings of Individuals with Disability." Moscow, ID: Idaho Center on Developmental Disabilities, The University of Idaho. 1991.

Cleveland, D. W., and N. Miller. "Attitudes and Life Commitments of Older Siblings of Mentally Retarded Adults." *Mental Retardation* 15, 1977.

Coleman, S. V. "The Siblings of the Retarded Child." (Doctoral dissertation, California School of Professional Psychology, San Diego.) 1990.

Crothers, Bronson. "Education of the Handicapped Child," *American Journal of Public Health*, March 1938.

————. "The Appraisal of Children After Birth Injury." *The Pennsylvania Medical Journal*, September 1940.

De Vinck, Christopher. *The Power of the Powerless*. New York: Doubleday, 1988.

Dougan, Terrell. *We Have Been There*. Eds., Terrell Dougan, Lyn Isbell, Patricia Vyas. Nashville: Abingdon, 1983.

Ellifritt, Julia. "Life with My Sister." *Exceptional Parent*, December 1984.

Featherstone, Helen. *A Difference in the Family: Life with a Disabled Child*. New York: BasicBooks, 1980.

Fish, Thomas, and Frances Dwyer McCaffrey. *Profiles of the Other Child: A Sibling Guide for Parents*. Columbus, OH: The Nisonger Publication Dept.

Greenberg, Jan S., Marsha Mailick Seltzer, and Marty Wyngaarden Krauss, et al., "A

Comparison of Coping Strategies of Aging Mothers of Adults with Mental Illness or Mental Retardation." *Psychology and Aging* 10, 1995.

Grossman, Frances Kaplan. *Brothers and Sisters of Retarded Children.* Syracuse: Syracuse University Press, 1972.

Hornby, G., and T. Ashworth. "Grandparents Support for Families Who Have Children with Disabilities: A Survey of Parents. *Journal of Child and Family Studies,* 3, 1994.

Johnson, Julie Tallard. *Hidden Victims, Hidden Healers.* Edina, MN: Pema Publications, Inc. 1994.

Keeping the Balance. Videotape produced by the Department of Communications Media at the University of Calgary, Canada, 1992.

Klein, Stanley D., and Maxwell J. Schleifer. *It Isn't Fair.* Westport, CT: Bergin & Garvey, 1993.

Konstam, V., M. Drainoni, et al. "Career Choices and Values of Siblings with Individuals with Developmental Disabilities," *School Counselor,* 40, 1993.

Krauss, Marty Wyngaarden, and Marsha Mailick Seltzer. "Current Well-Being and Future Plans of Older Caregiving Mothers." *Irish Journal of Psychology* 14, 1993.

Kübler-Ross, Elisabeth. *On Death and Dying.* New York: Macmillan, 1974.

Lobato, Debra J. *Brothers, Sisters, and Special Needs.* Baltimore: Paul H. Brookes, 1990.

Luterman, David. *Deafness in the Family.* Boston: Little Brown, 1987.

McHale, S. M. and W. C. Gamble. *Journal of Children in Contemporary Society* 19, 1987.

McCullough, M. E. "Parent and Sibling Definition of Situation Regarding Transgenerational Shift in Care of a Handicapped Child." Doctoral dissertation, University of Minnesota, 1981.

McHugh, Mary. "Telling Jack," the *New York Times,* January 9, 1994.

————. "Loving Jack," *Good Housekeeping,* September 1995.

Markowitz, J. "Participation of Fathers in Early Childhood Education Programs." Unpublished manuscript, George Washington University, Washington, DC, 1983.

Meyer, Donald J. *Living with a Brother or Sister with Special Needs.* Seattle: University of Washington Press, 1996.

Meyer, Donald J. "Fathers of Children with Handicaps: Developmental trends in Fathers' Experiences over the Family Life Cycle." *Families of Handicapped Children: Needs and Supports across the Lifespan.* Austin, TX: Pro-Ed, 1986.

————. *The National Association of Sibling Programs Newsletter.* Number 3, Winter 1993.

Meyer, Donald J., and Patricia F. Vadasy. *Sibshops.* Baltimore: Paul H. Brookes, 1994.

Meyer, Donald J., ed. *Views from Our Shoes.* Bethesda, MD.: Woodbine House, 1997.

Moorman, Margaret. *My Sister's Keeper.* New York: W.W. Norton, 1992.

The Next Step. Videotape produced by the Nisonger Center at Ohio State University. Funded by the Columbus Foundation.

Perwien, Louis. "My Brother Artie." *Exceptional Parent,* August 1996.

"Planning for the Future." *News Digest,* National Information Center for Children and Youth with Handicaps, no. 11, 1988 (reprinted 2/91).

Powell, Thomas H., and Peggy Ahrenhold Gallagher. *Brothers and Sisters—A Special Part of Exceptional Families.* Baltimore: Paul H. Brookes, 1993.

Quittner, Alexandra L., and Lisa C. Opipari. "Differential Treatment of Siblings: Interview and Diary Analyses Comparing Two Family Contexts." *Child Development,* 1994.

The Rest of the Family, videotape produced by the Epilepsy Foundation of America, Landover, MD.

Rolland, John S. *Families, Illness, and Disability*. New York: BasicBooks, 1994.

Ross, Lydia (pseudonym). "I Could Not Love My Brother." *Glamour*, May 1991.

Sargent, Janice R. et al. "Sibling Adaptation to Childhood Cancer." *Journal of Pediatric Psychology*, vol. 20, no. 2, 1995.

Saylor, Annie. "Reflections of a Baby Boomer." *The Bond* (former newsletter of the National Alliance for the Mentally Ill. Now called *The Advocate*.) Winter 1993/4.

Seligman, Milton. "Siblings of Handicapped Persons." *The Family with a Handicapped Child*. Grune & Stratton, 1983.

Seligman, Milton, and Rosalyn Benjamin Darling. *Ordinary Families, Special Children*. New York: The Guilford Press, 1997.

Shillingburg, Donald H. "Sometimes It's Hard to Love." *Boy's Life*, December 1982.

Siegel, Bryna, and Stuart Silverstein. *What About Me? Growing Up with a Developmentally Disabled Sibling*. New York: Plenum Press, 1994.

Smith, Groves B. "Cerebral Damage in Children," read at 93rd annual meeting of The American Psychiatric Association, Pittsburgh, May 10, 1937.

Stoneman, Zolinda, and Phyllis Waldman Berman. *The Effects of Mental Retardation, Disability, and Illness on Sibling Relationships*. Baltimore: Paul H. Brookes, 1993.

Swados, Elizabeth. *The Four of Us*. New York: Farrar, Straus & Giroux, 1991.

Vadasy, Patricia F., Rebecca Fewell, Donald Meyer, and Greg Schell. "Siblings of Handicapped Children: A Developmental Perspective on Family Interactions." *Family Relations*, 33, January 1984.

Valdivieso, C., S. Ripley, and L. Ambler. National Information Center for Children and Youth with Handicaps, *News Digest*, no. 11, 1988. Washington, DC: Interstate Research Associates.

Watson, James. "The Day My Silent Brother Spoke," *Reader's Digest*, November 1992.

Westra, Maryjane. "An Open Letter to My Parents." *Sibling Information Network Newsletter*, vol. 8, no. 1, 1992.

What About Me? Videotape produced by Educational Productions, Beaverton, OR, for The Kennedy Institute, Baltimore, 1990.

RESOURCES

VIDEOTAPES

Being Blind: Inspirational Stories. The Institute for Families of Blind Children. The Institute for Families of Blind Children, Mail Stop #111, P.O. Box 54700, Los Angeles, CA 90054-0700. (213)669-4649.

Brothers and Sisters: Growing Up with a Blind Sibling. The Institute for Families of Blind Children (see address above).

Equal Partners: African-American Fathers and Systems of Health Care, Father's Network, 16120 8th St., Bellevue, WA 98008. (425)747-4004, ext. 218.

Keeping The Balance. Department of Communications Media, University of Calgary, 2500 University Drive N.W., Calgary, Alberta, Canada T2N 1N4. (403)220-3705.

The Next Step. Ohio State University, Nisonger Center, 1581 Dodd Drive, Columbus, OH 43210. (614)292-9844.

The Rest of the Family. Epilepsy Foundation of America, 4351 Garden City Drive, Landover, MD 20785. (800)213-5821.

Special Kids, Special Dads. Father's Network, 16120 8th St. Bellevue, WA 98008. (425)747-4004, ext. 218.

They Don't Come with Manuals: Parenting Children with Disabilities. Community Services Information Group, Inc., P.O. Box 80552, Baton Rouge, LA 70898. (504)928-7175.

What About Me? The Kennedy Institute, 707 North Broadway, Baltimore, MD 21205, (410)502-9411.

For a list of videotapes on issues relating to developmental disabilities, contact the Sibling Information Network at the A. J. Pappanikou Center on Special Education and Rehabilitation at the University of Connecticut, 249 Glenbrook Rd., U-64, Storrs, CT 06269-2064.

NEWSLETTERS

Carlson, Janice, Audrey Leviton, and Mary Mueller. "Services to Siblings: An Important Component of Family-Centered Practice." *The ACCH Advocate,* Fall/Winter 1993. vol. 1, no. 1.

The Advocate (NAMI), Frieda Eastmann, editor. 200 No. Glebe Rd., Suite 1015, Arlington, VA 22203.

Coalition Quarterly. Federation for Children with Special Needs, 312 Stuart St. Boston, MA. 02116. (617)482-2915.

The Epigram, Laura Held, editor. Epilepsy Foundation of America, 50 East State St., Suite 212, Trenton, NJ 08608. (609)392-4900.

Families, Norman Reim, editor. The New Jersey Developmental Disabilities Council, CN 70032 West State St., Trenton, NJ 08625-0700.

Family Support Bulletin. "Tips for Dealing with Siblings of Persons with Disabilities." Spring/Summer 1988. Washington, DC, United Cerebral Palsy Associations, 1660 L St. N.W., Suite 700, Washington, DC 20036-5602.

Insights (spina bifida), Nancy Campbell, editor. 14323 Long Green Dr., Silver Spring, MD 20906, (301)871-3517.

NASP Newsletter. The Sibling Support Project, Children's Hospital and Medical Center, P.O. Box 5371, CL-09, Seattle, WA 98105-0371. (206)368-4911.

News Digest, The National Information Center for Children and Youth with Disabilities, P.O. Box 1492, Washington, DC 20013-1492. (800)695-0285.

Report. Mary Dolan, National Organization on Disability, 910 16th St. N.W., Washington, DC 20006. (202)293-5960.

Retinoblastoma Support News. Nancy Mansfield, editor. The Institute for Families of Blind Children, P.O. Box 54700, Mail Stop #111, Los Angeles, CA 90054-0700. (213)669-4649.

Sibling Forum. Susan Levine, editor. Family Resource Associates, Inc. 35 Haddon Ave., Shrewsbury, NJ 07702. (732)747-5310.

Sibling Information Network Newsletter. Lisa Glidden, editor. The A. J. Pappanikou Center, 249 Glenbrook Road, U-64, Storrs, CT 06269-2064, (860)486-0273.

MONOGRAPHS

"New Horizons, Father's Network." 16120 8th St., Bellevue, WA 98008. (425)747-4004, ext. 218.

"Circles of Care and Understanding." Association for the Care of Children's Health, (609)224-1742.

CHILDREN'S BOOKS

For a list of books about disabilities and illnesses for young readers, contact Erica Lewis Erickson, Sibling Support Project, Children's Hospital and Medical Center, P.O. Box 5371, CL-09, Seattle, WA 98105-0371. (206)368-4911.

For books especially for siblings 4–9 years old and 10 years and older, contact Susan P. Levine, Family Resource Associates, Inc., 35 Haddon Ave., Shrewsbury, NJ 07702. (732)747-5310.

REFERENCE MATERIALS

Exceptional Parent 1996 Resource Guide. *Exceptional Parent Magazine*, 209 Harvard St., Suite 303, Brookline, MA 02146-5005. (617)730-5800.

Janicki, M. P., et al. *Help for Caring–For Older People Caring for Adults with a Develop-*

mental Disability. Albany: New York State Developmental Disabilities Planning Council, 1996.

SIBLING SUPPORT GROUPS

For a complete list of sibling support groups throughout the country, contact:

Lisa Glidden, The A. J. Pappanikou Center, 249 Glenbrook Road, U-64, Storrs, CT 06269-2064. (860)486-0273.

Donald Meyer, The Sibling Support Project, Children's Hospital and Medical Center, P.O. Box 5371, CL-09, Seattle, WA 98105-0371. (206)368-4911.

The Arc's Family Support Project, P.O. Box 1047, Arlington, TX 76004. (817)261-6003.

INTERNET SITES FOR SIBLINGS

Rick Berkobien, The Arc.: rberkobi@Metronet.com

Don Meyer, Sibling Support Project: http://www.chmc.org/departmt/sibsupp

The Family Village Web Site: http://www.familyvillage.wisc.edu

Father's Network: http://www.fathersnetwork.org

SibNet: A place on the internet to exchange ideas with other siblings. From Don Meyer's Sibling Support Project: http://www.chmc.org/departmt/sibsupp

ORGANIZATIONS

American Foundation for the Blind, 11 Penn Plaza, Suite 300, New York, NY 10001. (212)502-7600.

American Paraplegic Society, 75-21 Astoria Blvd., Jackson Heights, NY 11370-1177. (718)803-3782.

Angelman Syndrome Foundation, P.O. Box 12437, Gainesville, FL 32604. (800)If-Angel.

The Arc, 500 East Border St., Arlington, TX 76010. (817)261-6003.

Autism Society of America, 7910 Woodmont Ave., Suite 650, Bethesda, MD 20814-3015. (301)657-0881 or (800)328-8476.

C.H.A.D.D. (Children and Adults with Attention Deficit Disorder), 499 N.W. 70th Ave., Suite 101, Plantation, FL, 33317. (305)587-3700 or (800)233-4050.

Cystic Fibrosis Foundation, 6931 Arlington Rd., No. 200, Bethesda, MD 20814. (301)951-4422.

Epilepsy Foundation of America, 4351 Garden City Dr., Landover, MD 20785.

Federation for Children with Special Needs, 95 Berkeley St., Boston, MA 02116. (617)482-2915.

Multiple Sclerosis Foundation, 6350 N. Andrews Ave., Fort Lauderdale, FL 33309. (305)776-6805.

Muscular Dystrophy Assoc. 3300 E. Sunrise Dr., Tucson, AZ 85718. (520)529-2000.

National Alliance for the Mentally Ill, 200 No. Glebe Rd., Suite 1015, Arlington, VA 22203. (703)524-7600

National Association of the Deaf, 814 Thayer Ave., Silver Spring, MD 20910. (301)587-1788.

National Spinal Cord Injury Assoc., 545 Concord Ave., No. 29, Cambridge, MA 02138-1122. (617)441-8500.

National Down Syndrome Society, 666 Broadway, New York, NY 10012-2317. (212)460-9330 or (800)221-4602.

Plan NJ, 1273 Bound Brook Rd., Suite 15, Middlesex, NJ 08846. (908)563-0300.

Siblings for Significant Change, United Charities Building, 105 E. 22nd St., New York, NY 10010. (212)420-0776.

Spina Bifida Association of America, 4590 MacArthur Blvd. N.W., Suite 250, Washington DC 20007-4226. (202)944-3285.

United Cerebral Palsy Associations, Inc., 1660 L St., N.W., Suite 700, Washington, DC 20036-5603. (800)872-5827.

For a complete bibliography of books and articles for families of those with developmental disabilities, contact the Sibling Information Network at The A. J. Pappanikou Center, University of Connecticut, 249 Glenbrook Rd., U-64, Storrs, CT 06269.

For a bibliography for the siblings of people with all disabilities, contact: Donald Meyer, Sibling Support Project, Children's Hospital and Medical Center, P.O. Box 5371, CL-09, Seattle, WA 98105-0371. (206)368-4911.

The author gratefully acknowledges permission from these sources to reprint the following:

Quoted material from *It Isn't Fair* by Stanley D. Klein and Maxwell J. Schleifer, copyright © 1993 by the Exceptional Parent Press reproduced by permission of Greenwood Publishing Group, Westport, CT; quoted material from *Ordinary Families, Special Children* by Milton Seligman and Rosalyn Benjamin Darling, copyright © 1997 by the Guilford Press, reproduced by permission of Guilford Publications, New York, NY; excerpt from *The Four of Us* by Elizabeth Swados, copyright © 1991 by Elizabeth Swados, reprinted by permission of Farrar, Straus & Giroux, Inc., New York, NY; excerpt from *We Have Been There* by Terrell Dougan, Lyn Isbell and Patricia Vyas, copyright © 1979, 1983, used by permission of Abingdon Press, Nashville, TN; excerpts from "I Could Not Love My Brother" from the May 1991 issue of *Glamour* are printed with permission of the author Lydia Ross (pseudonym); excerpts from "The Day My Silent Brother Spoke" by James Watson, *The Reader's Digest*, November 1992, reprinted with permission from *The Reader's Digest* and James Watson; excerpt from "Open Letter to My Parents" by Maryjane Westra from vol. 8, no. 1 of the *Sibling Information Newsletter* is reprinted with permission from the author; quoted material from the videotape *Keeping the Balance* used with permission of The Department of Communications Media of The University of Calgary, Canada; quoted material from the videotape *The Rest of the Family* used with permission of the Epilepsy Foundation of America, Landover, MD; Paul Shaugnessy's poem reprinted by permission of Paul and his family; Theresa Basile's poem "My Brother" is reprinted by permission of Theresa and her parents; excerpt from *My Sister's Keeper* by Margaret Moorman, copyright © 1992, is reprinted by permission of W.W. Norton & Company; quoted material by Annie Saylor from *The Bond*, newsletter of the National Association of Mental Illness, Winter 1993/4, is used by permission of the author; excerpts from "Life with My Sister" by Julia Ellifritt, published in *The Exceptional Parent*, December 1984, are reprinted with permission of the author; quoted material from *Brothers and Sisters: A Special Part of Exceptional Families* by Thomas H. Powell and Peggy Ahrenhold, copyright © 1993, reproduced by permission of Paul H. Brookes Publishing Co., P.O. Box 10624, Baltimore, MD 21285 and the author Thomas Powell; quoted material from the videotape *Brothers and Sisters: Growing Up with a Blind Sibling* used with the permission of the Institute for Families of Blind Children, Los Angeles, CA; quoted material from *Views from My Shoes* by Don Meyer, copyright © 1999, reproduced by permission of Woodbine House, Bethesda, MD; quoted material from *The Sibling Bond* by Stephen P. Bank and Michael D. Kahn, copyright © 1982, reproduced by permission of BasicBooks, HarperCollins Publishers Inc., New York, NY; quoted material from *Families, Illness and Disability* by John S. Rolland, copyright © 1994, reproduced by permission of BasicBooks, HarperCollins Publishers Inc., New York, NY; quoted material from the videotape *What About Me?* reproduced by permission of the Kennedy Institute, Baltimore, MD.

INDEX

McHugh, Mary. Special Siblings: Growing Up with Someone with a Disability. Feb. 1999. 256p. index. Hyperion; dist. by Little, Brown, $23.95 (0-7868-6285-8). DDC. 362.4

McHugh's brother Jackie suffered from cerebral palsy, apparently caused by a badly managed birth. When he was 37, the parents put him into a residential home, but family damage had already been done. In her book offering help to parents, relatives, teachers, and neighbors of disabled children who have siblings as well as to those siblings, McHugh is often highly personal when discussing feelings, seemingly minor events, and the failure or inability of persons supposed to be "in charge" to come completely to grips with the situation. Describing growing up with Jackie, she mentions how his disability affected her relations with him and her parents, pointing out, for example, that her parents accepted her high grades without comment or praise, whereas they gave Jackie loud praise for handling a bowling ball. She forcefully lays to rest the supposition that a child with a disability can live in a family without affecting the siblings. For although she describes a few cases with positive results, she doesn't gloss over any problems, short or long term. —*William Beatty.*

YA: *Reassuring insights for teens in similar situations.* CS.